North American

Super Sabre

NO SMOKING
WITHIN 50 FT.

OSPREY AIR COMBAT

North American F-100 Super Sabre

David A Anderton

Published in 1987 by Osprey Publishing Limited
27A Floral Street, London WC2E 9DP
Member company of the George Philip Group

Sole distributors for the USA

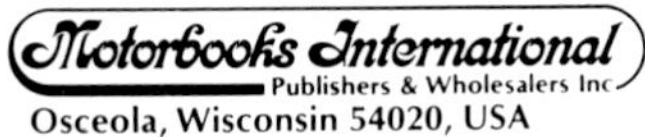

Osceola, Wisconsin 54020, USA

British Library Cataloguing in Publication Data

Anderton, David A
North American F-100 Super Sabre—
(Osprey air combat)
1. Super Sabre (Jet fighter plane)
I. Title

623.74'64 UG1242.F5
ISBN 0-85045-622-2

Editor Dennis Baldry

Designed by Gwyn Lewis

Filmset in Great Britain by
Tameside Filmsetting Limited, Ashton-under-Lyne, Lancashire, and printed by BAS Printers Limited, Over Wallop, Hampshire

FRONT COVER
CP 881, an F-100D (serial 0-55-2881) of the 531st TFS 'Ramrods' of the 3rd TFW, heads out of Bien Hoa in early 1970 headed for a distant target. Warload is four Snakeye high-drag bombs. Oleg Komarnitzky is at the controls
(Komarnitzky Collection)

TITLE PAGES
With afterburner howling, the Pratt & Whitney J57-P-7 powerplant of the 24th F-100A (53-1529) runs at full thrust. This aircraft was part of Phase VI tests at AFFTC; the photo may have been taken there, at North American's facilities
(Rockwell International)

Contents

This book is dedicated, with all my love and thanks, to my wife, Krin, and our sons, Bruce and Craig

Acknowledgements

This book is the product of a horde of Hun drivers, wrench-turners, observers, and enthusiasts. A simple request for help was published as a letter in *Air Force* magazine; the response swamped me. It should not have been a surprise; practically every living USAF and ANG fighter pilot past the age of 40 has flown the Super Sabre.

The biggest problem was choosing whose experience to tap, because so many shared the common experience of a tour of duty in Vietnam, dropping ordnance on targets designated by FACs. It was a tough decision, and I hope that the people cited here will be seen as acceptable surrogates by the many who offered to help.

Initial inputs came from long-time colleague Earl Blount, of Rockwell International, who dusted off archival material and tracked down elusive documentation. Without him, no book.

As things took form, I received major contributions from members of the Super Sabre fraternity identified earlier in these pages and here arranged in alphabetical order without rank or title, then or now: Bob Baker, Al Blackburn, Jack Broughton, John Downey, Jed Erskine, Jim Foster, Don Fraizer, Bruce Hanke, Richard Hartman, Doug Henderson, Bud Hillman, Don Joy, George Laven, Jr, Wallace Little, John Maene, Merrill McPeak, Don Schmenk, J C Seymour, Ken Shealy, Ron Standerfer, Randy Steffens, Joe Vincent, Ed White, Willie Wilson.

Additionally, these folks helped with an introduction, a lead, photographs, or collected material: Bill Austin, Pete Bowers, Robert Breckel, John Campbell, Bob Dorr, Robert Ellis, Bill Flower, Dick Hallion, Paul Hoiness, Bob Jones, Gerald Key, Oleg Komarnitsky, Larry Lofton, George Macri, John Mannings, Jim Mesko, Bob Mikesh, Maurice Miller, Larry Montgomery, Dave Musikoff, Ron Nickel, Terry Panopolis, Nancy Paull, Bob Pickett, Denny Swanstrom, Robert Tucker, Gurney Ulrich, Chuck Whitley.

A special acknowledgement is due to three people who know why I'm thanking them here and now: René Francillon, Dave Menard, and Jay Miller

Finally, personal thanks to Dennis Baldry, Osprey's point man for the colonies, whose patience passeth all understanding. Dennis, I owe you.

David A Anderton
Ridgewood, NJ, April 1987

Introduction

The North American F-100 Super Sabre—the Hun, familiarly—was the first supersonic aircraft in the inventory of the United States Air Force. Designed for an air superiority mission, it was the first of the Century series, a group of aircraft developed for the USAF as fighters, interceptors, and fighter-bombers.

It originated in a time-honoured, evolutionary manner, within the NAA organization. Company engineers studied ways to modify the F-86 Sabre, then barely out of flight test, to gain speed performance. The basic features of the Sabre—its sweptback wing and tail, nose inlet with straight-through flow to a single jet engine, power control systems—held the potential for a new layout using updated technology. Those potentials coalesced, and led to the first of a new generation of combat aircraft capable of supersonic speeds.

The F-100 was off to a brilliant start when unpredictable problems suddenly stopped the programme dead in its tracks. The losses of several early aircraft and their pilots in rapid succession, including the ninth F-100A with North American's chief test pilot George Welch, trigged an investigation that was thorough and, finally, fruitful.

The Super Sabre was not welcome at first in the Air Force. The F-100A day fighters were in active service a relatively short time before being transferred to Air National Guard units which were, by long tradition and standard practice, equipped with the castoff aircraft of the active forces. The later F-100C was more acceptable to the USAF, but only because it was capable of fighter-bomber missions. And in that role of an air-to-ground weapon, the Super Sabre finally came into its own.

By that time, a decade had passed since the first models had been declared operational with the USAF, and war raged in a remote part of the world. Inevitably, the Super Sabres went off to fight.

First used on combat air patrols, they were tasked to protect fighter-bombers from possible MiG attacks deep in enemy territory. But they were slower than the Republic F-105s they escorted, and seldom saw enemy MiGs, or fought with them.

So the Huns became fighter-bombers, carrying Snakeyes and CBUs, rockets and napalm tanks, lifting them off runways at Tuy Hoa, Phan Rang, Bien Hoa and Phu Cat, and dropping them on targets marked for them by a forward air controller (FAC). Then they returned to their bases, were refuelled and rearmed, and did it again. And again, and again.

Calls for support came from US and Vietnamese troops, were relayed through communications nets to FACs and to the pilots on cockpit alert, their F-100s armed and ready to go. They scrambled, flew to the coordinates, found their FAC, watched for his smoke rockets that marked the target, rolled in and pickled the bombs or the napalm, or roared in on a long slanting dive, firing rockets and cannon.

They also carried one group of daring pilots who acted as high speed forward air controllers, and used the radio call sign of Misty. Another group of brave souls, crews of Wild Weasel I Huns, deliberately drew the fire of enemy surface-to-air missile batteries.

But for most of the war, they were artillery on wings, firepower to hit enemy troops, bunkers, strongpoints, ambushes, infiltrations. Over and over they made the trips. Their pilots logged combat sorties, completed tours, went home. Others replaced them, to repeat the cycle.

And all the time, underneath its disguise as airborne artillery, was a fighter wanting to be set free.

It happened, once in a while, in the years after war had ceased and F-100s once again armed ANG units. Guard pilots seized the chance to fly the Super Sabres as they had been designed to fly. They climbed to lofty rendezvous and started from there, using the potential energy in that weighty and solid airframe, adding the kinetic energy of its speed. They zoom-climbed, made gut-racking turns followed by steep dives, and—frequently—a final low-level run in burner, whistling across the water or the flatlands just as fast as they could go.

Pilots who had more than a few hundred hours in the F-100s loved them. Today, years after they last climbed out of those cockpits, they remember the first of the Centuries with an emotion bordering on love. It was not an easy airplane to fly, they remind you. If you flew the Hun well, you were by God an aviator, not just another pilot.

And after you knew it well, was it fun to fly?

'I'll tell you the truth,' said one former F-100 aviator, 'and I'll look God straight in the eye and tell Him the same thing. It was more fun than sex.'

Chapter 1
Supersonic Search

On 14 October 1947, high above the desert and dry lakes northeast of Los Angeles, California, USAF Captain Charles E Yeager flew the bullet-shaped orange Bell XS-1 through the speed of sound, demolishing a myth.

The myth was that an invisible wall, a 'sound barrier' in the sky, prevented supersonic flight. To add substance, there was theoretical evidence: calculated drag curves rose toward infinity at sonic speed. Further fortifying the myth, British test pilot Geoffrey de Havilland was killed on 27 September 1946, when his D.H.108 aircraft disintegrated at high speed during practice runs for an assault on the world speed record.

The XS-1 proved supersonic flight possible in an airplane designed for that specific purpose. To achieve such performance in a military aircraft, with entirely different design requirements, might be very difficult indeed. But at North American Aviation, Inc, designers were about to try.

North American, an industry giant now part of Rockwell International, was incorporated in 1928, and in 1935 built its main plant and corporate headquarters in Inglewood, California, on a site now adjacent to the Los Angeles International Airport. During World War 2, the company's B-25 medium bomber and P-51 fighter had gained immortality for exceptional combat performance in every major theatre.

On 3 February 1949, NAA engineers began to explore the possibilities of achieving supersonic performance with the F-86 Sabre, a subsonic day fighter first flown 1 October 1947. They hoped to increase its maximum speed to at least Mach 1, because the Sabre had reached Mach 0.87 while setting a new world speed record on 15 September 1948.

(And also about then, engineers in the aircraft design bureau led by Artem Mikoyan and Mikhail Gurevich began development of the I-350 prototype, the Soviet Union's first aircraft with supersonic potential. After major design modifications, including installation of two afterburning engines, the I-350 evolved into production MiG-19 fighters that served in numerous air forces, and were formidable opponents in air-to-air combat.)

Previous experience at near-sonic speed was the domain of aircraft built purely for research, like the Bell XS-1 (later X-1) series and the Douglas D-558-I Skystreak. The aerodynamics of high-speed flight were imperfectly understood, with more data gaps than data. John Leland (Lee) Atwood, then NAA President, said that when the company began its studies to boost F-86 performance to Mach 1, 'Relatively little was known. No aircraft had been flown at supersonic speeds except momentarily in dives by aircraft such as the F-86, and systematic instrumentation to determine the forces, pressures, drags, lifts had not been well worked out; in fact, the knowledge was rudimentary. Certain wind tunnels of small size had been developed and built to blow air at supersonic speeds, and . . . small-scale model tests had been made . . . We had no tunnel, at least none that we had access to, which would maintain steady flow and what we might call transonic speeds or, say, Mach one; we had fragmentary data.'

Atwood can be forgiven for not citing the XS-1 accomplishment of supersonic flight months before design work began on the 'sonic' F-86. He may have been thinking in terms of operational military aircraft, not research types. Further, the first and second XS-1 had completed only about 20 flights at supersonic speed between 14 October 1947, and 3 February 1949. The total of all XS-1 supersonic flight time was less than one hour, hardly a firm foundation for technology.

Steps toward the Supersonic

Given an existing aircraft, little can be done to

The mid-day California sun glints off the faired contours of the first YF-100A (52-5754) in flight high above the desert floor near the Air Force Flight Test Center, Edwards AFB. Notice the vertical tail layout, with its high aspect ratio, narrow-chord rudder almost the full height of the fin, and the fuel system vent hooking downward from the fin tip fairing
(AFFTC)

achieve major performance gains without major design changes. NAA's first study—increasing the F-86 wing sweepback to 45°—showed little gain; fuselage drag rise was the governing factor. Modifying the fuselage reduced its drag a bit, but even a substantial reduction would have made little difference, given the steep drag rise near sonic speed. Further, the Sabre lacked power to overcome that drag increase, then common to all aircraft.

Traditionally, airplane designers always look for more engine power, or thrust, preferably with a concomitant reduction in fuel consumption, to assist in reaching the goal of improved performance. As experience with the relatively new jet powerplants increased, and research uncovered more about the factors that determined performance, designers did achieve higher thrust and lower fuel consumption in lighter engines.

The Allison Division of General Motors, a major producer of jet engines, was first to offer a potential powerplant for the F-86 redesign: an upgraded J35 turbojet (itself originally a General Electric Co design rated at about 4,000 lb (1814 kg) thrust, and later built in second-source production by both Chevrolet and Allison Divisions of GM). The 9,000-lb (4082-kg) thrust rating of the Allison J35 nearly doubled the thrust of the standard GE J47 engines in the Sabre. It encouraged NAA to begin new studies in April 1949.

In August, GE proposed an advanced J47 turbojet, with 9,400 lb (4263 kg) thrust and with afterburning, a relatively new phenomenon, to increase maximum thrust to about 13,000 lb (5896 kg). (Afterburning is an accurate description. Fuel injected into the tailpipe of the engine immediately ignites and burns fiercely, adding its thermal energy to that of the hot engine exhaust. It produces a major increase in thrust, at the expense of a big increase in fuel consumption. It pays off in maximum-weight

Prototype airplanes are clean and show purity of line, with never a hint that in a few years they will be festooned with bombs and rockets and napalm tanks, and their smooth and polished skins hidden by coarse gray, green, and brown camouflage paint. In the background, the chase pilot in an F-86 Sabre reassures George Welch in the first YF-100A that all doors are tightly closed and it's okay to begin the next test run
(AFFTC)

takeoffs, and in combat performance.) The new engine, about the size of standard J47s, did not require that the Sabre fuselage cross-section be enlarged.

But by then, designers had decided that the F-86D all-weather interceptor—a quite-different version of the standard F-86A Sabre—was a better bet for sonic performance. On 14 September 1949, they began new drawings and studies around the advanced J47. Their calculations predicted a speed of Mach 1.03 in level flight at 35,000 ft (10,670 m) altitude.

Then followed a cycle of designs, proposals, rejections and redesigns that culminated in the final layouts and performance calculations that defined the Super Sabre. There were three important phases.

First was the Advanced F-86D. An unsolicited proposal to the Air Force (Report NA-50-859, of 25 August 1950) described it as a single-place, transonic, all-weather interceptor, with a 45-degree wing sweep angle and an area-ruled fuselage. The Air Force rejected it, suggesting that NAA design an advanced day fighter instead.

Second was the Advanced F-86E, proposed in January 1951. It retained wings, tail and powerplant of the earlier Advanced F-86D, but had a redesigned slimmer fuselage and a nose inlet. The Air Force rejected this one also, but indicated that NAA might want to rework it into an air-superiority fighter. (The air-superiority defensive mission was to clear the air of attacking enemy aircraft. The offensive mission was to clear the air above areas of tactical operations, preparing for forward movement of air-ground combat operations.)

Third was a further reworking of both first and second proposals, retaining the 45-degree sweepback of earlier studies, and leading to the new designation of Sabre 45. It combined features from both the Advanced F-86D and F-86E with a new and

promising Pratt & Whitney turbojet, the J57-P-1, rated at 15,000 lb (6803 kg) thrust in afterburner. Report NA-51-451 of 14 May 1951, described an air-superiority fighter armed with four 20mm T-130 cannon. Estimated combat gross weight was 23,750 lb (10,771 kg); takeoff gross weight, 28,632 lb (12,987 kg). Performance calculations predicted a speed of Mach 1.3 at 35,000 ft (10,670 m), and a combat radius of 580 nautical miles (1073 km). This third redesign was the true basis for the F-100 Super Sabre.

NAA asked the Air Force to fund two prototypes, one for aerodynamic testing, the other for armament development. That way, the company argued, production could follow rapidly and operational USAF squadrons would have early availability of combat-ready airplanes.

The Air Force Council, meeting that October, strongly suggested that a further revision of the Sabre 45 be ordered, even though there were reservations about its relative complexity and cost. The Aircraft and Weapons Board thought two prototypes were too few to achieve early operational dates, and recommended that the airplane be bought in quantity before its flight-testing was completed. This procedure—known variously as the Cook-Craigie plan or the principle of concurrency—ran the risk of a major modification programme down the line. But because there was a hot war in Korea and the Cold

The YF-100A, coasting above the AFFTC, typifies a first-generation supersonic fighter: sweptback wings, low-set tail, powerful engine, inboard ailerons. It was almost the correct formula; but one factor was missing from the equations
(AFFTC)

RIGHT
Chase pilots saw this view of the YF-100A as they flew tight formation to check the condition of landing-gear doors, speed brake, access panels and other closures. It makes you realize what a pretty airplane the designers had created
(AFFTC)

War was well underway, early operational dates were a driving requirement for new weapons systems. The Air Force Council agreed with the Board's recommendations.

Concurrency was a scheduled, deliberate overlap of research and development with production. During the late 1940s and early 1950s USAF Generals Laurence C Craigie, Deputy Chief of Staff/Development, and Orval R Cook, DCS/Materiel, had studied ways to reduce the lead time between programme starts and initial operational capability (IOC) date. They suggested building prototypes from the start with production

USAF

tooling, but limiting production aircraft quantities. Faults found during test flights could be fixed early, it was argued, and production could easily be accelerated.

It's accepted now that concurrency didn't work as planned. The risk became actuality, resulting in expensive modifications after many airplanes had been built, or were well along in production. And concurrency did not necessarily accelerate delivery of operational aircraft to user units.

The Air Force decision-making process for ordering the Sabre 45 took about six months. Meantime, NAA continued engineering design in a company-funded effort. It paid off; on 1 November 1951, the USAF issued letter contract AF33(600)-6545 authorizing NAA to build two Sabre 45 prototypes, and to begin engineering design, production tooling, and purchasing of long lead-time items needed for eventual production of about 94 more.

Eight days later, the Air Force completed its formal inspection of the mockup. Attending officers asked for three major changes: single-point refuelling to reduce turnaround time, modifications to the artificial feel of the control system, and 275 rounds of ammunition for each 20 mm cannon instead of the 200 in the mockup. The Mockup Board decided against the first, recommended continued studies of the second, and made the third mandatory. Two mandatory changes were added: hydraulic control systems were to be separated to reduce the chance of simultaneous battle damage, and the tailskid was to be removed, saving 60 pounds (27.2 kg).

On 7 December 1951, the Air Force officially designated the Sabre 45 as the F-100A, first of the Century Series of fighters.

Honing the Super Sabre

A North American document states '. . . it was necessary to redesign the prototype' after the mockup inspection. The fuselage was reshaped with an even-higher fineness ratio and an extended clamshell canopy. The horizontal tail was lowered below the chord plane of the wing. On 23 June 1952, the Air Force approved the alterations, but told NAA to study the installation of external bombs and rockets, and to substitute non-self-sealing tanks for existing bladder tanks to save 400 lb (181 kg) in weight.

(It is dumbfounding that a military service, buying military airplanes, often eliminated the very features that made those airplanes more combat-worthy: self-sealing tanks from the F-100; cannon, fuel-tank explosion suppressors, and passive electronic countermeasures from the F-105; guns from the F-4, among other examples.)

Meantime, generalized wind-tunnel tests and theoretical studies at NACA (National Advisory Committee for Aeronautics, predecessor of today's NASA, the National Aeronautics and Space Administration) and elsewhere hinted at further performance gains. NAA was eager to learn anything that might help, because some of those new tests also indicated the F-100A probably could not meet its guaranteed speed of Mach 1.3.

NAA engineers made three significant changes to reduce drag and increase thrust. First, they thinned the inlet lip to a fine edge, in line with NACA research, to improve the intake flow and deliver higher-energy air to the engine. Second, they lengthened the nose by nine inches, further increasing fineness ratio to reduce drag. Third, they halved

The eighth production F-100A (52-5763), with AFFTC insigne below the cockpit, rests on the hard lakebed at the Center between flight-test assignments. It has the vertical tail of early production A models, changed from the geometry of the YF-100A to be shorter, with lower aspect ratio and smaller rudder of greater chord and shorter span. The fuel vent has been moved, with its fairing, from the tip to a point further down the vertical surface. Note also the non-retractable tail bumper. Sometimes the angle of attack input required with sweptback wings was large enough, or sudden enough, to bang the tail on the runway. Hence the bumper
(AFFTC)

the thickness/chord (t/c) ratio of horizontal and vertical tails, to three and one-half percent. The third change, scheduled for production aircraft, was made too late to be incorporated on the two YF-100A prototypes.

The Super Sabre's wing aerodynamics derived from the attempts to make the F-86 supersonic. On the drawing board, designers had studied a further sweep of the basic F-86 wing box structure, that portion bounded by upper and lower wing surfaces, and the front and rear spars. They gained 10°, increasing the sweep to a 45° angle measured at the quarter-chord line. Increasing the sweep that way also thinned the airfoil aerodynamically, reducing the Sabre's 10 per cent t/c ratio to the Super Sabre's 8.2 per cent. The addition of a glove airfoil section to the leading edge reduced the wing t/c ratio further to seven per cent. With these changes, the wing area increased to 376 sq ft (35 m^2). Wing span was 36.78 ft (11.2 m^2) and the taper ratio (tip chord/root chord) was 0.25.

Inboard ailerons reduced wing twist from aileron deflection, and gave the F-100 a high roll rate at Mach 1, approximating 200°/sec. No wing flaps were used, but the leading edge had five-segment automatic slats, actuated by air loads. The slats increased lift for takeoff, delayed wing buffet, improved lateral control near the stall, and permitted tighter turns.

An oval nose inlet and intake duct improved the pilot's view for landing, and passed beneath the pilot without producing an abnormally large fuselage cross-section. The thin inlet lip reduced the drag and increased engine efficiency, adding about 50 knots (92.5 km/h) to the F-100A maximum speed, and emphasizing the importance of design details.

Some sweptwing aircraft had a dangerous, even deadly, tendency to pitch up suddenly and violently following a stall, because the usual location of the horizontal tail placed it in the disturbed wake from the wing and reduced its effectiveness. The F-100 one-piece, all-movable horizontal 'slab' tail was deliberately placed very low on the fuselage to prevent pitch-up by keeping the tail clear of the wing wake at high angles of attack. (A low tail had been used earlier on the French Sud-Est 2410 *Grognard* close-support aircraft prototype that flew in April 1950. The slab tail had been developed and tested on a Curtiss XP-42 by NACA in 1943 and later was specified by NACA for the XS-1.)

The speed brake, faired into the fuselage belly ahead of the main landing-gear well, could be used at any flight speed with little trim change in pitch. In

29 October 1953: 'Pete' Everest, flying the YF-100A to establish a new world speed record, zips through a timing trap on the Salton Sea, California, course. He's little more than 100 ft above the desert floor and speeding at more than 750 mph
(Smithsonian Institution Photo No 87–740)

combat manoeuvres, the brake decelerated the F-100 rapidly so that it could turn more tightly. A drag chute reduced landing rolls, and lessened the wear on brakes and tyres.

The powerplant was a single Pratt & Whitney J57-P-7 turbojet with afterburner. Military power rating at sea level was 9,220 lb (4182 kg) of static thrust (measured on a test stand, not in the airplane installation). Afterburning increased that thrust to 14,800 lb (6713 kg). The afterburner had a two-position variable-area nozzle for best efficiency: closed for normal operations, opened for afterburner use. Main fuel supply was in the fuselage; five non-self-sealing bladder tanks held a total of 750 US gallons (2838 litres). Two underwing drop tanks held 275 US gal (1041 lit) each.

Armament for production airplanes was four T-160 (later M39) 20-mm automatic cannon, two on each side of the fuselage below the cockpit, each with a 275-round supply of ammunition. The A-4 gunsight computed the lead automatically, aided by range information from a simple radar antenna mounted on the inside of the upper nose inlet lip.

On 26 August 1952, the USAF increased its order to 273 airplanes and a static test article. Three days later, an NAA status report noted that the engineers had spent 984,369 hours to date on design of the prototype YF-100A, and were ready to release 4,118 drawings to manufacturing. At the same time, work was progressing on the design of the F-100A, the production configuration. On 30 January 1953, the second batch of drawings—5,701 of them, including YF-100A drawings that were applicable—was released. As the scheduled first flight drew near, NAA and the Air Force agreed that two prototypes would not suffice for the test programme, so the first ten production F-100As were designated as test aircraft. Experience had taught that flight-test time was logged slowly, because of instrumentation requirements, data reduction time—this was in the days before computers—and aircraft and engine maintenance. USAF's Wright Air Development Center (WADC), programme overseers, estimated the tests would require about 540 flight hours, at a rate of about six hours per month per test airplane; so 12 would be needed to complete the programme before December 1954. By then, North American should have delivered 88 production aircraft.

The two prototypes were assigned to obtain initial engine performance, check stability and control characteristics, and validate the armament installation. The third, fourth and fifth test aircraft—actually production numbers 1, 2 and 3—were to test the production powerplant installation, stability and control, and performance and cruise-control, respectively.

Two Beers for Mach One

Completed on schedule 24 April, the first YF-100A

Wheels throwing fine sand from the dry lakebed, the first YF-100A begins a takeoff run at the Air Force Flight Test Center . . .
(Maene Collection)

was readied for flight at North American's flight-test operation at the North Base of the Air Force Flight Test Center (AFFTC), Edwards Air Force Base. Edwards lay in the Mojave desert 100 miles northeast of Los Angeles and the North American plant, and west of Rogers Dry Lake, an enormous area of clay and silt baked to concrete hardness by the California sun. The lakebed bore a number of five-mile long runways and one that stretched more than eight miles, necessary for the rocket-propelled experimental aircraft then in flight-test. Further, AFFTC was far from any population concentration, contributing to the safety and security of USAF flight operations.

25 May 1953, like most days at Edwards, was bright, clear, cloudless. The Super Sabre was ready, and so was NAA test pilot George S ('Wheaties') Welch. (On 7 December 1941, Welch was one of five young lieutenants from the 47th Pursuit Squadron at Hawaii's Haleiwa airfield. Off base when the Japanese struck, they drove to Haleiwa and managed their own air battles in Curtiss P-36 and P-40 fighters. Welch claimed four victories.)

Lieutenant Colonel Frank K (Pete) Everest, Jr, Chief of AFFTC's Flight Test Operations Laboratory, planned to fly a Sabre to chase the YF-100A's maiden flight. At the briefing, he and Welch discussed exceeding Mach 1 on the first flight; each was confident it could be done. Welch said that if he did it, he'd buy the beer. And then, as if to underscore his confidence, he raised his offer: 'Buy you two beers, Pete!'

Airborne first, Everest circled to watch Welch make taxi runs preparatory to takeoff. Then he closed on Welch's wing as the Super Sabre, afterburner roaring, began its takeoff roll from Rogers Dry Lake. It lifted off at about 150 knots; the duo climbed to 20,000 feet (6100 m) and levelled off while Welch checked the speed brakes. Then they climbed to 35,000 ft (10,670 m); Welch lit the afterburner, and Everest pushed his power control to get full thrust for his F-86. Both accelerated side-by-side briefly, until Everest noted that he had reached Mach 0.9, maximum speed for an F-86 in top condition. He watched Welch and the YF-100A pull away and speed out of sight.

He continued to monitor Welch's transmissions, waiting for the signal of success. And then Welch shouted, 'Bingo!', the agreed code indicating that the YF-100A had passed Mach 1. Everest thumbed his mike switch and answered laconically, 'OK, two beers.'

That first flight lasted 57 minutes; the second, later that day, lasted 20. The YF-100A passed Mach 1 in level flight during both. Enthusiastically, NAA boasted that the YF-100A was the world's first operational supersonic airplane, a claim founded on the loose interpretation of 'operational'.

On 27 May, Welch flew the YF-100A twice; on 29 May, four times. The first flight that day ended with the first landing on the hard-surface runway; all previous takeoffs and landings had used the lake bed. On the eighth and ninth flights, Welch sensed some rudder flutter, anticipated because of a similar encounter on F-86s. Hydraulic rudder dampers, added after the flight, solved the problem, and later dive tests (Flights 37 and 41) exceeded Mach 1.1 speeds without any flutter. By the end of June, flight tests had included a preliminary evaluation of both lateral and directional (rolling and pitching) dynamic stability.

But by then, top USAF officers at both WADC and AFFTC suspected the YF-100A was not as good as contractor reports indicated. NAA had aroused Air Force suspicion by what was perceived as a shorter-than-usual Phase I test programme at the isolated North Base, by reporting only minor maintenance, and by submitting reports of spectacular performance. It also appeared to the Air Force, according to official documents, that North American was not just saying the YF-100 was ready for production; it

. . . and rolls past the photographer on its way to liftoff (Pickett Collection)

actually was accelerating production at the factory. The Air Force wanted to uncover any deficiencies as soon as possible, to avoid an expensive modification programme, and to deliver operational aircraft as rapidly as possible, consistent with safety.

Suspicions aside, the first YF-100A actually was achieving spectacular performance, and by 5 July had demonstrated satisfactory handling in high-speed dives from 30,000 ft (9145 m), at speeds as high as Mach 1.4. The following day, Welch's test flight reached Mach 1.44 in a long dive from 51,000 to 20,000 ft (15,545–6096 m), as fast as the prototype ever would go.

Although Welch was the designated contractor test pilot for Phase I flights, the prototype also was flown by NAA pilots Daniel Darnell and Joseph Lynch. Together, they logged 43 flights.

On 11 August, WADC commander Major General Albert Boyd made the first USAF flight, joining Lieutenant Colonels William F Barnes, Richard Johnson, and 'Pete' Everest in preliminary evaluations of the YF-100. It was an unofficial beginning of Phase II flight testing by that service (Appendix 5 details the phases of flight test for a new USAF military aircraft).

Boyd and his counterpart at AFFTC, Brigadier General J Stanley Holtoner, insisted that Air Force Phase II testing begin as soon as possible, and finish before May 1954. Everest was project pilot; his team included Boyd, Colonel Horace A Hanes, Majors Arthur Murray, Robert L Stephens, and Charles E Yeager. Captain Herbert Z (Zeke) Hopkins was Everest's deputy. The Phase II programme—scheduled to begin 11 August 1953—actually began 3 September and lasted through 17 September. It required 39 flights—19 hr 42 min of logged time—on the first YF-100A (AF52-5754).

Fast, Fun to Fly, But . . .

The USAF test pilots said that the Super Sabre outperformed any other production fighter in the USAF. They believed it had good potential, and could be made into a useful weapon system. But, they added, it's unacceptable operationally for three major reasons: poor visibility over the nose during takeoff and landing, neutral and negative static longitudinal stability in high-speed level flight, and poor low-speed handling.

It climbs slowly, said the pilots; it takes 16 min to get to 40,000 ft (12,190 m) without afterburning. Visibility forward in the climb is poor. Lateral and directional damping are unsatisfactory at all altitudes. It wants to yaw and pitch near the stall, and the left wing drops uncontrollably. Landing is more difficult than with any other production fighter; response to control inputs is slow, touchdown speeds are high. Approach and landing are dangerous at night. It's a poor gun platform, and difficult to fly in formation.

Everest personally was not happy with the Super Sabre, and said so in his official assessment of the YF-100A's flying qualities and potential for development as a weapons system. The experienced USAF engineering test pilot team had found many problems, and Everest recommended that the F-100 not be delivered to operating commands until fixes had been made.

North American, stung by the criticism, objected vigorously. So did some USAF officers. It was then suggested—by whom is not known—that the YF-100 be flown by pilots from Tactical Air Command, future operator of the F-100, to get their views. They flew it, loved it, and only complained that it wasn't fast enough. Everest's report was pigeon-holed, and USAF Headquarters ruled procurement would continue as planned.

As soon as the Air Force returned the first prototype to NAA, the company began an accelerated development programme to evaluate new components and modifications. The first production F-

100A was completed by the factory three weeks ahead of schedule, on 25 September 1953, accepted by the Air Force 26 October, and first flown 29 October. Welch again was the pilot, and during the 30-minute test flight, he accelerated through the speed of sound. Now three Super Sabres were flying: the first prototype YF-100A, the second prototype—which had made its first flight 14 October—and the first production airplane.

Run for the Roses

Although the supersonic Super Sabre was the fastest US military aircraft, the official world speed record was held by the Douglas XF4D-1 Skyray, made by a rival company for a rival service, the US Navy. Lieutenant Commander James B Verdin had flown the Skyray at 753.4 mph over a three-kilometre straight course, beating by a substantial margin the previous British-held records.

The Air Force and North American wanted that record. To gain it, the Super Sabre had to top the existing mark by at least one per cent, which meant averaging more than 760.9 mph during two runs in each direction over the course. The Air Force assigned the record attempt to Everest, the most experienced USAF pilot on the type, and the first prototype YF-100A was groomed for the runs. The three-kilometre course was flown over the Salton Sea in California's Imperial Valley. Everest made the required four runs at the best possible speed, faster than the XF4D-1, but not enough faster.

Then North American suggested an attempt over a 15-km straight course because, for that distance, the official record of 707 mph was held by an F-86. The F-100 could easily exceed that speed and set a new world mark. And under the rules of the *Federation Aéronautique Internationale*, the certificating agency of record flights, the fastest speed over either course was the official world speed record. So a 15-km course was planned for the Salton Sea. Old automobile tyres were piled beyond each end of the course, to be set afire to generate smoke markers for Everest's runs.

On 29 October, the same day the first production F-100A flew, Everest and the record crew waited until the temperature had topped 85°F and began to drop. (Record attempts were helped by a hot day. On a 59°F day, the speed of sound at sea level is about 763 mph; on a 90°F day, it's about 786 mph. Aircraft speed is limited by an abrupt drag rise at a specific Mach number, say, 0.9. Multiply the speed of sound by the limiting Mach number of the airplane to find out how fast it might go. Because 786 × 0.9 is higher than 763 × 0.9, a hot day is better for speed record attempts.)

Everest took off, lined up on the column of smoke from the burning tyres, and lit the afterburner to accelerate into the first speed trap. He flew at about 75 ft (23 m) altitude, buffeted by low-level turbulence, and flashed across the finish line and the second speed trap which recorded his time off the course. Rules prohibited a climb to a safe altitude in order to make his turn to re-enter the course; the intent was to keep pilots from diving to pick up speed. He made a wide and flat turn, still just a few dozen feet off the ground, and headed for the entry trap. About 42 seconds later he flashed over the exit, and zoomed into a series of victory rolls.

By mealtime that evening, Everest had been told that he had set a new world speed record: 755.149 mph (equivalent to Mach 0.97). One run exceeded 767 mph (Mach 0.98), faster than the Skyray's mark. Before 1953 ended, Everest's record had in turn been exceeded, although not officially, by the first production F-100A, in all respects but one a stock production model. That one exception arose out of concerns about the potential for flutter of the thin horizontal tail designed for production airplanes. It was a one-piece slab surface with only three-and-one-half per cent thickness ratio. 'Inadequately tested,' said NAA engineers, and changed back to a seven-per cent-thick surface on this one airplane.

The tail drag didn't make much difference. NAA had guaranteed a top speed of Mach 1.3 for production F-100As with thin tails. On 8 December, during USAF flight tests, the first F-100A—with its thicker tail—reached Mach 1.345 in afterburner in level flight at an altitude of 35,000 ft (10,670 m), and met its guarantee.

The shell of the second YF-100A prototype, camouflaged and improperly numbered—its tail could read 0-25755—is perched forlornly on brick pylons at Keesler AFB, Mississippi
(USAF/Nancy Paull)

Chapter 2
Prototype to Production

Many lessons of the Korean war have been forgotten, but some were still fresh in the minds of Air Force leadership in 1953. The war had ground to a halt on 27 July that year; within a few months, reviews of the conflict spurred 'new looks' at the doctrines of air power. That air war had become a tactical one soon after the B-29 Superfortresses of Strategic Air Command had pounded the very few major targets into rubble. Eventually, air superiority, interdiction, and close support of ground troops became the three major airpower tasks, influencing the thinking and action of USAF leadership long afterwards.

President Dwight D Eisenhower's administration also reconsidered its policies. On 12 January 1954, Secretary of State John Foster Dulles said that local defences '. . . must be reinforced by the further deterrent of massive retaliatory power.' Dulles' combat pointed to increased emphasis on nuclear-weapon delivery, a mission then exclusive to SAC. Now, it was politic for Tactical Air Command, re-created on 1 December 1950, to develop its own force to deliver nuclear weapons.

For that, TAC needed a fighter-bomber with major performance gains over the Lockheed F-80C and Republic F-84G that had borne the interdiction burden in Korea. Additionally, the US Mutual Development Assistance Program required fighter-bombers to re-arm the air forces of friendly countries. Had it been available, the new Republic F-84F, with sweptback wings and superior performance, might have filled both needs, and this story would have been different. But the Thunderstreak was seriously delayed because of problems with its Wright-built J65 jet engine.

Except for the F-100, there was no immediate candidate for a fighter-bomber that could deliver nuclear weapons. And so, on 31 December 1953, the Air Council redirected Super Sabre production; the last 70 F-100As on order were to be modified to fighter-bombers and redesignated F-100C. The fourth production F-100A (52-5759) was chosen for modification to the 'dry-wing' prototype of the F-100C.

Production of the F-100A was well along. NAA engineers had gained more confidence in the new thin horizontal tail with its 3.5 per cent t/c ratio. But calculations had shown that its critical flutter speed was about 90 knots (167 km/h) lower than for the 7 per cent section. They surmised that tail flutter, if it occurred, would be sudden and catastrophic.

NAA and the Air Force developed a test programme to 'fly' the horizontal tail on a rocket-propelled sled on the 10,000-ft (3050 m) high speed research track at AFFTC. The complete horizontal tail assembly, including its hydraulic system and the connecting torque tube, was tested at speeds as high as Mach 1.216, and was, after some failures and modifications, proven free from any tendency to fail catastrophically in flutter. That hurdle was cleared during December 1953, and the thin surface was scheduled for installation on all production F-100 models.

It also was retrofitted to the first production F-100A and, on 11 March 1954, that plane was flown faster than any Super Sabre before then. Entering a steep dive from an altitude of 50,000 ft (15,240 m) and a speed of Mach 0.97, and with full afterburner thrust, the F-100A touched Mach 1.55. The tail stood up to the high stress of that flight test.

The production jump from the F-100A to the F-100C bypassed the B model, planned to have a more powerful engine, more efficient engine aerodynamics, and an improved airframe. Eventually, it became such a different airplane that it received a new designation; as the F-107A, it led a short but interesting and productive life (Chapter 10).

Six nearly complete F-100A aircraft were pulled off the production line and modified during September 1954, with installations of photo-reconnaissance equipment. Without armament, but

with cameras in awkward fuselage blisters, the six 'Slick Chicks' also led productive lives (Chapter 10).

The seventh production F-100A (52-5762) poses in profile during an engineering flight test above the California mountains near Palmdale
(Smithsonian Institution Photo No 87–743)

RIGHT
In a steep climb away from the North American base at Palmdale, the fifth production F-100A (52-5760) shows its modified vertical fin, extended as part of the fixes incorporated after the Welch accident. This plane was assigned to NAA Engineering Flight Test, then flew in Phase I and III tests at AFFTC
(Rockwell International)

First Signs of Trouble

TAC accepted its first F-100A on 18 September. By then, Air Force pilots had experienced stability and control problems with the airplane. The vertical tail didn't seem large enough to maintain directional stability, and there were differences of opinion within NAA on its required dimensions. Both YF-100As had been designed and built with large vertical tail surfaces; when the Super Sabre went into production, the area was reduced. But now, North American engineers were concerned about the Air Force reports and, worried about the potential for serious trouble, had begun a series of experimental flights on F-100As with different and modified control systems, trying to find solutions.

Company engineering test pilots had reported more than a year earlier that the F-100 had stability problems. North American pilot Joseph Lynch, after returning from his first flight of an F-100A equipped with wing tanks, commented acidly, 'The only time the ball was in the centre was when it was passing through to go to the other side.' Complaints about inadequate stability also were voiced in the final report of USAF Phase II flight tests.

By August 1954, NAA had extended the wingtips of the dry-wing prototype F-100C (-5759) 12 inches (30.4 cm) on each side, improving its roll characteristics and decreased stalling speed somewhat. By 4 October, flight tests had shown those extensions to be desirable for all production airplanes.

Meantime, company engineers had recommended a series of flight tests on a production F-100A equipped with a taller and enlarged vertical tail surface. The schedule called for the new surface to begin its inflight validation programme on 27 September.

The first TAC F-100A airplane was delivered 1 October, just as it had been built, with the smaller vertical tail, and entered operational service with the 436th Fighter-Day Squadron of the 479th Fighter-Day Group, George AFB, California. It was clearly understood that they were for nothing more than an introduction to the experience of supersonic flight. There were tacit assumptions: the F-100As would not be flown to the limits of performance envelopes, they were only interim aircraft, and they would be replaced by modified F-100As.

From Disaster, New Knowledge

On the morning of 12 October 1954, George Welch

FW-760
U.S. AIR FORCE
25760

walked out to the ninth production F-100A (AF52-5764). He and that aircraft had been assigned to one of the continuing tests to demonstrate maximum-G at maximum Mach number for the production airplanes. His flight test card called for a maximum-G symmetrical pullup at 23,700 ft (7224 m) from a supersonic dive at the highest attainable Mach number, imposing an airload more than seven times (probably 7.33) the force of gravity. That condition is one of the worst possible; it burdens the airplane with an extraordinary loading that stresses the structure severely. If an airplane gets through the test smoothly and controllably, engineers feel that the worst is over. But the worst lay ahead.

Welch taxied out, called for takeoff clearance, lifted the plane off the Palmdale runway at 1046 hr, and climbed to altitude. He called the ground station at 1100 hr to say that he was over Mojave at 45,000 feet (13,720 m), beginning the dive toward his reference point, Rosamond Dry Lake.

The copilot of a Boeing B-47 cruising at 25,000 feet (7620 m) above Palmdale spotted a high contrail, and he and the B-47 pilot estimated its altitude at 45,000 ft (13,720 m). The sun glinted off the banking wing of the tiny aircraft just visible ahead of the condensation trail as it rolled to begin a hurtling dive toward the bright sands of the valley. The bomber crew watched as it passed to their right, several miles away, still diving. In this area, they knew, that's somebody's routine test flight. And then, to their horror, the distant airplane suddenly blossomed orange and black. As they reached for mikes to call in the accident, the B-47 crewmen were looking for good chutes, and saw one as they called. But a dying pilot hung in the shroud lines.

Palmdale tower called North American flight test to report that two chutes (one later turned out to be the brake parachute) had been seen at 20,000 ft (6098 m) above Rosamond Lake. Fearing a mid-air collision, Murray O'Toole called the NAA pilots' ready room on the intercom: 'Welch is in trouble; two parachutes reported.' NAA test pilots Bob Baker and Bud Pogue ran to a Navion and were airborne within a few minutes. They spotted the descending chutes and saw Welch's body hit the ground. Landing alongside, they ran to help. Welch was still alive, but had been fatally injured; the airplane had broken at the cockpit area, and chunks of metal like shrapnel had torn his body.

The wreckage was in tiny pieces, scattered over acres. North American teams searched the area, photographed it from the air and from eye level. They

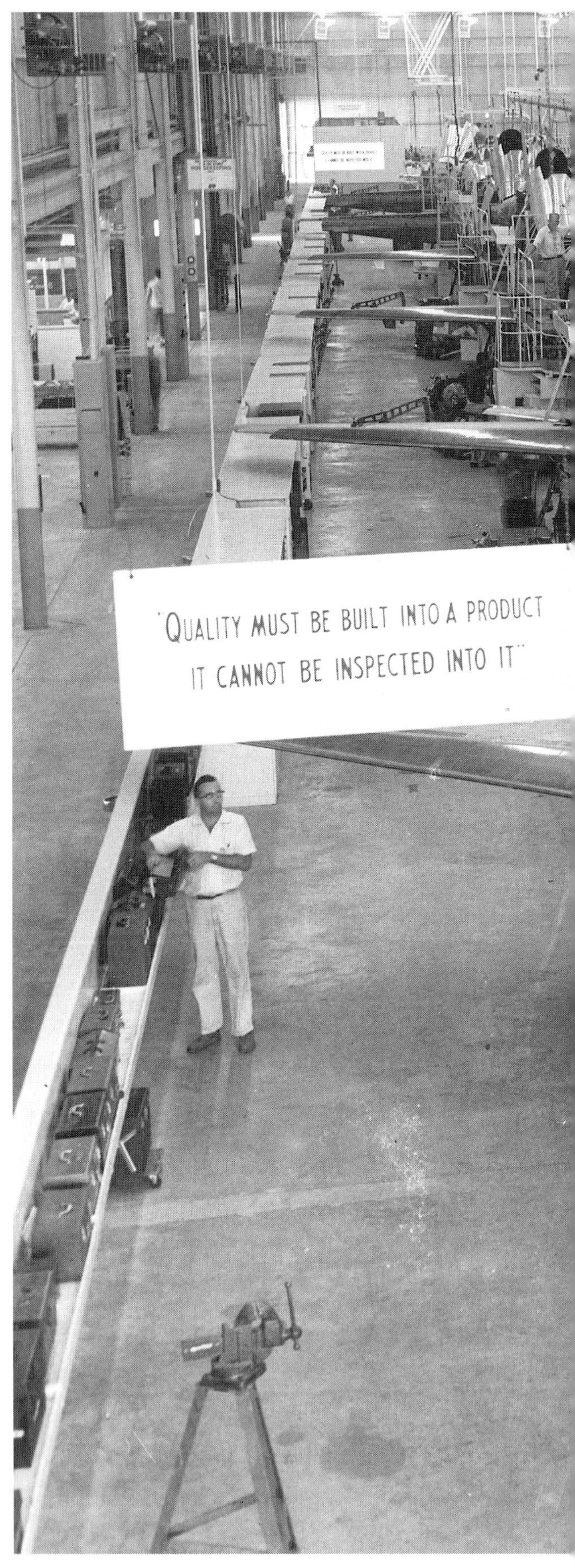

'QUALITY MUST BE BUILT INTO A PRODUCT
IT CANNOT BE INSPECTED INTO IT''

F-100A No 140, complete with recently modified vertical tail, is shown at the head of the production line. A censor obliterated the number 140 on the fuselage side, but missed the number on the protective paper on the windshield. None of the Super Sabres on the rear production line has yet received its modified vertical tail
(Rockwell International)

The 20th production F-100A (52-5775) was assigned to the Wright Air Development Center of the USAF Air Research and Development Command for engineering flight tests. It has the low tail of early production A models (Peter M Bowers/Maene Collection)

identified and plotted positions of pieces, interviewed people who said they had seen what happened, talked long with the B-47 crew. Then they loaded the wreckage into trucks and took it back to study.

On 8 November, a noted Royal Air Force officer—Air Commodore Geoffrey D Stephenson—crashed and was killed at Eglin AFB, Florida, when his F-100A went out of control. The following day, Major Frank N Emory's Super Sabre (52-5771) went wild during a practice gunnery mission, part of the Phase IV testing, over Nevada. Emory ejected and landed safely.

On 10 November, the Air Force grounded the entire fleet. There had been six major accidents with two fatalities, and the answers were no closer than when the first was reported.

In a Shadow a Clue

Welch's airplane had been heavily instrumented for the test flight, as were all of the NAA test fleet. All instruments were running when the plane disintegrated. One ciné camera, recording images of the horizontal tail during the pullup, continued to operate briefly on its own inertia after the airplane began breaking up and camera power was lost. When its film was processed and projected, it revealed the first evidence of what might have happened. The shadow of the vertical tail raced across the horizontal surface, as if the airplane had yawed violently and rapidly, or as if there had been a catastrophic case of tail flutter.

There was no way to be certain; but it might be possible to simulate whatever gyrations produced the motion of that shadow. So the engineers first checked solar astronomical data, and recreated the Sun's position relative to the airplane. With a spotlight to replace the Sun, and a scale model of the F-100 to manipulate and photograph, they painstakingly positioned and repositioned the model until they had reconstructed the shadow of the vertical tail, and its motion across the horizontal surface.

After the investigators had exhausted their lists of items to check, one engineer suggested that NAA photo-lab technicians take another look at the film from the recording oscillograph mounted in the cockpit. That film had been badly light-struck when the recording camera smashed into the ground, shattering its case. The talented NAA darkroom crew had obtained usable results in the past from bad cases of under- and over-exposed film. This time, they had only five inches of light-struck film to work with, and those precious inches could be priceless. Sliver by

This short-tailed Super Sabre (53-1539) was the 34th production aircraft. Assigned to the Wright Air Development Center, it was photographed at McConnell AFB, Kansas
(USAF/Pickett Collection)

sliver, using stronger and stronger developers, they meticulously processed the strip and printed the results, copying and recopying until useful prints were obtained. The oscillograph had monitored control positions and forces; it had filmed the recording instruments which now could be read, analysed and interpreted.

It has been widely reported that Welch's accident was due to the then-new phenomenon of inertial roll coupling. Although the F-100 did demonstrate that characteristic, and often violently, that was not the case in Welch's accident; post-accident analysis showed that roll angle at the pull-up was not a factor.

Welch had rolled into his dive from level flight, a routine procedure. But as he did so, the ball of the turn-and-bank indicator went off centre, indicating that the F-100 was yawed. And although Welch levelled his wings for the dive, the ball never returned to centre.

Remember that NAA engineering test pilots had reported deficiencies in the directional stability of the F-100. The aerodynamic forces that provide directional stability decrease as Mach number, lift coefficient, and yaw angle increase. When Welch began his pull-up, every parameter of disaster came together in a split second. The F-100 was at a high Mach number, a high angle of attack, and was still yawed. Inexorably, the airplane yawed further, beyond the ability of the vertical tail to compensate and then, suddenly and wildly, swung out of control. The supersonic airstream blasted the Super Sabre, literally blowing it apart.

The fix was classically simple, and tragically ironic. The F-100A needed a larger and taller vertical tail, to improve its high speed directional stability. The YF-100A originally had a larger tail, but its size had been reduced for production F-100A aircraft.

On 17 December 1954, while the Super Sabres were still grounded and the flight-test evaluation of the modified airframe was proceeding, North American and Douglas jointly received the Collier Trophy for their development of operational supersonic military aircraft.

Increased Areas Made the Difference

Out of the losses and the investigations came major recommendations for changes in the design of the F-100A. First, 27 per cent more vertical tail area was added to delay the onset of instability above Mach 1.4. It also increased the aspect ratio of the vertical tail, an aerodynamic improvement with effect equal to, or even greater than, the effect of the area increase.

With those changes in area came an increase in airplane height by six inches (15.2 cm), from the 14.94 ft (4.5 m) height of the YF-100A to the 15.34 ft (4.6 m) height of modified F-100A models.

Second, the wingtips were extended to increase both wing span and area, and to move the wing centre of pressure aft to compensate for a change in centre of gravity (CG) due to a change in the engine's CG. These changes increased the span from 36.78 ft to 38.78 ft (11.2–11.8 m), and the wing area from 376 square feet to 385.21 sq ft (34.94–35.80 m^2).

Finally, the artificial feel systems for the aileron and stabilizer powered controls were modified.

These changes were incorporated as rapidly as possible in the F-100A models, and the first three completed were assigned to NAA, the Air Force, and NACA for thorough and extensive inflight evaluations. Bob Baker, now NAA chief test pilot, USAF Captain Milburn Apt (later to be killed in the Bell X-2 research aircraft), and NACA pilots including Joe Walker, put the modified Super Sabres through a series of carefully planned and controlled manoeuvres.

During the investigation, North American had compiled and analysed an enormous quantity of data on the stability and control problems of supersonic aircraft. It had cost untold sums of money, and uncounted man-hours. Possession of that body of knowledge gave the company an immediate technical advantage over all its competitors. But North American, in a gesture still remembered and greatly respected by older observers of the industry, distributed its carefully collected data on the accident and the solution of the problem to the rest of the country's aircraft companies for their use, with no strings attached, and nothing asked in return.

Raymond H Rice, NAA Vice President in charge of Engineering, had underscored the importance of that knowledge in a summation of the tragedy prepared for the company magazine *Skyline*: '. . . the simple fact is that we are now on the brink of being able to fly past the limits of our available research data.

'But because of Welch's priceless contributions we are now aware of some of the new problems—we have tangible things to determine answers. The future of all of aviation owes George Welch a debt of gratitude for leaving us this insight.'

The grounding order was lifted early in February 1955. The Super Sabres were back in the air, and the programme moved on. Production rate restrictions were lifted on the F-100As, and NAA technicians began to install the fixes on the entire fleet. And before the month was out, manufacturing had begun on the F-100D models, the airplane that was to become the definitive Hun, the tough trooper of Southeast Asia.

Modified with the taller vertical tail, F-100A-10-NA (53-1565; the 60th production airplane) is assigned to AFFTC. Note the nose position of the national insigne, and the retractable tail bumper
(Peter M Bowers/Maene Collection)

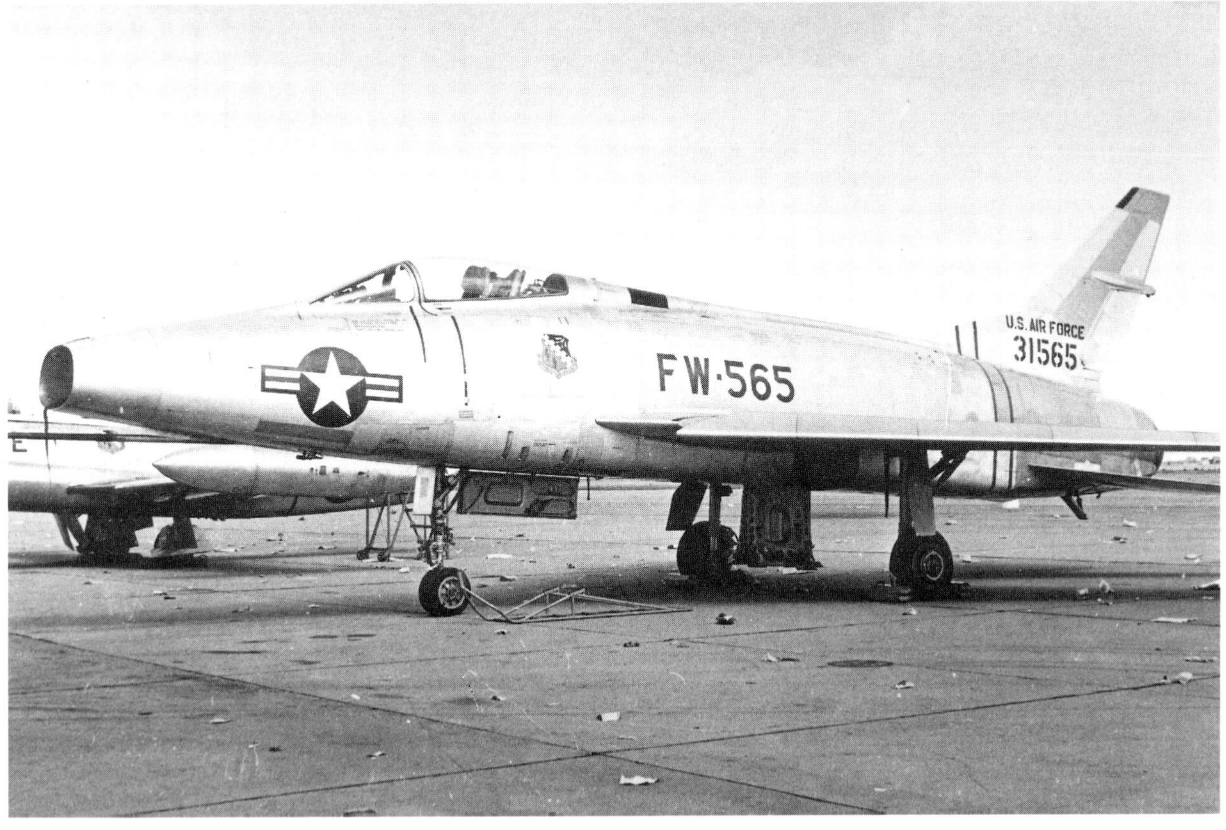

Chapter 3
Building and Developing the Super Sabre
Interlude A: First Deployments

The Super Sabre pioneered in an almost-unknown region of flight to give the Air Force a weapon system of great potential and versatility. But to fly and fight at unfamiliar speeds and altitudes required a different kind of structure, using new materials, manufacturing methods, and processes. No longer would combat aircraft be built in the traditional way, with light frames to give form to a thin shell that carried the loads. From this first fighter of the Century Series on, military airplanes were formed from massive blocks of steel, aluminium alloy and titanium.

The quest for performance was the driver. Higher speeds meant higher air loads on structures, requiring heavier, more complex, and stronger parts. Massive jigs and rugged tooling were needed to hold alignment during assembly; more care was demanded to match the closer tolerances required. Bending brakes, sheet-metal rollers, rubber presses, and hand-operated rivet guns moved toward obsolescence, as massive forging presses, precision machine tools, horizontal millers and automatic drilling machine bore the burden of building the brute.

Further, for the first time in the experience of the US aircraft industry, titanium was specified for structural use in the earliest stages of a new aircraft design. Titanium, light and strong, also tolerates high loads at high temperatures. It was a natural choice for F-100 structure, specifically for the aft fuselage section. There, outside the inferno of jet engine combustion processes, temperatures ranged from 1,700°F at the combustors to as high as 2,900°F at the exhaust nozzle. Designers specified titanium skin and frames to delay the melting of structure in the event of an engine fire. The heat resistance of the new material was the same as that of stainless steel, but titanium weighed about 40 per cent less.

The high rejection rate of the raw stock complicated the early use of titanium delivered to North American. Impurities often ruled out its use for aircraft parts even before they were fabricated, and frequent cracks caused during fabrication made it necessary to remake or replace parts at a higher-than-normal rate.

Besides that, titanium was difficult to work; drilling and riveting required special tools and extra care. Machining it was like machining stainless steel; tools had to be extra heavy and rigid so that they didn't chatter during the cut. They had to be ground to specific angles, and required special coolants during the cutting process; the old-fashioned 'pigeon milk' lubricant/coolant wouldn't do. The tools were run at constant feeds and speeds to avoid work-hardening the metal, but even with the best of care, the useful life of the tools was short.

NAA's production F-86D interceptors had used some titanium parts after trying them on the 1,400th F-86 built. But the F-100 used six times as much titanium as did the F-86D (650 lb against 100 lb), and thus accounted for a major share of all the titanium alloy produced in the US. In fact, NAA used about 95 per cent of the titanium alloy produced in 1953 and about 60 per cent in 1954, by which time, both the production rate and the quality of the metal had increased substantially.

North American had a policy then, which continues today, of pioneering in design and manufacturing and thus advancing the art of aircraft fabrication. In addition to the extensive use of the relatively untried titanium, NAA designers specified aluminium honeycomb sandwich components in the F-100. These were made of formed upper and lower metallic skins, sandwiching a thin aluminium foil honeycomb that separated the skins and was bonded to both of them. The honeycomb pieces used in the F-100A added up to more than 77 sq ft (7.1 m^2), compared to only 18 (1.6 m^2) for the F-86D. These components were stiff, strong, and light; but they had to be heat-formed, and that meant that more heat-forming tools were required.

The Techniques of Tooling

At the time the Super Sabre entered production, much of the industry was still using tooling techniques that had been developed and refined during World War 2. Assembly jig frames were built of steel tubing several inches in diameter, with steel bars and smaller tubes used to position steel fittings that held pieces rigidly for assembly. The conventional aluminium alloy subassembly made at workbenches and fitted to jigs for final assembly was often light enough to be warped into place if it had been built a little out of its prescribed tolerances.

But the F-100 parts were rigid and made precisely to fit into the jigs. In fact, they were strong enough to warp the jigs out of line if an attempt were made to force them into their fittings. And the close specified tolerances were so demanding that normal daily temperature changes in the factory could cause dimensional changes in tooling and jigs too great to accept without special provisions to maintain accuracy. Such jigs took longer to build, also. The most complex was the wing outer panel master jig, which on the F-86D had taken 3,600 hr from start to finish. For the F-100A jig, that figure more than quadrupled, to 16,173 hr.

The F-100 wing was probably the best example of the new construction techniques. It was designed as two removeable wing panels, with their ailerons and slats, bolted together at the centreline and attached to the fuselage with four bolts. The tip panels were removeable. The structure was a multi-spar aluminium-alloy assembly, with aluminium-alloy tapered plate skins that carried the bending and shear loads.

With the thin (seven per cent t/c ratio) airfoil section of the F-100 wing, internal volume, especially depth, was lacking. The strength usually developed by deep spars and ribs was carried by upper and lower wing planks, integrally stiffened by structure machined in the thick plank. Longerons and ribs were machined out of aluminium plate nearly two inches thick, and then the plates themselves were cut to tapered thicknesses, all these operations being done on huge horizontal milling machines.

And what was learned fabricating the wings for the F-100A had to be relearned in part for the F-100C and D, which had even heavier wing structures because of their integral fuel tanks and the hard points for external stores, absent in the A model. As

'Well, we got 12 of 'em in the air, and a few more on the ground, and that should convince the Russians that we're operational with the world's fastest fighter!' Maybe. These are among the first modified F-100As, and they're assigned to the 479th Fighter-Day Wing, at George AFB in the California high desert country. But these Super Sabres lacked a cutting edge, and it would be some years before they became effective weapons
(Rockwell International)

31680
FW-680
FW-656

Jet exhaust searing the air behind her, the fourth F-100A (52-5759) roars into the air loaded with paired auxiliary fuel tanks and four 750-pound bombs. She's been converted into the 'dry-wing' prototype of the F-100C, with added fighter-bomber capabilities
(Rockwell International)

RIGHT
The 'dry-wing' F-100C prototype, originally the fourth production F-100A (52-5759), streams the brake parachute while her pilot taxis her off the runway at AFFTC. The vertical tail has again been redesigned, and is approaching the shape of its final configuration
(Rockwell International)

an example, the F-100C wing spar weighed 60 lb (27 kg) when ready for installation. It was sculpted from a single piece of bar stock that weighted 800 lb (363 kg); simple subtraction shows that 740 lb (335 kg)—93 per cent of the bar—became chips.

There was some compensation. Super Sabre wings took less time to assemble than the wings of the F-86D, which had a primary structural box fabricated from 462 individual pieces of metal fastened with 16,084 bolts, rivets, and screws. The F-100A wing box had only 36 pieces and 264 fasteners, which made for faster assembly.

Structural testing was both conventional and unconventional. NAA test engineers performed the usual laboratory checks on everything from samples of raw materials to static load tests on a complete airplane. They also tested a complete F-100A with realistic localized temperatures to simulate engine operations. For example, the inside of the rear fuselage was heated to 550°; the forward, to 200°F. The simulated engine was an assembly of heaters fitted inside the static test airplane. The heat could be varied along the thrust line of the engine as well as radially. Cooling ducts replicated the effects of blast air on certain internal portions of the airplane; in other areas, heaters clamped directly to components raised the temperatures to those expected in powered flight at high speed.

It was a new experience for both North American and the US aircraft industry. Suppliers and vendors, sub-contractors and machine shops, all needed education in the Super Sabre's advanced manufacturing technology. Gradually a capability spread throughout the industry, forming a solid foundation for subsequent military airplanes that required high technology to meet the demands for high performance. But remember: it began with the Super Sabre. The F-100 not only pushed performance to new limits; it also moved manufacturing and materials out of the reference frame of World War 2 and toward today's methods.

There was one other attempt to establish a precedent; a clause in the initial production contract for the Super Sabre would have assigned all patentable features of the design to the US government. Further, it would have allowed the government permission to assign production of the F-100 to other companies. North American dug in its heels. Lockheed had rejected outright a similar provision in its May 1952 letter contract for the XF-104 prototypes and, partly on that precedent, North American, Convair (on the F-102) and McDonnell (on the F-101) held out and eventually obtained government agreement to delete the provisions in their contracts.

Aftermath of an Accident

When the Super Sabre fleet was grounded following the accident to the ninth F-100A, the Air Force had accepted 70 airplanes and North American had completed 108 others. When the modification programme began in January 1955, one additional acceptance had been made, and 165 airframes completed. The first aircraft to complete its modification programme was the 34th Super Sabre, and the first batch of 11 modified airplanes was delivered to NAA Engineering Flight Test.

Because of the rate of production, it wasn't until the 184th airframe that modifications arising from the accident could be incorporated in normal assembly. Earlier aircraft—68 accepted and 112 completed—were retrofitted in hangar areas. Parallel to those, other modifications were cranked into production aircraft. From the 11th onward, all F-100As were fitted with a retractable tail skid. From the 24th, a yaw

Loaded at all six stations with 'slicks'—low-drag bomb shapes—this F-100C banks into what might be a bombing run on a test range in the western United States. Note the straight air-refuelling probe, and the sway braces on the inboard side of the pylons
(Rockwell International)

TOP RIGHT
The first F-100D (54-2121), resplendent in a special paint job for the occasion, takes off from Los Angeles International Airport, next to the North American production plant. It has the final vertical tail design, and the characteristic cranked wing, altered by the added trailing-edge flap
(Rockwell International)

RIGHT
Now that the wing flaps have been added, ailerons moved outboard a bit, and the definitive vertical tail designed, F-100D-15-NA (54-2281)—161st production D—can show all the characteristic contours of the model. The boxy housing on the vertical tail holds position lights, and a fuel vent. Later, it also will hold tail-warning radar antennae
(Rockwell International)

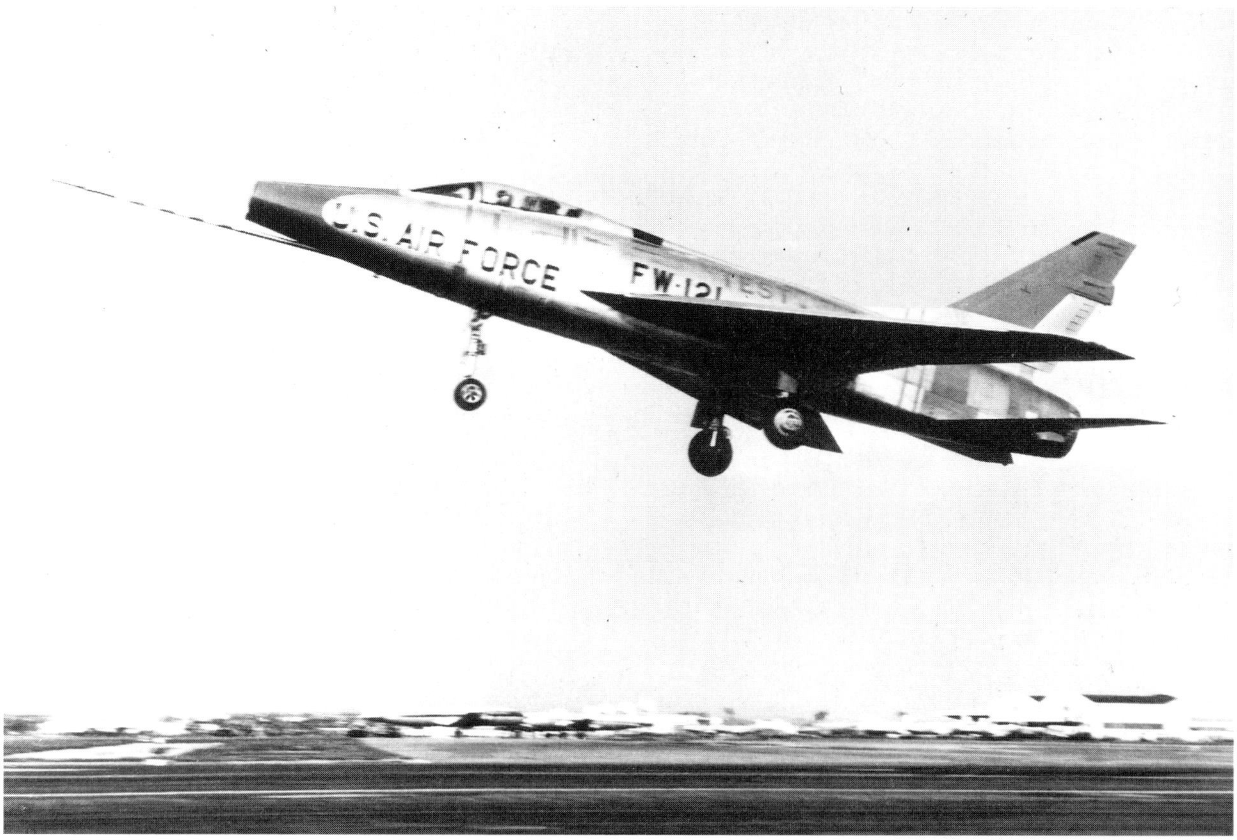
U.S. AIR FORCE
FW-121

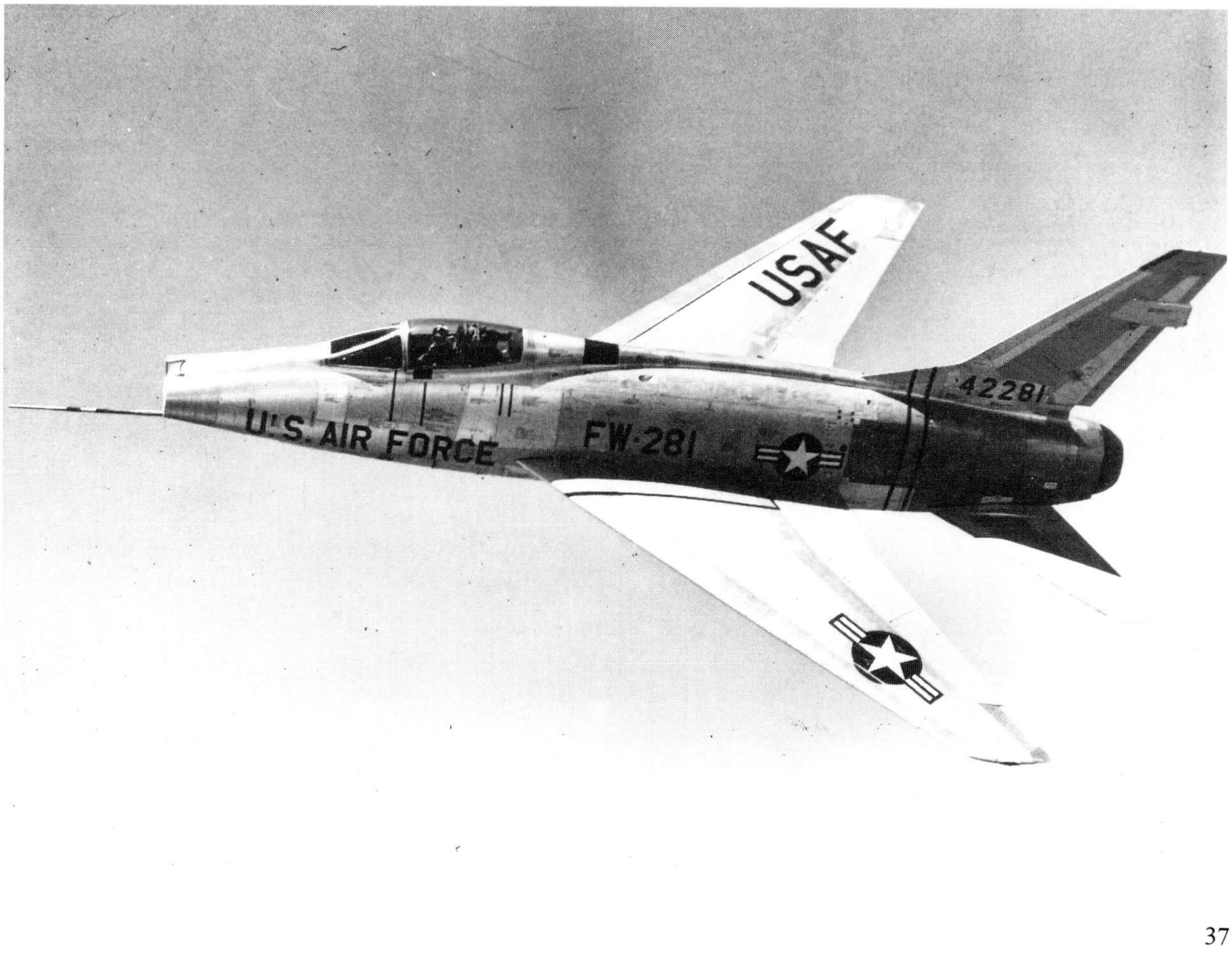
USAF
U.S. AIR FORCE
FW-281
42281

damper system was incorporated. The 12-inch (30.4-cm) wingtip extensions, originating before the accident, went on the 101st aircraft and subsequent. Provisions for a pitch damper were installed on aircraft 154 and subsequent.

(Author's note: the engineering and manufacturing technologies that North American developed in the Super Sabre programme applied directly to all models in the line. So this seems like a good place to summarize briefly the stories of all the production F-100s.)

F-100A Super Sabre (Design NA-192, Spec No NA 51-594)

These production versions were designed to requirements for an air-superiority fighter, armed with guns to destroy hostile aircraft. The F-100A was intended to be geometrically identical to the YF-100A prototypes; but as Chapter 2 described, NAA engineers made several significant changes in the design as a result of stability problems, and of Welch's fatal accident in the ninth airplane.

But design changes could not make the airplane into the air superiority fighter the Air Force wanted and needed. Late in 1955, pilots from the USAF Air Proving Ground Command at Eglin AFB, Florida, flew F-100As in Project Hot Rod to evaluate operational suitability. The conclusions were similar to those drawn from earlier evaluations by the engineering test pilots at AFFTC: the F-100A had great performance, but major functional and operational deficiencies.

The Super Sabres did achieve initial operational capability (IOC) in September 1955, a year after they entered service with the 479th Fighter-Day Wing at George AFB. Similarly, other squadrons with assigned F-100As experienced, typically, six-month delays in IOC. The Air Force accepted a total of 203 F-100As, the last 23 being delivered in July 1955.

Beginning in 1958, the A models were phased out of active USAF inventory and went into the Air National Guard, or into storage, with the exception of 15 sent to Nationalist China. But in 1961's Berlin Crisis, both the Air National Guard and the Air Force Reserve were mobilized, bringing some of the F-100As back to active duty with ANG units. By early 1962, USAF Headquarters made the decision to extend the service life of the A models. Tactical Air Command, which had gained ANG units during the Berlin Crisis, kept the airplanes after the Guard personnel had been released.

More transfers to Nationalist Chinese units further depleted the active F-100A fleet; ultimately, 118 aircraft were shipped to Taiwan, more than 58 per cent of the accepted A models. Approximately another 50 had been destroyed in accidents, leaving only about 35 which TAC retained for crew training. The last operational F-100A left the active inventory in early 1970; the ANG had lost its remaining A models to attrition by 1967.

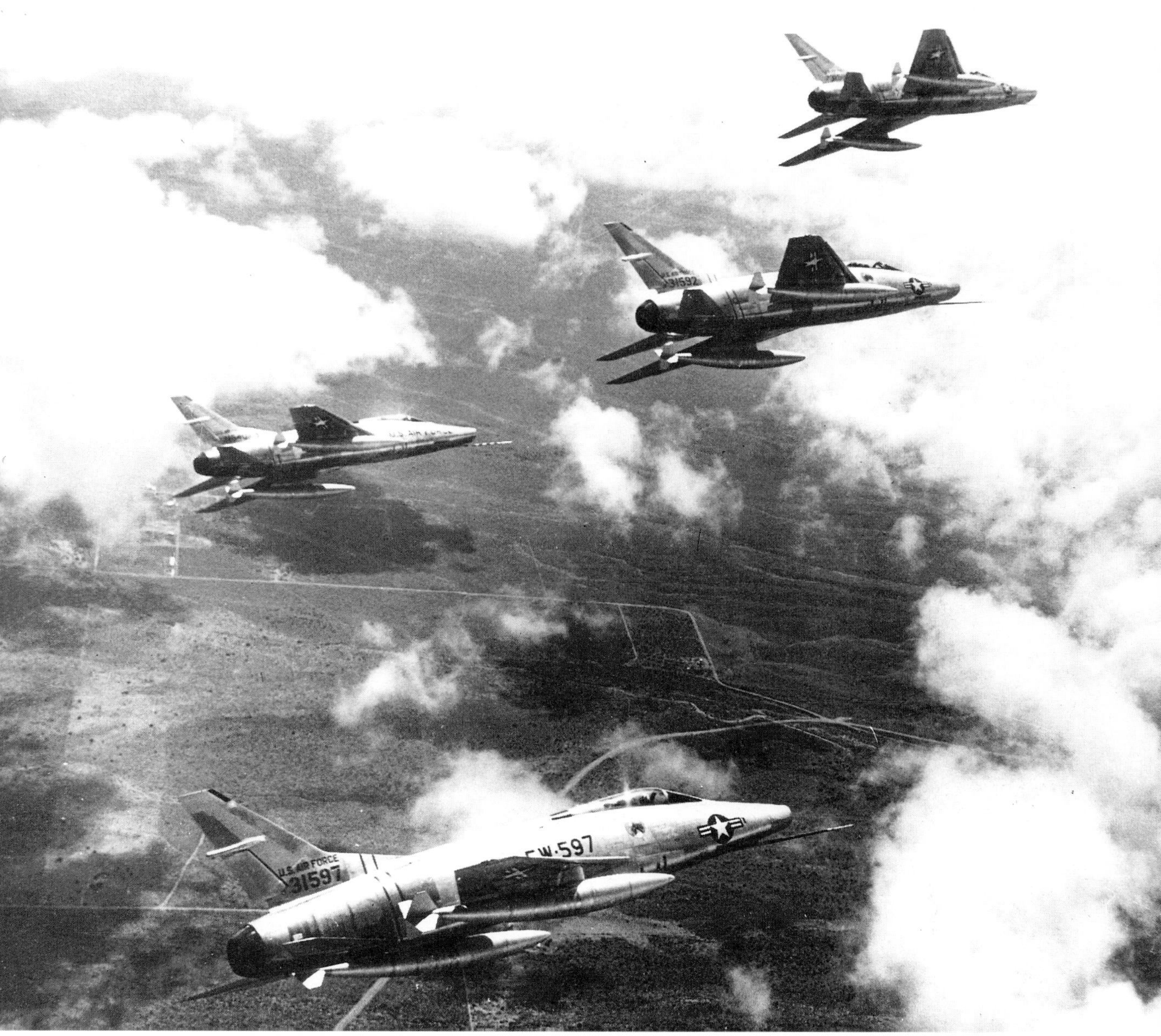

LEFT
These hills mark the region around the Mojave desert and are familiar sights to pilots flying out of Palmdale and Edwards AFB. Put yourself in that cockpit, with the dark cerulean sky overhead in sharp contrast with the stark beige desert floor and nearly black hills. You'd be flying 56-3122, an F-100D-70-NA, fresh out of the factory and rarin' to go
(Rockwell International)

ABOVE
Four modified A models from the 479th F-DW, George AFB, fly a loose formation above the low cumulus near their high desert home. In the foreground is 53-1597, the 92nd production A model
(Rockwell International)

F-100C Super Sabre (Design NA-214, -217, -222; various specs)

The C model was North American's answer to two urgent Air Force requests. The first, for fighter-bomber capabilities; the second, for more fuel capacity.

The Air Force had wanted more fuel in the F-100A almost from the start of design. Pilots know there is no such thing as too much fuel, and they know that preliminary data on fuel consumption are often wide of the mark and subject to later correction, generally upward. And what good is afterburning, however fuel-hungry, if it can't be used freely in combat?

In October 1952, well before the YF-100A had flown, the Air Force asked NAA to study the possibility of incorporating 'wet' wings containing integral fuel tanks. In March 1953, NAA engineers confirmed it was feasible. In July, the Air Force asked

Except for modern jet fighters, the flight line at George AFB in the mid-fifties was a relic of World War 2. Note that these modified F-100As carry the US star-and-bars insigne on each fuselage side forward of the cockpit, and the buzz number amidships. The 436th Fighter-Day Squadron insignia on the first airplane (53-1706, third from last model A built) is a black ace of spades on a USAF-blue disc, with yellow winged sword and the Latin motto Semper Primus, *Always First*
(Rockwell Industries)

RIGHT
The first production F-100C, 53-1709, has a white-painted underbelly, once a standard finish for nuclear-capable bombers. In theory, it was some protection against the intensely bright flash of the explosion; but white paint couldn't stop radiation effects. Note also the distinctive decoration on nose and vertical tail, probably in red paint
(USAFE/Pickett Collection)

if the new wet-wing structure could be further strengthened to carry additional external stores. On 4 August, NAA again responded affirmatively.

The Air Council revised the production order for F-100As on 30 December 1953, specifying that the last 70 airplanes in that contract should be produced as air-superiority fighters with fighter-bomber capabilities and be redesignated as F-100C (NAA Design NA-214). The Air Force, impatient to augment its fighter-bomber strength, issued letter contract AF33(600)-26962 on 24 February 1954, authorising production of an additional 230 F-100C models, raising to 300 the total under contract.

On 7 March, NAA machinists began fabricating parts for production F-100Cs. Five days later, engineering took delivery of the fourth production F-100A (AF52-5759) to begin modifying it to the prototype F-100C. But because it was nearly impossible to incorporate integral fuel tanks into a completed airplane to make it a 'wet-wing' bird, -5759 became the 'dry-wing' F-100C prototype. That prototype was delivered with the vertical tail of initial production F-100A models; later, the modified taller tail was fitted.

The fighter-bomber F-100C required specialized equipment that an air-superiority fighter didn't need. Wing modifications added hard points on the lower surface for removeable pylons to hold weapons, and strengthened the wing locally to withstand the sudden shock of stores release. New 'black boxes' improved the stability and control in yaw and pitch.

Because of the 'wet wing' requirement, NAA engineers redistributed the wing's integral systems to make room for fuel, and devised a leak-proofing system. All bolts that fastened skin to spars were sealed with injected material forced at 7,000 psi (580 *bars*) into a series of holes that channelled the sealant through a groove cut in the spar. Even when the wing deflected and distorted slightly under load, sealant flowed into any space created temporarily, and maintained the fuel-tank integrity.

In the final design, the F-100C integral wing fuel capacity totalled 451 US gal (1707 lit). There was provision for single-point ground refuelling, a major operational advantage over the outmoded gravity filling of the fuselage tank in the F-100As. A wing-mounted detachable refuelling probe was added for inflight tanking. The new wet-wing structure could hold—on six underwing stations—a wide variety of stores including external fuel tanks, chemical tanks, bombs weighing between 500 and 2,000 lb (227–907 kg), up to a dozen five-inch HVAR (high-velocity air rocket) weapons, and special stores (nuclear weapons).

But sometimes, adding external stores causes performance problems, as happened with the C models. Provision had been made for an additional pair of 200 US-gallon (757 lit) tanks to supplement the paired 275 US-gal (1041 lit) tanks normally carried, substantially increasing combat radius. But the smaller tanks decreased the longitudinal stability, especially at high cruise speeds, a problem the F-100 did not need. Curiously enough—well, maybe not, given the vagaries of aerodynamics—larger tanks eliminated the problem, and that's why both 275- and 200-US gal tanks later were replaced by a single pair of 450-US gal (1703-lit) units. But the bigger tanks were costly and scarce, and a change to 335-US gal (1268-lit) units was approved.

Engineering released 6,934 old and new drawings to manufacturing, detailing the F-100C, on 26 March, signalling the start of production. Before then, some parts had been fabricated, others ordered. But until the actual release of engineering drawings, production hadn't officially begun.

It was only a matter of days before the prototype F-100C was ready for flight. In March 1954, she lifted off the runway at Edwards AFB on her first flight. By mid-April, the USAF had completed Phase II flight-tests on the F-100C.

TOP
There's still some snow on the peaks of the Sierras, as this F-100C banks to clear the tops. A picture like this makes one envy the birds
(Rockwell International/Maene Collection)

ABOVE
A quartet of F-100Cs, in stepped-down left echelon, cruise above the California landscape
(Rockwell International/Maene Collection)

TOP
F-100A 52-5759, prototype for the F-100C, taxis out past the North American plant at Palmdale on an engineering flight-test assignment
(Rockwell International/Maene Collection)

ABOVE
Here's an oddity; 53-1733 is the 25th production F-100C, but it is fitted with an F-100D tail. It has just come off the runway at Palmdale and is taxying to an area where the pilot can jettison the drag chute
(Rockwell International/Maene Collection)

Another one of those photos that makes you want to be there, looking into deep blue sky, feeling the quiet roaring of the J57, and hearing your own breathing. It's F-100D 56-3122
(Maene Collection)

RIGHT
The cockpit of F-100C No 259 (54-1952) looked pristine when it was photographed on 12 December 1955. Note the light-coloured panel, the basic six instruments grouped near the upper centre, and the size of the 'steam gauges' common to cockpits 30 years ago
(Rockwell International/Maene Collection)

On 27 May, USAF contract AF33(600)-26962 increased the total of C models to 564, more than double the number sought by the earlier letter contract. The contract was amended later by a change notice of 27 September, specifying that the last 224 aircraft of the 564 be completed as F-100D aircraft. At nearly the same time, Tactical Air Command asked for more capabilities, and the USAF responded with studies that led to the F-100D.

In September, the Air Force decided to build Super Sabres at a second source, and North American opened an available plant at Columbus, Ohio. Letter contract AF33(600)-28736 authorized production of 25 F-100Cs at Columbus, to be followed by 221 F-100D models. Aircraft built at Columbus were to use the letters NH in their block numbers, instead of NA (for those built in Los Angeles).

Meantime, Pratt & Whitney had developed an upgraded version of the basic J57-P-7 afterburning turbojet that had powered all the Super Sabres until then. With more thrust at higher altitude, the J57-P-21 engine became the powerplant for the bulk of F-100Cs produced. It improved the speed by about 35 knots (65 km/h) at altitude, and reduced the time to

OXYGEN WARNING
FLIGHT CONTROL
UTILITY
CLIMB
FUEL FLOW
EXHAUST
°C X 100
FUEL QUANTITY
PUSH TO TEST
RADIO
COMPASS
RESET
BATTERY
INSTRUMENT
INVERTER
NULL CHECK
STOP
(GEN)

USAF

climb to 35,000 ft (10,670 m) by about ten per cent.

The first production wet wing F-100C was rolled out on 19 October 1954, and conditionally accepted by the USAF on 29 October, because all Super Sabres were grounded at the time. The first 'wet wing' production airplane flew on 17 January 1955, with NAA's Alvin White at the controls. F-100C deliveries to TAC began in April, and the F-100C became operational with the 450th Fighter-Day Squadron at Foster AFB, Texas.

North American built 451 F-100Cs in California, and 25 in Columbus. All 476 were accepted by the Air Force, the last in July 1956.

By the end of the year, almost one-third of the fleet was deployed with USAFE (United States Air Forces in Europe) squadrons. The 'Skyblazers' aerobatic team, formed by pilots of the 36th Fighter-Day Group in Europe, was attracting much public attention and praise on their round of air shows. The Air National Guard began receiving its first C models in mid-1959, reaching its authorized peak strength of 210 Super Sabres seven years later.

But the F-100C still wasn't a full-fledged fighter-bomber; by 1966, almost ten years after the last C model had been delivered, only 125 ANG Cs had been equipped to carry CBUs (cluster bomb units), and also to fire Sidewinder air-to-air missiles. TAC's F-100Cs could do neither. To remedy the latter, the Air Force assigned six F-100Cs to a modification programme with the eventual goal of arming Super Sabres with infrared homing missiles. Both the Hughes IR Falcon and the Philco Sidewinder were tested in early 1956 and, in September, Sidewinder was selected. The system finally was installed beginning with the 184th F-100D, because the F-100C already was out of production.

As with the As, so with the Cs; their active-duty life was short. Cannibalising, accidents, priorities assigned to ANG aircraft, and the re-equipping of the Thunderbirds reduced the active inventory to unacceptably low levels, and so eventually the Air Force retained only a few for crew training. The last USAF F-100Cs flew their last mission in March 1970, ending the gradual phaseout from active units and the beginning of transfer to Guard units.

F-100D Super Sabre (Design Nos. NA-223, -224, -235, -245)

In the F-100D, the Air Force finally got the fighter-bomber that had been required from the beginning. It was developed as a dedicated fighter-bomber, with no attempt to call it an 'air-superiority fighter with fighter-bomber capabilities'.

And this is one for every modeller who wants to replicate an authentic natural metal finish on an F-100C in 1/72nd scale! The words are, I think, 'Good luck!'
(Maene Collection)

The F-100D had the increased wing and tail areas required to cure earlier problems, plus a little extra on the vertical surface just in case. It had an autopilot and an inflight refuelling system, and a 'buddy' system for air-refuelling that also used the probe-and-drogue technique originally developed by Flight Refuelling in England. It carried a pair of huge 450-US gal external tanks that could be refilled in flight through the internal fuel system, as well as combinations of the earlier 200-, 275- and 335-US gal drop tanks. There were more 'black boxes' for fighter-bomber purposes. And, because the final result was inevitably heavier, the wing was modified to add landing flaps. The added flap area created the cranked-wing trailing edge, the familiar recognition feature of the F-100D.

It had the same underwing hard points for weapons as the C, but instead of gravity release, the pylons featured force ejection of the stores.

The first F-100D first flew 24 January 1956; deliveries began in September to the 405th Fighter-Bomber Wing, Tactical Air Command, at Langley AFB, Virginia.

Operational problems were relatively few, although serious enough to cause considerable concern at TAC Headquarters. And, following the pattern then—and now—making the fixes for these problems was delayed. TAC was not eager to deploy unfixed D models; but USAFE had such a pressing need for the airplanes, as did Far East Air Force (FEAF) that the operating commands won the arguments and F-100Ds left the country for Europe and the Far East.

In addition to fixes, several modification programmes began. Bullpup air-to-surface missiles, later to prove almost valueless in Vietnam combat, were adapted to 65 F-100Ds. The last 148 production aircraft had built-in zero-length launch (ZEL) capability.

But when the Air Force realised it was operating F-100 aircraft with few common systems, one answer was Project High Wire, a major standardization and upgrading of about 700 F-100D and F models. It was planned to extend the variety of non-nuclear weapons that could be carried and delivered, to remove excess weight and original wiring, standardize the cockpit, rewire it completely, and add a simple, spring-steel tailhook.

The High Wire modifications were so extensive that a separate set of manuals was necessary, identified by a Roman numeral I in parentheses; for example, the familiar Dash-One manual was designated T.O. 1F-100D(I)-1. The airplanes modified by High Wire—not all Cs and Ds went through the programme—were singled out by advancing the block number a single digit; for example, F-100D-25-NA became F-100D-26-NA.

High Wire began in April 1962, and was completed in mid-1965. It was expensive, its $150 million cost then equivalent to buying 215 complete new F-100D airframes, and it required as much as 60 man-days of

How do we know this is a low-time, perhaps even factory-fresh F-100D (54-2122)? Look at the fuselage tail area; the titanium shell is unrippled, untinted, and undistorted by radiated heat from a red-hot tailpipe. Truly your basic, plain vanilla D
(Peter M Bowers/Maene Collection)

RIGHT
The 13th production F-100F (56-3737) stands on the compass rose at the North American plant adjacent to Los Angeles International Airport. In the background are rows of F-86Ds, and a pair of F-100D models, 56-2903 and -3090. Note the extended wing slat, and the deflected stabilizer
(Rockwell International/Maene Collection)

labour on each aircraft. But in the end, it was worth it; the USAF had a fleet of F-100Ds that was, at last, standardized, and just in time for the war.

(Sidelight: all airplanes undergo modification programmes, some done in the field, some at factories or other industrial facilities. Nit Picker, for example, modified 658 F-100Cs and Ds. It was completed in April 1958, at Seymour Johnson AFB, and included the installations of independent oil systems, the Minneapolis-Honeywell MB-3 autopilot—the first developed for a supersonic jet—and new brakes that featured automatic anti-skid operation. In March 1965, Project Yellow Grain offered hope of curing, finally, the long-standing flameout problems of the J57 engines. Yellow Grain included 13 modifications of fuel pump, transfer valve, shutoff valve, and fuel-flow transmitter.)

In 1966, the Air Force decided to extend the combat life again, anticipating that the F-100 would stay in the inventory longer than originally planned. Its design life was then at the 3000-hr level: ten hours a day for less than a year, or about one-tenth the current design life of typical airliners and business jet aircraft. The first planned increment was another 2,500 hr; that later was raised by 1,500 hr more to a final level of 7,000 flight hr.

Concomitant studies of wing strength were made more urgent when the wings failed during Captain 'Tony' McPeak's solo Thunderbird routine (Interlude 7). His pull-up, by then, was being duplicated dozens of times daily as Super Sabre pilots hauled their aircraft up and away from their targets in Vietnam. The resulting fleet grounding was followed by temporary repairs made with external straps reinforcing the wings of in-service aircraft. Late in 1967, a complete structural modification programme was imposed by the Air Force, and completed on 682 F-100D models.

As the sorry war in Southeast Asia wore down, the USAF began sending its F-100s back to the US and transferring them to ANG squadrons. By mid-1972, the USAF operated only a dozen Ds, the Guard, 335. The last F-100D (56-3333) left TAC 19 June 1972, and the last ANG F-100D (56-2979) was retired 10 November 1979.

F-100F (Design NA-243)

The in-service accident rate of the F-100 was deplorable. There was a clear and urgent need for a two-place training aircraft in which pilots could learn the tricks of handling the F-100. A few hours of dual time in the logbook, it was argued, would lower the accident rate.

On 10 May 1954, NAA began design studies of a supersonic trainer and, on 2 September, submitted its proposal to the Air Force, offering to modify a standard single-seat F-100C to trainer configuration at no cost to the USAF. The offer couldn't be refused; USAF authorized the modification, loaned F-100C 54-1966 to the company, and awarded an initial production contract for 259 TF-100Cs.

The prototype first flew 3 August 1956. The following 9 April, the TF-100C spun into the ground and was destroyed during demonstration spin testing. NAA chief engineering test pilot Bob Baker ejected safely.

From the TF-100C prototype to the first F-100F two-seater was a relatively simple step. F-100F production engineering drawings were released to the shop on 7 September 1956. The first production airplane was completed the following 7 January and first flew on 7 March, with NAA pilot Gage Mace at the controls. At the end of May, the first F-100F arrived at Nellis AFB, assigned to an operational training squadron less than eight months after the start of production.

A special production model, F-100F-20, was developed at the specific request of Pacific Air Forces, the potential user command. The -20 was equipped with a navigational system including an AN/ASN-7 dead-reckoning computer, PC-212 Doppler radar (also known as RADAN), and a standard J-4 compass system. It also had modified flaps, with a spanwise duct built into the leading edges to direct air from the lower surface over the upper to reduce wing buffet in the landing configuration. The flaps had a full deflection of 40°, compared to the 45-degree full deflection of the standard flaps on the F-100D and F.

PACAF furnished an experienced pilot who flew almost 43 hr of flight tests at AFFTC. The command also suggested the missions that would best simulate user requirements: overwater runs to evaluate Doppler performance, and low-level runs at 500-ft (150-m) altitude.

It was not quite as successful as hoped. The final report said that, if the system were used correctly, it would increase the probability of reaching the target, even in adverse weather. But the -20 was not an all-weather aircraft; at best, its systems took the

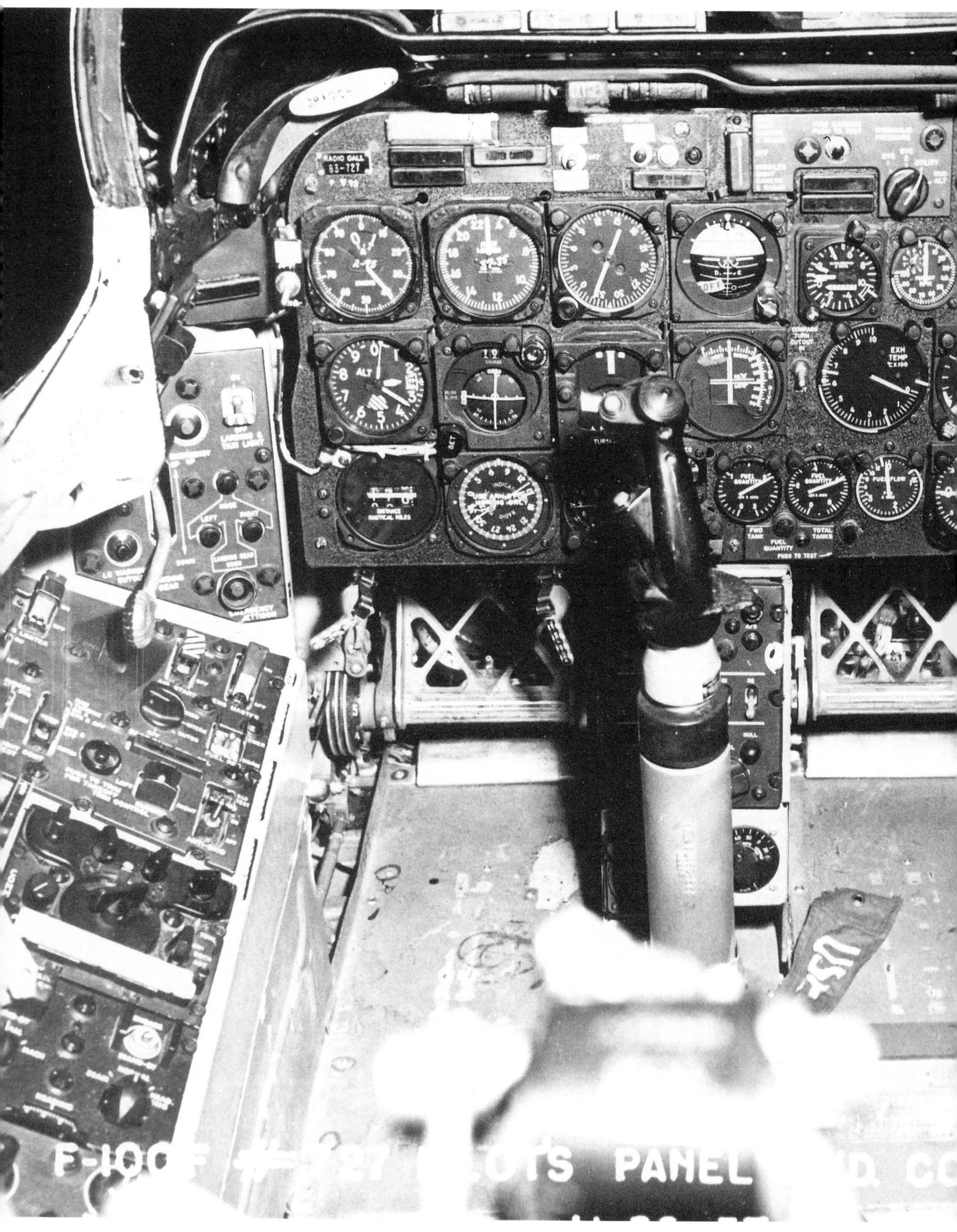
RADIO CALL
63-727
ALT
EXH
TEMP
°C X100
FUEL QUANTITY
FUEL FLOW
FWD TANK
TOTAL TANKS
PUSH TO TEST
DISTANCE NAUTICAL MILES
LANDING & TAXI LIGHT
NOSE
LEFT
RIGHT
PANEL

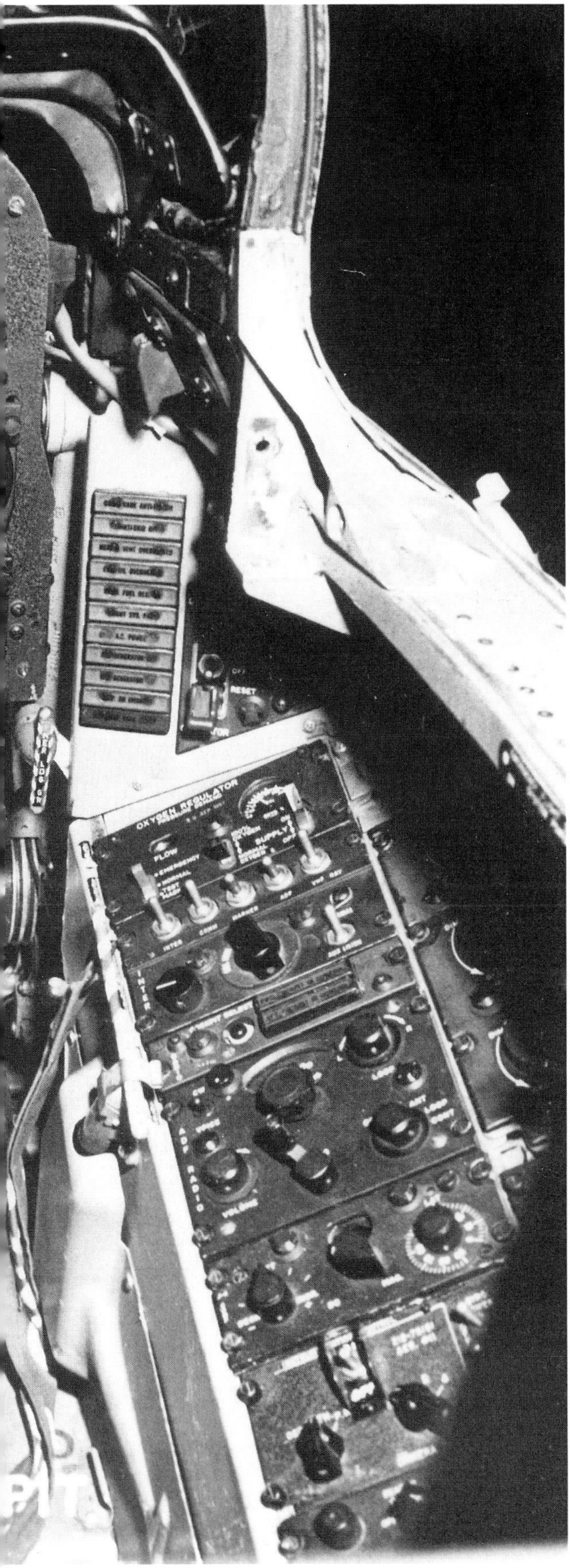

The 28th production F-100F, 56-3752, cruises above the low cloud and haze of central California. Note that the production number (ship number, in factory parlance) is stencilled on the lower tail cone
(Pickett Collection)

LEFT
This is the front office of the third production F-100F (56-3727) taken on 22 November 1957. Among other sights, it contains an object lesson in aircraft safety. There are stains from coffee or soft drink cups on the left floor panel. Were the cups or cans removed, or are they under the floor somewhere, waiting to jam something? That kind of carelessness occasionally causes a mysterious aircraft loss
(Rockwell International/Maene Collection)

guesswork out of navigation in the absence of radio ground aids, i.e., over water or enemy territory. Missions also had to be flown straight and level at high altitudes, because the PC-212 and J-4 systems had limited performance.

Neither was the two-seat trainer itself as successful as had been hoped. It also had a high accident rate and, at its phase out, about one-quarter of the fleet had been thus destroyed.

Greatness Thrust Upon Them

If, in reading the above condensed summary, you get the impression that the F-100 was really a dog, hang on a minute. To paraphrase an old saying, 'Some airplanes are born great, others have greatness thrust upon them.' The Super Sabre was of the latter ilk. It was great because it was in the right place at the right time, like the Curtiss P-40 and the Grumman F4F at the start of World War 2.

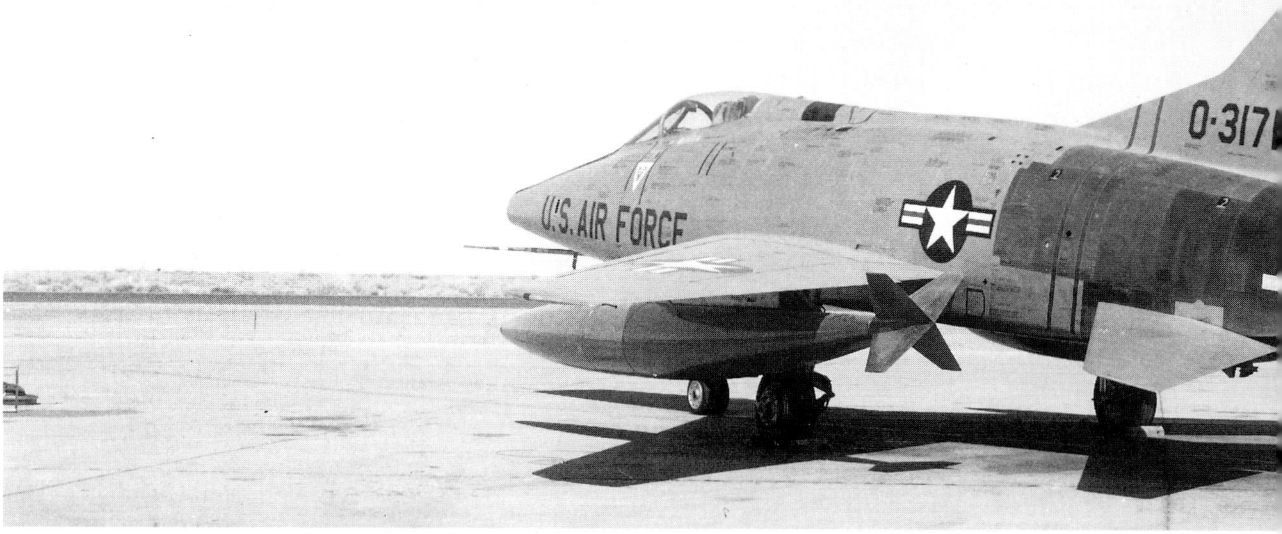
0-317
U.S. AIR FORCE

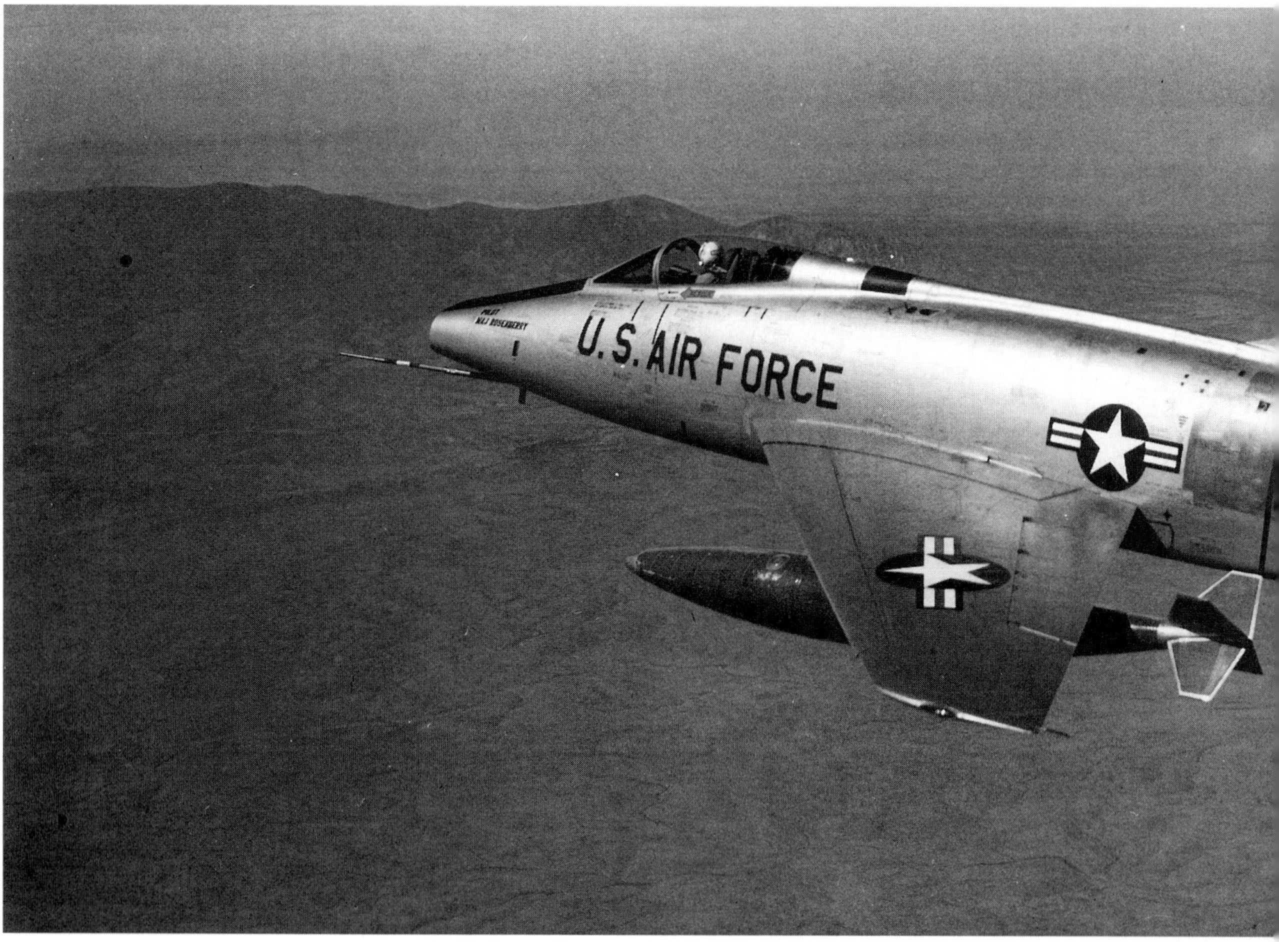
U.S. AIR FORCE

TOP LEFT
The tenth F-100C (53-1718) stands on the ramp at Holloman AFB, New Mexico, waiting for something to do. She's assigned to Air Defense Command, wears an Outstanding Unit ribbon on her fin, and a squadron insigne that a tedious search has failed to identify. Judging by the amount of scorched and discoloured fuselage tail area, she's spent a lot of time in afterburner
(USAF KE26 384)

LEFT
Maj Rosenberry of the Air Defense Command, his name displayed forward of the cockpit, drives F-100C (54-1951) near Holloman AFB, NM. The plane is immaculate; only the grungy auxiliary tank mars the overall sleek finish
(USAF KE26 388)

ABOVE
OK, Lieutenant, let's get 'er parked so I can get in off this hot damn apron. The crew chief, the pilot, and the F-100As are part of the 479th Fighter-Day Wing at George AFB, California, lucky recipients of the first supersonic fighter in the USAF inventory
(Maene Collection)

The war in Vietnam required a fighter-bomber for accurate close air support of troops on the ground. The F-100 responded nobly, with all that a great airplane could have given.

Remember also that experienced F-100 pilots like to claim that the airplane separated the men from the

A camouflaged F-100D eases up toward the tanker, waiting for the basket to come within lunging range. Looks like water down there, wide water maybe, but certainly deep, and the fuel will be welcome
(Montgomery Collection)

RIGHT
Sixteen Super Sabre Cs soar swiftly, surmounting sun-soaked sands
(Steffens Collection—damn that single hard C)

boys, the aviators from the pilots. Of course, the proponents of any airplane often make that same claim, because it reinforces their egos to think that they alone can handle the toughest mother in the inventory.

But when push came to shove, the F-100 proved itself in the one place where a military aircraft must prove itself—battle. Read on, and see how.

Interlude A: **First Deployments**

The F-100C was the first truly operational version of the Super Sabre. It entered service with the 450th Fighter-Day Squadron (F-DS), 322nd Fighter-Day Group (F-DG), at Foster AFB, Texas, on 14 July 1955, and stayed in active duty with regular and Guard squadrons, although in small quantities, right through the war in Vietnam. It was popular with pilots, because it was lighter and had a margin of speed and performance over the D models. But it was not as popular with mission planners, because it had fewer capabilities than the later F-100D.

On 20 August, Colonel Howard A Hanes, an AFFTC pilot who had flown phase tests on Super Sabres, flew an F-100C to a new world speed mark. Flying above a 15–25 km course laid out on the Mojave Desert near Palmdale, Hanes averaged 822.135 mph (1323.094 km/h), a new record and the world's first at supersonic speed.

On 4 September, Colonel Carlos Talbott won the Bendix Trophy in an F-100C that traversed the 2,325-mile (3742-km) transcontinental distance at an average speed of 610.726 mph (982.865 km/h).

During July 1955, Tactical Air Command had organized the 19th Air Force, a new type of unit to provide the planning and command structure needed by the Composite Air Strike Force (CASF) concept. The 19th AF, which came to be called 'The Suitcase Air Force', selected potential trouble spots and planned how to go there with what aircraft, if called. Pre-selected package forces were developed that could go to combat in widely different environments.

Mass deployments, featuring numbers of F-100Cs based in the United States, flew lengthy missions to test the concepts. Bendix winner Talbott led 16 Super Sabres of the 452nd F-DS, 322nd F-DG, from Foster AFB to French Morocco. It was the vanguard of a 40-plane CASF unit, the first complete air strike force to make a full-scale intercontinental deployment with aerial refuelling. A similar deployment moved another batch of Super Sabres from Foster to Landstuhl Air Base, in Germany, on a non-stop, 13 hr 30 min flight. The F-100Cs carried the big 450-US gal auxiliary tanks, and were refuelled in flight.

On a smaller scale, six F-100Cs left London on 13 May 1957, to fly to Jamestown, Virginia, near Langley Air Force Base, in an airborne replay of the three-ship Atlantic crossing that established the Jamestown colony in the early 17th century. Three F-100s landed to celebrate the event; the other trio continued to Los Angeles, completing a flight that lasted just over 14 hr. One of the six (54-1753) is now in the Air Force Museum, Wright-Patterson AFB, Dayton, Ohio.

Then, in November that year, 1st Lieutenant James Foster climbed into his F-100D, one of 16 Ds and 16Cs that were departing Cannon AFB, NM, on an operation designated Mobile Zebra. The Super Sabres were part of a composite force that included Douglas B-66s and McDonnell RF-101s, deploying to the Philippines. Each of the F-100s carried a pair of 450-US gal auxiliary tanks, and they were to refuel from Boeing KB-50 tankers, slow and lumbering piston-engined aircraft.

Far out over the Pacific, Foster and his group lead, M D Ulrich, were refuelling simultaneously from a KB-50, each probe deep in the basket trailing from left and right underwing points. The tanker suddenly hit the wake of another; it bucked up, suddenly rolled left, then right. Foster lost contact; the drogue whipped around, shattering his canopy. Ulrich had bent his probe badly during the wild and brief ride, and it was obvious that both F-100s needed to get on the ground as soon as possible. Midway was nearby, and both pilots landed safely.

Foster had great affection for the rugged airplane that saved him that time. When he saw it for the last time, it was being modified into a drone at Sperry's Phoenix Litchfield Airport (Chapter 10).

The CASF concept got a real test in 1958, when the Middle East erupted with an insurrection in Lebanon, and a coup in Iraq. President Eisenhower ordered a CASF to the area, and within 12 hours, the first F-100s were landing at Adana, Turkey, ready to go to the aid of the President of Lebanon who had requested the aid.

There was one establishment unique to the early deployment of the F-100. The 45th Fighter-Day Squadron was organized at Sidi Slimane, in French Morocco, to establish and operate the transition school for F-86 pilots based in USAFE to fly F-100s. New pilots assigned to European bases first checked in at Sidi Slimane, where the 45th put them through 50 hours of ground school and simulator flights before turning them loose in real F-100s to learn the finishing touches.

After completing the check-out in F-100s, the pilots flew the same familiar airplanes to their units in Europe. Replacement F-100s arrived at Sidi Slimane via 'High Flight' routes over the North Atlantic, down through Europe, above Gibraltar and across into North Africa.

And, given the performance of the airplane, and the location of the 45th, and the proclivity of fighter pilots to imagine new and novel names for their units, is it surprising that the 45th was widely known as the 'Mach One Camel Corps'?

Stars and stripes on the tail, and a red chevron on the nose mark this F-100C-5-NA (54-1792) from the 450th Fighter-Day Wing, Foster AFB, Texas. Why is there a Snark missile in the right background? (Peter M Bowers/Maene Collection)

Chapter 4
First Strikes
Interlude B: Soliloquy

In mid-1950, a US Military Assistance Advisory Group (MAAG) went to French Indo-China (as it was then called). USAF technicians also were ordered to the country to support French aviation units. Some returned home in August 1953, but in February 1954 several hundred more returned to Indo-China and its last days.

The French surrender at Dien Bien Phu on 7 May was followed by a July armistice that split Indo-China. North of the 17th parallel of latitude was the Democratic Republic of Vietnam, led by Ho Chi Minh, once a staunch friend and ally of the United States. South of it was the State of Vietnam, later widely called the Republic of Vietnam (RVN) or South Vietnam.

The RVN's small air force flew Cessna L-19 Bird Dog reconnaissance aircraft and Grumman F8F-1 Bearcat fighters, both American-built, both inherited from the departing French. With experience of past USAF assistance, the Vietnamese Air Force (VNAF) turned to the United States for training. USAF pilot instructors arrived in May 1957, and opened a basic training school at Nha Trang. Advanced training was done at Clark Air Base in the Philippines, and at bases in the US.

That spring, Viet Cong irregulars began acts of terrorism which quickly escalated to small-scale combat actions. And over the border in neighbouring Laos, a three-sided civil war pitted conservatives, neutralists, and leftists—largely the communist Pathet Lao—against each other.

John F Kennedy came to the presidency of the United States in January 1961 with Nikita Khrushchev's statements ringing in his ears: the USSR would wholeheartedly support wars of national liberation, such as the action in Vietnam. On 23 March, Kennedy announced during a press conference that the Russians '. . . have been conspicuous in a large-scale airlift (in Laos) . . . and heavier weapons have been provided (to the Pathet Lao Communist forces) . . . with the clear object of destroying by military action the agreed neutrality of Laos.'

That same day, Pathet Lao forces shot down an American SC-47 from Vientiane, Laos. It was flying an electronic intelligence mission to monitor radio frequencies used by the Russians at the airport at Xieng Khouangville, a Pathet Lao base. One survivor baled out; he was captured and repatriated after 17 months.

First Alerts, First Responses

An alert (code-name: Moon Glow) followed these events. Tactical Air Command responded by alerting, but not deploying, a Composite Air Strike Force (CASF) package. But six Super Sabres were moved on 16 April, in Operation Bell Tone, from the 510th TFS at Clark Air Base, in the Philippines, to Don Muang International Airport near Bangkok, Thailand. Their mission was air defence; they were the first F-100s to enter a combat zone.

Detachment 2A (code name: Farm Gate) of the 4400th Combat Crew Training Squadron (earlier code-named Jungle Jim), numbering 151 officers and men, left Eglin AFB Auxiliary Field No 9 (now Hurlburt AFB, Florida) on 11 October 1961 for Bien Hoa airbase in South Vietnam. Farm Gate included eight North American T-28 trainers, four Douglas SC-47 transports, and four Douglas RB-26 light reconnaissance bombers, all modified for counter-insurgency operations, all marked with VNAF insignia, at the specific request of US Ambassador (to the RVN) Frederick E Nolting.

Four McDonnell RF-101C aircraft from the Japan-based 45th Tactical Reconnaissance Squadron deployed on 20 October to Tan Son Nhut airport, to fly reconnaissance missions over Vietnam and Laos. Four more replaced them in November, at Don Muang airport. The 346th Troop Carrier Squadron,

FW-724
53724

from Pope AFB, North Carolina, was detached on temporary duty (TDY) and sent to Vietnam with its Fairchild C-123s, in operation Mule Train. With them came six C-123 Ranch Hand aircraft from the Philippines, to begin systematic defoliation missions.

The first complete F-100 squadrons to move were part of Operation Saw Buck, numbered TAC/CASF deployments. Beginning on 18 May 1962, Saw Buck rotated F-100 squadrons from Cannon and England AFBs in the US to Takhli Royal Thai Air Base (RTAFB), Thailand, on TDY. The first unit, the 428th TFS, from Cannon, was deployed in Saw Buck I as part of a Composite Air Strike Force, and was joined in Thailand by three Douglas WB-66D weather reconnaissance aircraft from the 9th Tactical Reconnaissance Squadron at George AFB, California. Saw Buck II began on 3 September 1962, and replaced the 428th with a sister squadron from Cannon, the 430th. Saw Buck III relieved the 430th with the 522nd, beginning on 13 December 1962.

On 22 January 1964, a Joint Chiefs of Staff memorandum to Secretary of Defense Robert S McNamara suggested a ten-step force escalation, tantamount to taking over the war from the Vietnamese. It included bombing North Vietnam, mining its waters, sending in large-scale commando raids, extending ground operations into Laos, and increasing reconnaissance flights. About two months later, McNamara went much further in a memo of his own to President Lyndon B Johnson: let the Farm Gate unit fly combat strikes, and strengthen the USAF presence with three squadrons of Martin B-57Bs. Clandestine operations and targeting studies followed. The USAF began supporting air operations by the Royal Laotian Air Force. There was pressure from RVN leaders for US airpower to strike North Vietnam.

First Combat Strike for the F-100

In May, the Pathet Lao overran the Plaine des Jarres area. American reconnaissance flights continued, and occasionally the aircraft—most of them Navy Vought RF-8As—were fired upon. On 22 May, an unarmed RF-8A, piloted by Lieutenant Charles F Klusmann, was hit but not shot down, and returned safely to the USS *Kitty Hawk*. On 6 June, Klusmann's luck ran out; he ejected near Pathet Lao troops, twisted his

This is the way they were lined up, probably at Tan Son Nhut Air Base, Republic of Vietnam, in 1964 before the Viet Cong rocket and mortar attacks began (nobody—except the VC—remembered Pearl Harbor). The three nearest are F-100Ds, 55-3724, -2921, and -3628, respectively, and they are undoubtedly Tactical Air Command assets, now under Pacific Air Force, on deployment to Southeast Asia. They're loaded with rocket pods and auxiliary tanks
(USAF 94569)

U.S. AIR FORCE
FW-674
53674

With rocket pods full and armed, a trio of F-100Ds lines up for takeoff on a strike against the Viet Cong sometime in 1964. Serial numbers are, respectively, 55-3674, -3628, and -3738
(USAF 94566)

LEFT
Under guard, an F-100F (56-3923) of the 481st TFS 'Crusaders' on deployment from Cannon AFB, NM, spends a quiet night at Tan Son Nhut AB, RVN. Note the open gun bay, the open leading-edge slats, and the pre-camouflage finish
(USAF K19578)

ankle on landing, and was abandoned by Air America rescue helicopters when they ran into a flak trap that badly wounded two crewmen. Klusmann was captured, but escaped after three months. On 7 June, flak downed an armed Navy F-8 escorting an unarmed RF-8A over the Plaine.

A decision was made at the 'highest national levels'—a euphemism for the President and Cabinet officers—to strike back. The mission was assigned to the 405th Fighter Wing at Clark AB; wing commander was 49-year-old Colonel George Laven, Jr, veteran of nearly 1,000 combat missions in World War 2, and an ace with victories in the Aleutians and the Southwest Pacific.

(Sidelight: Colonel Laven was 479th FDW Wing Commander in 1954; as senior commander at George AFB, he went to North American, picked out a new F-100C, and flew it back. Its serial was 54-2076; the last four digits were the same as those on his P-38 he flew in the Aleutians during 1942 and 1943. From the day he climbed into F-100C 2076, no one ever flew the airplane except Laven, until it was time to send it to Sacramento for modification. He logged more than 2,000 hr in 2076 in a little over four years. After 2076 completed years of service with a training unit at Luke AFB, it went to the New Mexico ANG, and Laven again flew the airplane on occasion in his capacity as Senior Air Adviser to the Guard. When the NMANG went to Vietnam, so did 2076. It came back home again, was sold to Turkey, and went through the invasion of Cyprus. In 1983, on a visit to Turkey, Laven was allowed to go on base and see, once again, 2076. It was still flying, and was then 30 years old.

Laven himself did considerably better. In a letter from a distant shore, he wrote: 'I still fly here, and only front seat, and only first-line fighters, and I can still fly and I am 68!')

Laven described the mission in a letter as, '. . . one of the worst I had ever flown. The pilots of the TDY squadron (the 615th TFS) had been at Clark for less than a week and had never flown in the Vietnam area. Some had never flown combat. My instructions were to carry ordnance needed to attack an undefined ground target in Laos. We were eight pilots, flying F-100Ds; I briefed and led the flight from Clark to Da Nang (the northernmost RVN air base).

'The target was in the Plaines des Jarres. There was no photo intelligence on the approaches, but good information on the target itself. It was an enclosed fortress area, with a thick wall about four or five feet high around a small motor pool with vehicles, a single building, and a covered shelter with what looked like a single .50-cal machine gun.

'I was allowed to choose takeoff time and the weapons load, 38 rockets (two pods) and four 500-lb (227-kg) bombs for each airplane. I also decided we'd need tankers for refuelling after takeoff, and on standby, if we needed them on the way back.

'We were to go around dawn, so I went to bed early, only to be called at about 2300 hr by the Commander of the 2nd Air Division, changing our ordnance to a loading I didn't think suitable for the target. This load changing continued for three days and, by the third evening, I was beginning to feel that the squadron commander was LBJ, McNamara was ops officer, and (USAF Chief of Staff General Curtis E) LeMay was flight leader.

'I had selected a time over target between the burnoff of the morning fog and haze, and the buildup of the afternoon thunderstorms. Instead, the attack times were changed on orders from above, so that they would put us over the target at the height of thunderstorm activity.

'We briefed, with explicit instructions to the second flight of four to follow me. If I found the target, my flight would hit it and then I would call in the second flight. If I missed, we'd all miss, and it would be my responsibility.

'We took off (on 9 June) and hit our rendezvous with the tankers, to find them way off the course we'd been told they'd be holding. Besides that, they were in and out of bad weather. There was a KC-135 for each pair of fighters and we all eventually hooked up. I checked that all eight had been refuelled, and then asked the tanker commander for a vector to the target. "What target?" he asked.'

(With respect to the tanker commander, he and his crew were on the first combat deployment of the Yankee Team Tanker Task Force, sent from Andersen AFB on Guam just two days earlier. Also based at Clark, they were as unfamiliar as Laven's pilots with the territory.)

'Fortunately, I'd kept track of time and approximate distance, and so I headed for where I thought the target was. My only instructions to the second flight were as before: follow me. Flight lead answered and said he was following.

'When I was about at bingo fuel (fuel required to get back to base), I spotted the target, called my flights and said I was going in. Each of us in my flight made two passes, and we felt we had done about 40 per cent damage, not bad for visual bombing in lousy weather. After my last man pulled off the target, I called the second flight lead and told him to make his passes. One of my bombs had hung up, so I dropped it; then my wing man radioed he didn't have enough fuel to get back to Da Nang. We headed for Udorn RTAFB, the first base in Thailand south of the Mekong river. I blew a tyre landing, and we had to wait for a crew to change it, then refuel and head back to Da Nang.

'The runway at Da Nang was then only about 6,000 ft (1830 m) long and was being lengthened. I landed and again blew a tyre; my F-100D had a faulty anti-skid system. I turned off the runway, ran over the wires to the runway lights, cut them and left my wing man with no runway lights. I positioned my airplane with the landing lights on, and asked for some trucks to help me give him some lights and perspective, and he landed safely.

'By the time we got to operations for debriefing, the second flight was reporting in. When we compared notes, not all of them matched, but that wasn't too unusual. Three days later, when RF-101s came back

Four fighter-bombers from the 481st TFS head out from Tan Son Nhut AB to drop napalm and strafe enemy positions. The nearest is F-100D 55-3569; she carries the green triangle on the vertical tail that marked the 'Crusaders' aircraft, and her starboard auxiliary fuel tank has '481 TFS' stencilled on the nose
(USAF 95475)

with photos, there were 17 bomb craters not in the target area. One was my hung bomb, and the other 16 had been dropped by the second flight about 25 miles (40 km) away from the assigned target. Photos showed we had done about 40 per cent damage, as we had claimed, and had hit the building which was an ammo storage area. We destroyed some vehicles and knocked a hole in the wall.

'There was an investigation, and I was blamed. For some years, before things were finally cleared up and I was completely exonerated, I was "the guy that bombed the wrong target". My tour as Wing Commander was cut short by a couple of months, and I was given my choice of any job in the USAF, if there was a vacancy. I knew I wouldn't make Brigadier General, so I chose an ANG slot as Senior Advisor to the Colorado Air Guard.'

Laven had led the first F-100 combat strike, the prototype of most of the sorties for the rest of the war: brief, takeoff, refuel, find and bomb the target, go home.

Backdrop for Escalation

Late in July 1964, the Navy began steaming near the coast of North Vietnam on missions overtly a show of force and covertly a gathering of electronic intelligence. On 2 August, in late afternoon, the Navy destroyer USS *Maddox* was attacked by a trio of North Vietnamese patrol torpedo boats, and drove them off after a brief engagement. President Johnson ordered the patrols to continue, and directed a second destroyer—USS *Turner Joy*—to sail with the *Maddox*. He also protested to the government in Hanoi.

On 4 August, after sunset and during bad weather, the *Maddox* again reported enemy fire (controversy surrounds that reported action; the full story is beyond the scope of this book). In retaliation, Johnson ordered a single maximum-effort strike by the Pacific fleet against North Vietnamese patrol boat bases and their supporting fuel supplies, and approved the movement of additional forces to Southeast Asia. Planes began arriving on 5 August.

The 405th TFW at Clark sent ten F-100s to Takhli RTAFB and eight from the 615th TFS, temporarily deployed to Clark, to Da Nang. Strike Command, that short-lived joint rapid deployment task force of the early 1960s, moved F-100s to compensate for the drawdown of inventory at Clark, and F-100s from TAC's 27th TFW at Cannon AFB, NM, and from the 401st TFW at England AFB, Louisiana, continued their rotational deployments to and from Da Nang. They were joined by tankers, F-105s, RF-101s, F-102s, B-57s and C-130s.

The RF-101s, flying routine reconnaissance missions north of the border, brought back a series of pictures taken 7 August of Phuc Yen, Hanoi's major air base (some sources say it was a U-2 overflight that produced the pictures; it may have been both). There were 39 enemy MiG-15s and 17s, just in from China, parked in revetments. General Hunter Harris, commanding PACAF, wanted to use the F-100s on alert at Da Nang to strike the MiG base in a surprise attack. The plan was to send the F-100s in at high speed and low level to drop cluster munitions (CBU-2A bombs) and then strafe the MiGs while suppressing the defences. But Harris' plan, although endorsed by Admiral U S Grant Sharp, Commander-in-Chief, Pacific, was turned down at higher levels in Washington.

A Laotian T-28 was shot down on 18 August 1964, at the northwest corner of the Plaines des Jarres. Air

Finned napalm bombs and SUU-7/A bomblet dispensers decorate the lower surfaces of this F-100D (55-3535) from the 429th TFS, 474th TFW, deployed from Cannon AFB, NM. She's turning into a bomb run sometime during October 1965. The heavy deposit of gun gases on the forward fuselage belly indicates either recent firing, or a neglected task
(USAF 95463)

Flaps and gear down, slats extended, this late model F-100D (56-3448, 16th from the end of the D production line) turns onto the final approach. Flight could be local training, ferrying, or a deployment, because no ordnance pylons have been fitted
(Rockwell International)

America, then coordinating rescue efforts, relayed the call for help. At Takhli, four F-100s scrambled in a Rescue Combat Air Patrol (RESCAP) to protect an Air America helicopter. It was a first, and a new and different mission for the Hun pilots, untrained for it. They couldn't save the helicopter; Pathet Lao gunners shot it down, and hit one of the Huns. Its pilot nursed it to a safer altitude across the Mekong River into Thailand, and ejected, to be picked up by another Air America helicopter.

An F-100 pilot (call sign: BALL 03), one of two escorting a reconnaissance mission on 18 November 1964, attacked an enemy anti-aircraft artillery position, and was shot down in central Laos near the North Vietnamese border. His loss triggered the first large-scale search and rescue effort of the war, involving 13 F-105s, eight Huns, six Navy A-1Es, two Air Rescue Service HH-43s, two Air America H-34s and an HU-16 before darkness ended the first day's hunt. On the second day, another HU-16 worked with four Thuds, four T-28s, two H-34s and a second HU-16. They saw a chute and wreckage; one Air America helicopter hovered over the scene while its copilot rode a cable down. He found the pilot dead from injuries suffered during his emergency landing.

F-100s In Barrel Roll

Near the end of 1964, President Johnson approved the overt action of Operation Barrel Roll, a limited series of bombings in Laos near the NVN border. The first mission, flown 14 December, was an armed reconnaissance strike against Route 8 and the Nape road bridge. Eight F-100s flew MiGCAP (MiG Combat Air Patrol) for F-105s from Korat RTAFB that arrived in the target area short of fuel, made just one pass at the bridge, and missed it.

On 21 December, the 428th TFS despatched four F-100s on an armed recon strike along Route 8. They were lightly armed with cluster munitions and 2.75-inch rockets; the enemy was heavily armed with flak, and pounded the Huns. They lost their way briefly, couldn't find any secondary targets, and soon were at bingo fuel. The outcome of this and earlier foul-ups

A dirty D, with 500-lb bombs inboard, auxiliary fuel tanks on the mid-point pylons, napalm outboard, and gun blast gas smearing the underside of the nose, heads into battle in October 1966. The triangle marking on the vertical tail identifies one of the 'Crusaders' of the 481st TFS (PACAF/Pickett Collection)

was an unsubtle message from General LeMay telling 2nd Air Division commander General Joseph Moore that he had expected a higher level of professionalism from USAF pilots.

Two regiments of the Viet Cong captured Binh Gia, one of the government-controlled hamlets in South Vietnam. US Army helicopters air-lifted ARVN Rangers to the scene in an attempt to retake the hamlet, but were driven off with heavy losses. Post-battle criticism divided along service lines; the Air Force said Army gunship helicopters didn't have enough firepower, and the Army said Air Force fighters were never available when they were needed.

As one result of the fiasco at Binh Gia, General Westmoreland asked for permission to use (read: command and control) whatever in-country jet fighters were available. His request was approved in late January 1965, for emergencies only. From then on, there were many emergencies, and the in-country jets—which were, of course, the F-100s—became the Army's fire brigades.

The F-100s went into action again on 13 January 1965, against the Ban Ken bridge on Route 7 in northern Laos. More than 100 anti-aircraft batteries defended the bridge; 34 of the guns were 37- or 57-mm cannon. Eight Huns, carrying CBU-2A cluster munitions for defence suppression, accompanied 16 F-105 bombers. The tactical plan called for all eight F-100s to attack at low level in line abreast, suppressing all gun sites simultaneously.

The F-100s hit the guns, but didn't knock out all of them. The bridge was cut by the first wave of F-105s, so the remaining Thuds joined in striking the defences. One F-105 and one F-100 were shot down, the latter on its fifth run-in against the guns. Poor judgement, said General Moore in a post-mission critique; the force should have left after cutting the bridge. That's what it was sent to do.

On 8 February, Air Vice Marshal Nguyen Cao Ky led a force of 24 VNAF A-1s, accompanied by six Farm Gate A-1 pathfinders and 20 F-100s for defence suppression, on a mission to hit military barracks at Chap Le in North Vietnam. The Huns went in first and hammered the anti-aircraft positions, while the Farm Gate sextet bombed likely targets. Ky's force never showed, having diverted to another target.

The enemy counter-attacked at Qui Nhon, killing 20 Americans by blowing up a hotel. In retaliation, the US command ordered Flaming Dart II on 11 February. It sent 99 Navy planes to hit Chanh Hoa. A second force of 28 VNAF Skyraiders, supported by 28 F-100s, went back to Chap Le and pounded it again.

During February, an elite VC battalion moved into the central highlands of Vietnam; on the 24th, it surrounded South Vietnamese forces on Route 19 in the An Khe valley. General Westmoreland, now holding the authority to send USAF aircraft into emergency situations, acted. A mixed force of F-100s from the 613th TFS, plus B-57s and A-1Es, covered the arriving Army UH-1B helicopters that evacuated the surrounded troops in three round trips, with no casualties. They carried out 220 officers and men who otherwise might have been slaughtered.

First Peals of Rolling Thunder

Also during February, President Johnson decided it was time to begin a sustained series of air strikes against 94 primary North Vietnamese targets—military barracks, vehicles, ammunition dumps, and radar sites—chosen from a list prepared by Commander-in-Chief, Pacific (CINCPAC) for the Joint Chiefs of Staff. It was to be a limited air campaign, primarily a political and pscyhological weapon. It had a unique chain of command; Johnson and a few key administration officials made all decisions and gave all orders. They selected targets, specified times at which they were to be struck, and defined the armament to be carried, instead of coordinating the efforts with commanders in the field who knew local conditions and were abreast of changing developments. And they named it Rolling Thunder.

There was a 19-day quiet spell after the offensive strike of Flaming Dart II. Then on 2 March 1965,

One of PACAF's own F-100Ds, this camouflaged bird is arriving at Bien Hoa AB in November 1965. She's from the 510th TFS of the 3rd TFW and, like the other PACAF Ds and Fs, is equipped with Doppler radar for long-range navigation. The giveaway: the tiny air intake just above the fin leading-edge break
(USAF/Pickett Collection)

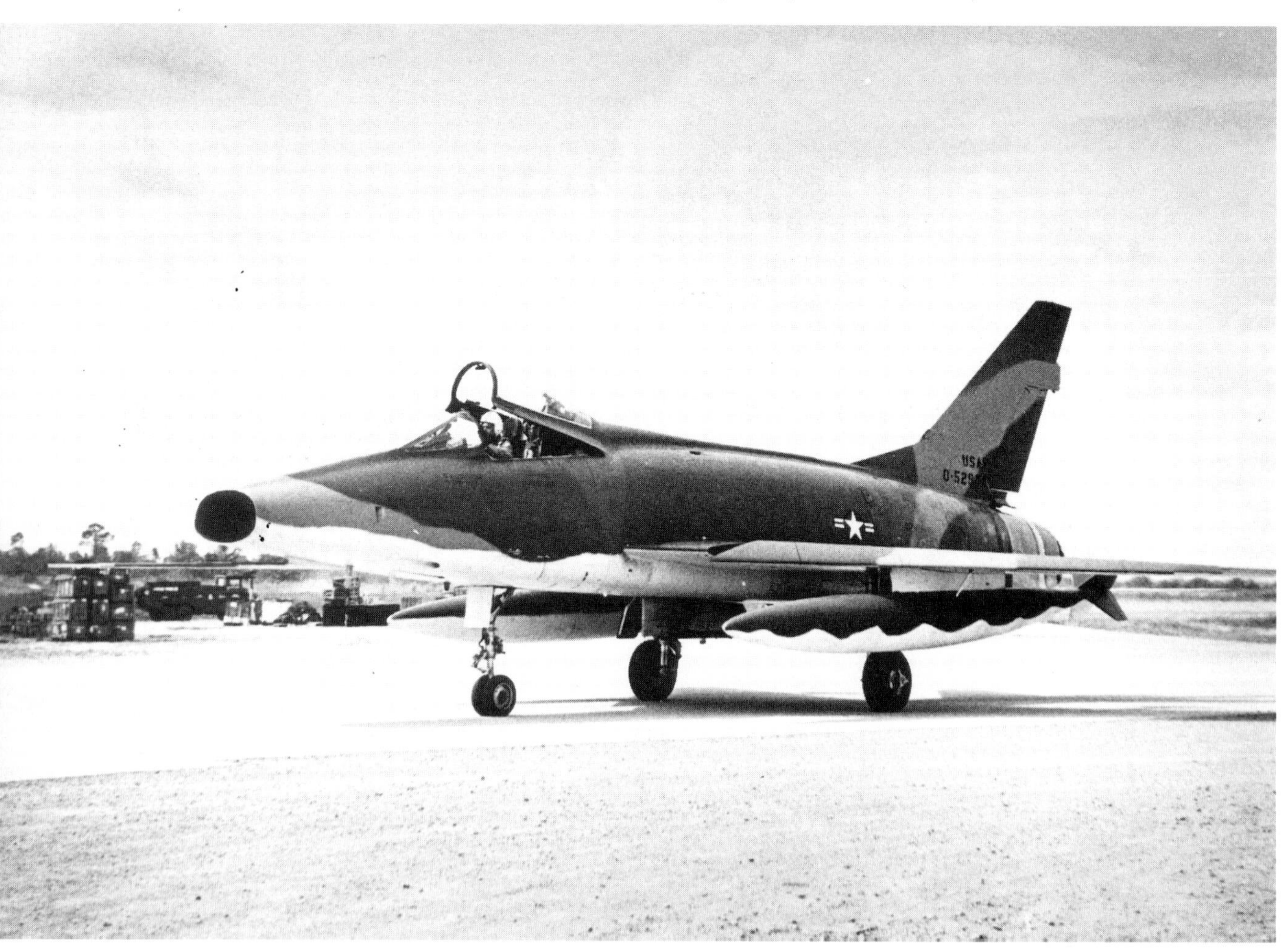

Rolling Thunder began with a strike against an ammunition depot at Xom Bong, 35 miles (56 km) inside North Vietnam. The mixed force included 44 F-100Ds from Da Nang, an equal number of Thuds from Thailand bases, and 20 B-57s out of Tan Son Nhut, supported by tankers and other aircraft.

The Hun pilots were first in, firing 2.75-inch rockets and 20-mm cannon to suppress the defences. One of the F-100s was hit, and its pilot, Lieutenant Hayden Lockhart, Jr, ejected. He was able to evade capture for a week, but on 9 March he had the dubious honour of becoming the first USAF pilot captured by the enemy.

Up to this point, the US planes that had participated routinely in air strikes had been marked with Vietnamese insignia and carried a Vietnamese airman. On 9 March, the JCS directed that US aircraft could fight autonomously within South Vietnam. Restrictions remained; the USAF could not launch strikes from airfields in Thailand, and could not fly missions that the VNAF was capable of completing. But from then on, American airmen and planes fought under their own colours.

Interlude B: **Soliloquy**

Jed Erskine did a combat tour of 288 missions in Vietnam with the Lucky Devils, the 614th TFS, 35th TFW, between the Aprils of 1968 and 1969, gaining the Distinguished Flying Cross and 15 Air Medals in the process. He had graduated first in his pilot training class, and chose the F-100 as his first assignment.

'Flying the F-100 in combat,' he wrote, 'was a dream come true to me. I think of her as a mischievous, but not malicious, joker who enjoyed deflating pilots' egos. And she did that very often. We loved her, but she was not nice to us. She would bite you, but always bring you home, even with large pieces blown away. Almost everything was faster, but we were proud to be flying her.'

Erskine's contribution is a poetic combat soliloquy that reads like this:

You're on the way, with a warload festooning the F-100's wings and a target in your mind. The sun is hot, your wingman is tucked in close, the tanks are full, and right now there is no better place to be and nothing you'd rather be doing. And soon you'll be wondering why the hell you ever took up this line of work, because you could get killed (Steffens Collection)

F-100D

This is beautiful,
Just airborne—on the wing,
Lead is frozen in the sun.
What a beautiful bird.
I can hear myself sucking on oxygen.
Gear is up . . . engine's humming,
5,000 foot check, disconnect the lanyard,
Settle down, move out to route.
Beautiful down there.
Armament safety check complete.
Wonder who will receive these today?
Between us we have four snakeyes and four napes,
plus 20 mike mike of course.
It's beautiful here, mountains below, puffy clouds above.
A cryptic message on the radio—ignore it.
We're there—start down; speed brakes . . . ready . . . now . . . air buffet
Refocus . . . Refocus
All mechanical and calculating now.
Emergency bail-out area.
Location of friendlies.
What's the target?
Set 'em up hot.
Red golf balls drifting up look soft and silly.
Lead's in hot . . . lead's off left.
I'm in . . . check the switches.
Check the target . . . airspeed . . . dive angle . . . pipper . . . release altitude
Forget all that now. Go for the feel of it.
Pickle button. EXCITEMENT ADRENALIN
PULL . . . HARD . . . LEFT . . . LOOK . . . CHECK SIX
Going up, airspeed down, ease off
look at the smoke . . . soft turn . . . then
Back in . . . there's a hooch—a truck—maybe that's a . . .
What the Hell . . . WAKE UP . . . PICK ONE
Keep turning—pulling—AIRSPEED . . . AIRSPEED
Off left 500 knots—Head this sucker home.
Snappy rejoin and I'm back on lead's wing—settle down
Bird's OK. Lead's OK, not like last time.
What a beautiful bird.
We really shouldn't make her do these things,
But she will survive it.
That's why I love her so.

A word or two of explanation may be needed. 'Snakeyes' are iron bombs with air brakes that deploy after release and slow the bomb so that it doesn't explode underneath the airplane. 'Nape' is short for napalm. A common ordnance load was called 'snake and nape' by the pilots. And '20 mike mike' is the phonetic treatment of 20-mm, the calibre of the F-100's cannon battery.

'Refocus,' said Erskine, 'describes the mental transition from the serenity of the peaceful cruise to the harsh demands on the pilot to descend from that safe environment to the target area.'

'Red golf balls' are enemy tracers. The 'pipper' is the target marker of a gunsight; when the pipper is on the target, that's where the bullets or bombs go when fired or dropped. The 'pickle button' is the push-button switch that releases the bombs; it got its name by association with the claims for bombing accuracy of the famed Norden bombsight of World War 2 that could put the bombs '. . . in a pickel barrel.' (Not really; but it was a good story.) A 'hooch' is a native house; it was easier to destroy a 'hooch' than a 'home', in a war where euphemism ruled.

Erskine added, 'Well, she didn't always bring you home . . . During my tour, our wing lost about 23 aircraft and 20 or 21 pilots. The bird was getting a little tired about then, and the bad guys got to be better shots.

'The J57 engine had a cable wrapped around the compressor section to reduce vibrations in the forward portion of the engine. They hoped that would stop the engines from blowing up as often. The strange thing was that it worked.

'Next, the wings started to come off, and we had a 4G limit on the Hun until each one had been put through the IRAN (Inspect and Repair As Necessary) facility in Tainan. There they rebuilt the wing box, and we had our 7.33G limit back. Most of us thought that a 4G limit was dangerous because that didn't give much to pull with when you were recovering from a dive. Especially if you pressed it a little and were a little low when you started your pull.

'The Hun had what was called "non-linear stick gearing". That was a linkage between stick and slab tail that resulted in an ever-increasing slab movement to stick movement as you pulled back. The stick was quite docile in normal flight, but when you had the stick back in your belly, a little movement would give you a great amount of pitch change. In the flare for landing, with the stick back, the engine was at idle and, if you pumped the stick a little, the demand on the hydraulic system exceeded the hydraulic pump output at engine idle, and the stick would freeze. That cured you of pumping the stick in the flare.

'The outboard ailerons on the D models had more leverage for adverse yaw. At high angles of attack, if you moved the stick left or right, the bird would snap-roll in the opposite direction. That cured you of moving the ailerons when you had a lot of G on the airplane.'

Erskine still remembers the F-100D the way one remembers an old love, now lost somewhere back in time, but still beautiful, unaged and unageing.

Chapter 5
Scenarios for Super Sabres
Interlude C: The Base at Tuy Hoa

A playwright sets the scene before writing a line of dialogue. So should I, because few of us knew then—and fewer now—what Vietnam was like, and what kind of an environment challenged the Super Sabres and other US weapons of war in that Southeastern Asian theatre.

Vietnam bends around the coast of Southeast Asia for about 1,000 miles (1609 km), looking like a surrealistic dumbbell with large, and approximately equal, land masses at north and south extremities, joined by a thin stretch on either side of the 17th parallel. The capital cities of Hanoi, in the Democratic Republic of Vietnam (DRVN), and Saigon, formerly in the State of Vietnam and now Ho Chi Minh City in the DRVN, are about 720 air miles apart, or approximately the airline distance between New York City and Charleston, South Carolina, or between London, England, and Bologna, Italy.

The land lies between the eighth and 23rd parallels, north of the equator, and its climate is tropical. Heat and humidity are oppressive, but some relief comes from monsoon rains, which fall during the winter in the North and the summer in the South.

A mountainous spine, the Annamite Chain, occupies much of the northern narrow section of the former State of Vietnam. The southern section is the broad, flat delta land of the Mekong rising into rolling hills and wide plains. The eastern coast is a long and narrow plain, once extensively cultivated and thickly populated.

Each of these regions had its characteristic warfare. In the delta, it was infantry and the 'Brown-Water Navy' against guerrilla forces. In the rising hills, it was 'search-and-destroy' operations against North Vietnamese troops. The coastal plains, which were to hold the primary operational airfields for the F-100s, were subject to single, sharp attacks by raiding parties intent on damaging US materiel and supplies.

Running along the border that separated both Vietnams from Cambodia and Laos was the infamous Ho Chi Minh trail, a footpath that turned into a major truck route for troops, supplies and munitions headed south from the Communist North. Because South Vietnam had a lengthy border for its size, enemy infiltration from the Trail was relatively easy.

Airfields had been built earlier by the French near or in centres of population: Bien Hoa, Binh Thuy, Da Nang, Nha Trang, Pleiku, and Tan Son Nhut. But in 1965, they were totally inadequate for contemporary warplanes, and only three—Da Nang, Bien Hoa, and Tan Son Nhut—held potential for military jet aircraft. Bien Hoa was marginal; Da Nang, the major French military airfield, could just about support F-100s. Tan Son Nhut was the commercial airport for Saigon; it needed a new runway, or a repaired and strengthened one, to handle military jets.

US engineers immediately began planning new jet airfields for coastal sites at Cam Ranh Bay, Phan Rang, Phu Cat, and Tuy Hoa, and an expansion of the strip at Pleiku for emergency recoveries of battle-damaged aircraft. The basic decision was to build a pair of 10,000-foot (3050-m) runways for each of the major jet airfields.

Four of these bases—Bien Hoa, Phan Rang, Phu Cat, and Tuy Hoa—were to become home to Super Sabre units during their combat tours.

The Packaging of the Routes

Coordinating air missions is one hell of a job, especially when you have conflicting requirements, demands, services, and personalities. Several methods were proposed, considered, and rejected. What finally evolved was an arbitrary division of the combat theatre into six areas called Route Packages (Route Packs or RP for short; Roman numerals defined the specific RP). The RPs began at the demilitarised zone (DMZ) and reached north to the border with China. Route Package VI, in the northeastern corner of North Vietnam, was further divided into two areas, VI A and VI B. Hanoi, Haiphong, and all the most lucrative targets were in RP VI A and VI B.

The Air Force controlled missions into RPs I, V, and VI A; the Navy, into II, III, IV, and VI B. But, because initially RP I was considered as a simple extension of the ground battle zone, air strikes into that RP were directed by Military Assistance Command Vietnam (MACV).

But what you really need to know is that the F-100s divided their time in the air among targets in Route Packages I and II, targets in Laos and Cambodia, and targets in South Vietnam. The latter were called in-country missions, and the others were, equally obviously, out-country missions.

When the Joint Chiefs of Staff began listing potential targets for air strikes, they placed a high priority on stopping, or at least choking, the southward flow of war materiel from the industries and depots around Hanoi and Haiphong. They hoped also to slow down infiltration of the south. And they thought one good way to do that would be to destroy the railroad network in North Vietnam.

Hanoi and Haiphong were rail centres. The French had built a major line in the northeast from Hanoi to Lungchow, just inside the Chinese border, as a commercial link to the markets and manufacturing of Canton. Another line ran northwest to the Kunming region, a resort area the French frequented to avoid summering in the Red River Valley.

North Vietnam's railroad system seemed most vulnerable at two key bridges. All rail traffic headed north traversed the Paul Doumer bridge that spanned the Red River in the outskirts of Hanoi. Everything headed south by rail and highway crossed the Song Ma river on a bridge at Thanh Hoa, a village about 75 miles (120 km) south of Hanoi. Knock out those bridges, and Hanoi's war effort would be seriously hindered. So it was decided that bridges in general, and those two in particular, would be early targets.

Busting Bridges with Bombs

Bridges are notoriously difficult targets, and the bridges of Southeast Asia were no different from bridges in Korea in 1951, or in Europe and North Africa and Asia in 1944. In those wars, aircrews had learned at high cost that bridges were hard to hit, harder to destroy, heavily defended, and easily bypassed. But lessons learned had not found their way into textbooks studied, and so the USAF and Navy set out to drop two bridges into the Red River. It was to become a terribly expensive demolition project and, in the end, an investment that gave a very low return.

The bridge at Thanh Hoa was called Ham Rung, Vietnamese for Dragon's Jaw, in reference to a folktale about the area. Don't think in terms of the Golden Gate or the George Washington bridges; the Ham Rung bridge was only 56 feet wide, just enough for a single one-metre gauge track flanked by cantilevered 22-foot wide concrete highways. Completed in 1964, it was a modern structure, well supported with heavy concrete underpinnings.

Push the pickle button, start the pullout, feel the G-suit inflate and watch the condensation trails from the jungle humidity as a pair of slick 750-lb bombs drops away from your Super Sabre (F-100D 55-3560). It's May 1967, more than two decades distant now
(USAF KE28228)

The Ham Rung bridge was targeted first, as an early mission in the Rolling Thunder campaign. Destroying that bridge, it was believed, should cause at least a temporary setback in the movement of supplies to the irregulars in the south.

After a 24-hour delay because of marginal weather and a shortage of tanker aircraft, the 79 aircraft of Rolling Thunder Mission 9-Alpha launched just after midday on 3 April 1965. In the mixed strike force were 46 F-105s, 16 carrying two Bullpup missiles, and 30 carrying eight 750-lb (340-kg) general-purpose (GP) bombs, with 15 of the 30 assigned to bomb the bridge.

There were 21 F-100s from several bases in the RVN. Seven of them, armed with two 750-lb (340-kg) bombs and two pods each loaded with 19 2.75-inch rockets, were assigned—along with 15 Republic F-105s—to suppress the anti-aircraft artillery defences at the bridge. Four more F-100s, armed with Sidewinder air-to-air missiles in addition to their four 20-mm cannon, were the MiGCAP (MiG Combat Air Patrol). Eight F-100s drew RESCAP (Rescue Combat Air Patrol), a job that could require orbiting above any downed airman, keeping him

Napalm and iron bombs aboard, this F-100D heading into combat in Vietnam also is carrying a centreline camera pod, used to record the accuracy of, and damage done by, a strike
(Steffens Collection)

protected from capture while a helicopter or two came to the rescue. A pair of Super Sabres flew weather reconnaissance.

The F-100s came up toward Thanh Hoa along the coast, and joined the F-105s flying in from their Thailand bases. The Huns rocketed and bombed the defences, and the Thuds launched 32 Bullpup missiles and dropped 120 bombs against the bridge. There were good hits, but when the smoke cleared away, the bridge showed some charred spots and a damaged roadway section on the southern side. On the ground near the bridge site lay the wreckage of an F-100 and one of the two RF-101s assigned to photograph the results.

There were three lessons learned that day. One, bridges were still a difficult target. Two, latter-day weapons technology was not perceptibly better than the iron bombs of an earlier era. Put bluntly, the Bullpup missiles were totally useless against a hard target. Three, the ground-based anti-air defences were really effective.

Go 'round and Try It Again

So a restrike was scheduled for the next day. But the F-100s were not assigned to defence-suppression; nobody was. The Super Sabres flew MiGCAP, RESCAP, and weather reconnaissance, as before. And 48 Thuds would drop 384 750-lb (340-kg) general-purpose bombs.

In flights of four, the F-105s passed over the IP (initial point) of their bomb runs, made the trip down the chute, and pulled off the target. Above the F-100 MiGCAP orbited. And above them, a quartet of MiG-17s nosed down and headed for the four Thuds of ZINC flight that had arrived a little ahead of schedule and were waiting to make their bombing runs.

Two of the MiGCAP Super Sabres were being flown by Lieutenant Colonel Emmett L Hays and Captain Keith B Connolly, from the 416th TFS. Connolly spotted the MiGs as they blew through on their way to their targets, and called a warning to ZINC flight. For whatever reasons, the warning didn't get through; the MiGs hit two of the F-105Ds, sluggish as they were with their heavy bomb loads, and kept on going. Connolly and Hays were in position to attack by then; Hays got a lock-on and launched a Sidewinder, which either missed, or malfunctioned and therefore missed. Connolly fired a burst from his cannon, but it didn't register on the fast-moving MiG he had held briefly in his gunsight.

In that first air-to-air jet combat experience for the Air Force in Vietnam (the Navy had their first the day before), as Connolly said, 'We lost.'

The sad truth was that the Super Sabre, however well flown and fought, was inferior to its enemy opposition in air-to-air combat. MiG-17s and -21s, operating in the outstanding air defence system established by the North Vietnamese, totally outclassed them. The F-4s arriving in the theatre were far better equipped to fight the air-to-air war, with powerful radar, advanced weapons, and an extra pair of eyes.

Please, people, label photographs with time and place! This lovely air-to-air study of an F-100D (O-55-3651) was obviously taken sometime after 1965. It's a camouflaged airplane, its two inner guns have been fired, but there are no weapons pylons fitted
(Montgomery Collection)

RIGHT
An F-100D (56-2955?) and a pathfinder F-100F-20 (58-1215) taxi on the AM-2 runway at Tuy Hoa AB, RVN, during December 1966. Note that the undersurface light grey camouflage paint has been extended upward and forward to wrap around the inlet. The dark patch on the upper lip is the antenna housing for the AN/ASG-17 fire-control radar
(USAF 101575)

The F-100, as a tactical bomber, was inferior to the F-105 and F-4. The Thuds could carry a larger bomb load further and faster, and—more importantly—could do that on the deck because the F-105 was built to take the extreme structural strains of low-level, high-speed flight. The versatile F-4s were good bombers, because they could haul a heavy load fast and far, and were formidable fighters after they had dropped their bombs.

In wars, those who do the actual fighting learn quickly to make the best of what they have, to improvize, to innovate, because that way leads to survival. Given a mixed batch of F-100s, F-105s, and F-4s, an air force commander assigns roles and missions on the basis of what each airplane can or can't do, not on whether he likes the design.

Transformation to Airborne Artillery

Thus, more modern airplanes with higher performance took over the long-range missions deep into enemy territory, and the Super Sabres concentrated their efforts on the in-country war, and an air war that was fought above Route Packs I and II, primarily, and on strikes into Laos, and—for its duration—the invasion of Cambodia.

(Note in passing: a neutral country has, under the laws of war, the obligation to maintain its neutrality by armed force if necessary. The Swiss, for example, did this during World War 2, intercepting and driving off Allied and Axis forces alike. Since Cambodia didn't do this very well, if at all, the invasion of Cambodian territory by Vietnamese and US forces was perceived, at high government levels, as legitimate under the accepted rules of war.)

The F-100s became the primary airborne artillery strength of the ground armies, hauling bombs from home bases to targets discovered by troops in contact and marked by airborne forward air controllers (FACs). And, while that job was as important as any in the war—and sometimes of overriding importance—it was not a very glamorous job. Read any of the histories of that war in Southeast Asia, and you will be disappointed to find, if you are an F-100 enthusiast, very few references to the airplane. For all an uninformed reader would know, Super Sabres were a small and unimportant part of the war in Vietnam.

That impression has been reinforced because there were no Super Sabre air-to-air victories over enemy aircraft, let alone a Super Sabre ace. One truly courageous F-100 pilot, George Day, received the Medal of Honor; but it was for his behaviour in captivity, not for daring feats in the air.

It's true that most missions flown by the F-100 pilots were predictable in form, if not in content. But, while it's not totally true to say that if you describe one Super Sabre strike, you've described them all, it is uncomfortably close to the truth. Brief, takeoff, cruise to target area, find the FAC, drop on his

smoke, strafe, climb out, cruise home, land, debrief. Next day, recycle that one.

It's a pity those missions did not get more recognition. It took much courage and skill—perhaps a bit more than usual—to hurl your pink body toward the ground, hoping that the VC gunners don't have you bore-sighted, that the bombs don't hang up, that the guns fire, that you'll miss the friendlies and hit the bad guys, that the tanker will be there on the way back, and that a few other factors will band together and make this one safe for you. And the next one. And the next, and the next.

Increasing the Pressure

The increasing demand for more airpower resulted in the deployment to Vietnam of additional F-100 squadrons, as well as the in-theatre formation of tactical fighter wings. Although the initial command structure was an inheritance of peacetime practice, by March 1966, all USAF units in Vietnam and Thailand were part of the 7th Air Force. In turn, 7AF was a subordinate command operationally to Westmoreland's MACV, and administratively to the Commander-in-Chief, Pacific Air Forces (CINCPACAF).

Two of the earliest F-100 wings were the 3rd and 35th. The 3rd was based at Bien Hoa, about 15 miles (24 km) north of Saigon. The 35th operated from Phan Rang, on the coast.

The 3rd TFW had been a B-26 (Douglas A-26, for those with shorter memories) unit in the Korean War, but moved to the US without personnel or equipment (a paper transfer of a headquarters) in January 1964 to begin training and rotating its squadrons to Southeast Asia. Home-based at England AFB, Louisiana, the 3rd began its move to Bien Hoa in November 1965, with the deployment of the 510th TFS (in-theatre tail code letters: CE). It was joined by the 531st TFS (tail code: CP) in December, and the 90th (tail code: CB) in February 1966.

The 308th TFS, part of the 31st TFW, deployed to Southeast Asia in December 1965, from Homestead AFB, Florida, its temporary home since the Cuban missile crisis of October 1962; it was assigned temporarily to the 3rd TFW before being moved to Tuy Hoa a year later and assigned to the 31st TFW there. The 416th TFS, fourth unit of the 3rd TFW, moved to Tan Son Nhut, but remained under the operational control of its parent wing. In June 1966, the 416th moved to Bien Hoa. It later was moved to Phu Cat and operational control of the 37th TFW.

During the first six months of combat, pilots of the 3rd TFW completed more than 13,000 sorties, and expected to double that after 12 months of fighting. For comparison, during its three-year tour in the Korean war, flying fighter-bombers, the wing logged 33,000 combat sorties, or an average of 11,000 a year. Thus, the intensity of action for the 3rd TFW in Vietnam was almost 2½ times its level in Korea.

North American, in its contemporary house magazine, *Skyline*, reported the projected figure of 26,000 combat sorties a year for the 3rd TFW. Since there are no days off in war, divide 26,000 by 365, and you get an average of 71.2 sorties each day. During the first six months of combat, the 3rd grew from an initial strength of approximately 20 F-100Ds and Fs to approximately 100. So the 3rd TFW sortie rate was probably about one per F-100 per day, a good figure for those times and a wartime environment.

The 35th TFW was inactivated in October 1957, after Korean combat and air defence roles in Japan. Then it was reorganized in April 1966 at Da Nang AB, moved in October 1966 to Phan Rang, replacing the 366th TFW there, and became an all-F-100 wing. Its squadrons were the 352nd (code: VM), the 613th (VP), the 614th (also VP), the 615th (VZ), and Detachment 1, of the 612th TFS (code: HS), the F-100F 'Misty FAC' unit. When the Air National Guard was recalled in early 1968 (Chapter 8), the 35th gained the 120th TFS (code: VS), Colorado ANG, with its 22 F-100Ds. That strength, added to the 80 to 120 F-100Ds and Fs already at Phan Rang, brought the wing to approximately 140 airplanes.

The 3rd and 35th were joined in theatre by the middle of 1967 by the 31st TFW, based at Tuy Hoa, and the 37th, based at Phu Cat. The 31st TFW, which was moved from Florida and the aftermath of the Cuban missile crisis to Tuy Hoa in the RVN, included the 'Emerald Knights' of the 308th TFS (code: SM), the 309th (SS), and the 306th (SD), with a total between 60 and 80 assigned F-100Ds. The 31st gained the 188th TFS of the New Mexico ANG ('The Enchilada Air Force'; code SK) and the 136th TFS of the New York ANG ('Rocky's Raiders'; code SG) in May 1968. Each Guard unit brought 22 F-100Cs with it, swelling the Tuy Hoa Super Sabre fleet to about 110 aircraft of the active USAF plus 44 Cs and Fs of the Guard units.

The 37th was originally a Combat Support Group, based at Phu Cat, and was activated as a Tactical Fighter Wing in 1967. Its initial unit was the 416th TFS (code: HE). It later gained the 355th TFS (code: HP) and, when Detachment 1 of the 612th became a full squadron (code: HS) in July 1968, it too was assigned to the 37th. Finally, the 174th TFS, of the Iowa ANG, joined the 37th TFW as a gained unit, with its 22 F-100s. Total strength of the 37th peaked between 80 and 110 F-100Ds, which included between 15 and 18 F-100F 'Misty FAC' aircraft.

So the F-100 units in the Republic of Vietnam grew to a maximum strength of about 490 aircraft with which to rollback, upon request, enemy forces. Of course, the 490 never were all ready at one time.

It's the popular conception that a war drains all available resources, and that every aircraft, ship, tank and gun that can be spared is sent to the fighting front. And yet, in September 1968, the total F-100 force in the Republic of Vietnam was 317 C, D and F

Coming home with empty pylons and partial fuel, this F-100C (53-1741) of the 188th TFS, New Mexico Air National Guard, banks into the pattern at Tuy Hoa AB. Note the open revetments and hardstands near the taxiway, the fuel farm (above the Hun's vertical tail), and the construction materials laid out on the beach (below the cockpit). There are cleared areas, indicating that the base is not yet completed. The time is around mid-1968, and the 'Enchilada Air Force' has been at Tuy Hoa for just a few weeks
(USAF K34357)

models, according to North American Aviation's Aircraft Location Record documents.

It's interesting to look at percentages here. There were 76 F-100Cs, or 31 per cent of the total USAF inventory of that model; 215 F-100Ds, or 41 per cent of the total inventory; and 26 F-100Fs, or 14 per cent. In terms of total production, the 76 F-100Cs represented 16 per cent; the F-100Ds, 17 per cent; and the F-100Fs, 8 per cent. At that time, the total USAF inventory of all F-100 models was 1,000 airplanes; adding in those that went to friendly nations raises that total to 1,215. The total built was 2,292. Perhaps that gives some idea of fleet attrition to accidents, combat losses, and all other causes. Out of 2,292 F-100s built, in September 1968, less than 14 per cent were in the combat theatre.

Runways and Revetments

You probably also ought to know about the base environment in which the F-100s lived and moved and had their being. In the old days of World War 2 and the Korean war, temporary runways were assembled from planks made of steel that was made lighter, but somewhat stronger, by a myriad of punched holes, each with a bent-down rim. These pierced-steel planks (PSP) interlocked, and were laid on grass, gravel, sand, and whatever to make operational runways. Their surface tore tyres, and was not very effective for wet-weather braking, but in general PSP was the closest thing to an instant runway and hardstand that Army or Air Force engineers had.

Enter the technology of the 1960s, in the form of AM-2, an aluminium matting replacement for PSP. Its planks also interlocked, were two feet (0.6 m) wide by either six or 12 ft (1.8–3.6 m) long, and had a flat, solid upper surface coated with an anti-skid material to improve wet-weather braking. They were laid on a sand base that had been wet down and then rolled flat, and they made an exceptionally good runway in lieu of a permanent concrete installation. The AM-2 runways were 102 ft (31 m) wide and 10,000 ft (3048 m) long, and their material cost to taxpayers was $3.83 million per runway. Originally regarded as temporary runways until concrete installations could be completed, the AM-2 runways stayed in use until the US left the country, even after a parallel concrete runway had been laid down.

A few minutes after midnight on 1 November 1964, the US air base at Bien Hoa was hit by 60 to 80 rounds of incoming mortar fire from a small enemy force that escaped without ever being seen or intercepted. The shells killed four Americans, wounded 30 others, destroyed five B-57 bombers, severely damaged eight more, and slightly damaged seven. It was a tremendous blow in terms of the effect on morale, and a severe blow to USAF airpower as well as to its ego. Never before had any ground troops attacked and badly mauled an Air Force base.

To add some protection for the aircraft, in August 1965, the Air Force began erecting three-sided revetments made of corrugated steel bins 12 ft (3.6 m) high and 5.5 ft (1.6 m) wide, filled with earth for stability and blast protection. These pre-fabricated revetments had been developed by the Air Force Logistics Command and the American Rolling Mill Co (ARMCO), and by the end of 1965, hardstands at Bien Hoa, Da Nang, and Tan Son Nhut had been enclosed by ARMCO walls.

But a revetment with one open side is no protection against the rocket that lands dead centre, or the mortar shell ditto. During the spring offensive by the North Vietnamese army supported by Viet Cong irregulars, their mortar and rocket bombardments destroyed 25 USAF aircraft and damaged another 251. That further setback spurred the installation of shelters, made of a double corrugated steel arch sandwiching an 18-inch (45.7 cm) layer of concrete, poured in place. A free-standing backwall to this shelter, suitably pierced by a hole to let out engine exhaust, gave protection equal to that of the roof shell. Some of the shelters were fitted with front closures, but they were a minority. The first cover was poured in October 1968, and the last was capped at Tuy Hoa on 13 January 1970. Most of them were built by Air Force RED HORSE engineering units (RED HORSE = Rapid Engineer Deployment, Heavy Operational Repair Squadrons, anything for an acronym!) aided by troop labour. The total under 7th Air Force jurisdiction was 373 shelters and about 1,000 revetments.

Finally, a brief word about air traffic. An F-100 base, with its alert scramble aircraft standing ready to go, and its remaining strength in revetments or under shelters, waiting for their assignments, was a busy, busy place. In January 1967, Robert R Rodwell, of *Flight International* reporting from Vietnam, called the 3rd TFW base at Bien Hoa the world's busiest airport. It logged an average, said Rodwell, of 64,000 'runway actions' a month, which is, if you work it out, one every 42 seconds, around the clock, seven days a week of a 31-day month.

That is busy. But it was always a busy war for the F-100s.

Unfinished business: the Ham Rong bridge. To emphasize the earlier point about the difficulties of bridge-busting, consider that the bridge at Thanh Hoa was finally dropped into the Song Ma river on 13 May 1972, a little more than seven years after the first attack against it. During those years, the bridge received 873 air attacks; its defences chewed up 11 aircraft and their crews; its structure resisted the explosive force of nearly 2,000 tons (two kilotons, or the power of a small tactical nuclear weapon) of munitions. Whatever damage occurred was repaired within days, sometimes hours, and the bridge was never out of action for very long.

It was finally brought down by salvos of 2,000- and 3,000-lb (907–1360-kg) laser-guided bombs, dropped by USAF Phantoms. But by then, the ingenious North Vietnamese had built alternate routes that bypassed the bridge, and so the loss of the Dragon's Jaw bridge was not a serious blow. And also, by then, it was apparent that bridge or no bridge, the Democratic Republic of Vietnam had lost battles, but had won the war.

Interlude C: **The Base at Tuy Hoa**

With the largest number of assigned Super Sabres, Tuy Hoa was the busiest of the F-100 bases for a while during the war in Vietnam. It operated five full squadrons, three that were the regular organizational units of the 31st TFW, and two Air National Guard squadrons gained by the 31st. Located on the coast, Tuy Hoa was sometimes jocularly called 'The Atlantic City of the South China Sea.'

Bruce F Hanke, then an Airman First Class, was assigned to the 31st Armament and Electronics Maintenance Squadron of the 31st TFW at Tuy Hoa from May 1968 to November 1969. He wrote a detailed description of the base for this book, as well as contributing some memories of maintenance problems.

'The base was about four or five kilometres south of Tuy Hoa, a small, fairly quiet town of fishermen, farmers and a few VC. About two kilometres south was Phu Hiep Army Airfield, and just south of that was a Korean Army outpost. The Army's 91st Evac Hospital at Phu Hiep provided some of our medical care because we only had a small clinic. They used our exchange, which wasn't that big, but was bigger than theirs.

'The contract for Tuy Hoa construction was approved on 27 May 1966, and work began in June when the contractors built their tent camp. All materials were directly off-loaded on the beach right there, instead of being channelled through the already crowded ports.

'The first runway and parking facilities were AM-2 matting. (AM-2 aluminium matting replaced the earlier PSP—Pierced Steel Planking—as a pre-fabricated material for temporary runway construction.) Later, a concrete runway was added, but the AM-2 ramp was used until the base was abandoned in mid-1970.

'The first logistics aircraft—a C-124 and a C-130—landed on the AM-2 runway on 12 November, and on 15 November, the first F-100Ds arrived to open the

Vast facilities for a half-vast war, the sprawling base at Phan Rang heats up in the midday sun. Officers' and airmen's quarters lie at the left; in the right background you can see the runways. And in between, all of the infrastructure, soaking up infrared
(Ulrich Collection)

airfield. They were from the 308th TFS, which had been operating out of an overcrowded Bien Hoa, and they had just returned from a combat mission in the Central Highlands. The first combat mission from Tuy Hoa went on 16 November. On 12 December, the 306th and 309th TFS arrived from Homestead AFB, Florida, and made the 31st TFW fully operational.

'Construction on the parallel 9,500-ft (2895-m) concrete runway had begun in late November and was completed in April 1967. All the other facilities were completed by June to replace the early expeditionary tent camps. Almost all of the new buildings were pre-fabricated metal structures from the States, with the exception of a few wooden structures that had been used by the contractors as barracks. They also left behind a few air-conditioned trailer type buildings that were used as officer and senior NCO quarters, a source of hard feelings on the part of enlisted men. The difference in food quality also was noticeable; enlisted people actually hoped to pull KP in the officers' mess because it meant a decent meal; I know I did. The enlisted mess hall was so bad that most of us preferred C rations, and even found Vietnamese food preferable.

'There were two contractor-built hangars for sheltered aircraft maintenance, and in late 1968, the Air Force civil engineers built bunkers outside all barracks and shops.

'Standard revetments (pre-fabricated corrugated steel bins filled with earth) protected the aircraft, and were built with the open sides facing each other. There was a drawback to that convenient arrangement; once, cannon were inadvertently fired by a mechanic, seriously wounding an airman in the opposite revetment and damaging the airplane. It could have been worse. During the summer of 1969, "wonder huts" were built to house some of the alert aircraft.

'Our fuel was piped overland from Vung Ro Bay, about 20–25 kilometres away. The VC blew the pipeline occasionally, but it was repaired quickly. For fuelling operations, we used trucks and "hot-turn" bladder pits. After a flight, the aircraft was usually taxied to the pits, refuelled, and then towed to its revetment. All other times, they were fuelled by truck.'

Home away from home, for a bunch of guys from the mountains and cool streams of Colorado, was shuttered white barracks with tile roofs, sandbags around the foundations, duckboards and dirt. These buildings sheltered the men of the 120th TFS, Colorado Air National Guard, at Phan Rang AB, Republic of Vietnam
(Ulrich Collection)

Chapter 6
Tales of a Vanished Breed
Interlude D: Bombs, BLUs, and Bloops

War Zone C, a 1,000-square mile (2589-km^2) area, began about 30 miles (48 km) from Saigon, in the jungle. In late 1966 and early 1967, intelligence pointed to major enemy activity inside War Zone C; it indicated also that the zone held the Central Office for South Vietnam (COSVN), political and miltary headquarters for all the enemy activities inside the RVN. Those were most lucrative targets, and so plans were made for two major multi-division operations, code-named Junction City and Manhattan, to clear War Zone C and capture COSVN.

MACV planners chose to attack three months before the monsoon rains were expected. On 22 Februrary, the 173rd Airborne Brigade opened the Junction City operations with the only parachute assault of the entire war. The drop was supported by F-100s, attacking the perimeters of the drop zone to suppress the ground fire.

Junction City operations broadened, and by early March, it was clear that a major set-piece battle was in the making. The Army had established a fire support base at Suoi Tre, in an area of Michelin-owned rubber plantations about 20 miles northeast of Tay Ninh. Early in the morning on 21 March, six enemy battalions—about 2,500 troops from the 272nd Regiment—hit the base, and the defenders called for badly needed air support. Dau Tieng, just a few minutes by air, immediately scrambled an O-1 FAC, which was almost immediately shot down. Two more FACs scrambled to fill the recent vacancy, and F-100s were sent from Bien Hoa, as were F-4s from Cam Ranh Bay. Both air bases were within a few minutes' flying time from the fire support base, and soon aircraft streamed over the horizon like the US Cavalry at full gallop.

The attack had begun at 6:30 am; by 9:00 am more than 85 USAF fighters were hammering the enemy with 750-lb GP bombs and 20-mm cannon fire. One of the FACs later reported a 1,000-foot (305-m) ceiling and two miles (3.2 km) visibility above the battlefield, and said that he was talking attack aircraft down through the overcast to their targets.

There were other engagements during the Junction City operation, but none with the air support intensity of the fight around Suoi Tre. By mid-May, Junction City had run its course, and MACV claimed a major defeat of the enemy. The Huns and Phantoms had flown more than 5,000 strikes in that operation, the largest of the war. It was a major defeat for the enemy 9th Division, which retreated across the border into Cambodian sanctuary.

Why describe Junction City? It was typical of many Army operations that called for supporting air strikes, either Pre-Scheduled (like the initial airborne assault) or Immediate (like the fight over Suoi Tre).

Pre-Scheduled Missions generally were planned a day ahead of time, although for major operations like Junction City, they could be in the planning stages for a much longer time. Alert Missions (sometimes called Immediate) were flown by crews from the alert pad, on 15-minute notice. They required two aircraft and their crews, standing alert for a period of 24 hours, ready to go on 15 minutes' notice.

In either basic mission category, there were standard types of missions:

- Direct air support (DAS), flown against known or suspected enemy positions, facilities, or routes;
- Close air support (CAS), flown against enemy targets near friendly forces;
- Trail Dust, escorting C-123 Ranch Hand aircraft on defoliation missions;
- Bookie Escort, flying air cover for transport aircraft on resupply missions;
- Landing zone preparation (LZP), delivering ordnance to suppress enemy action during landing of friendly forces by helicopter or fixed-wing a/c;

● Landing zone construction (LZC), delivering blast weapons that clear a landing zone by flattening trees and vegetation.

Sortie Summaries

Wartime actions described by military sources have a flavour of their own. The words are standardized and censored military jargon, coloured by the locale, and generally make for dull reading. They mask the courage, the daring, the stupidity, and the anguish of war. For example, this piece from the 7th Air Force News around July 1968:

'Tuy Hoa—With the addition of two new Air Force F-100 Super Sabre squadrons (the ANG units) to the 31st Tactical Fighter Wing during June, the skies over the Republic of Vietnam were filled with Super Sabre pilots from Tuy Hoa AB.

'Flying a total of 2,175 combat sorties, the pilots accounted for 549 enemy fortificiations and 709 enemy bunkers destroyed or damaged and they were credited with killing 88 enemy soldiers.

'In addition, pilots from the 136th, 188th, 306th, 308th and 309th Tactical Fighter Squadrons cut heavily into the enemy's resupply capabilities, destroying more than 10 tons of supplies.

'Other bomb damage assessment include 10 sampans sunk or destroyed, 64 tunnels and caves damaged or destroyed, 200 foxholes destroyed, 13 bridges destroyed or damaged, and more than 1500 metres of trenches destroyed or damaged.

'The 31st TFW is commanded by Colonel Abner M Aust, Macon, Miss.'

Or read the pages of *Sand Blast*, published for Tuy Hoa personnel by the Information Division, 31st TFW. Under the title, '31st TFW's Dragon Report' in the 23 November 1968 issue, is this story:

'Super Sabre pilots from the 31st TAC Fighter Wing "Dragons" pasted many targets throughout all four corps areas in South Vietnam during the period Nov 10 through 16.

'On Nov 10, Lieutenant Colonel Fred J Fink, "Enchilada Air Force" (NMANG) commander, and Captain Dick Hardy, "Dragon" chief of flying training, struck an enemy location in Kien Hoa Province six miles east of the Truc Giang.

'A forward air controller credited them with destroying or damaging five enemy military fortifications and three bunkers and setting off two secondary explosions . . .

'Three military fortifications, six bunkers and two enemy sampans were destroyed and five fortifications damaged when other "Dragon" pilots hit an enemy

The USAF caption to this 1964 photo says, '. . . somewhere over Vietnam.' Wherever, this is F-100F 56-3934, taking on fuel. It's carrying rocket pods and auxiliary tanks
(USAF 95013)

FW-954
U.S. AIR FORCE

location in Vinh Long Province three miles east of Sa Dec. A FAC also credited the pilots with killing two enemy soldiers. . .

And these are the targets listed in other stories in *Sand Blast*: '. . . smashed an enemy base camp . . . destroyed 11 bunkers, one fortification, 50 metres of trench and damaged a tunnel entrance . . . struck an enemy fortification complex . . . a sampan . . . an enemy base camp . . . 15 bunkers . . . four fortifications . . . 10 fighting positions . . . set off two sustained fires.'

(Sidelight: one of my personal and continuing complaints about war coverage is the invented quotation in the material coming from the base Information Officer. Yes, he's doing his job, and his commander will have unkind things to say otherwise, but does anybody out there believe that fighter pilots really talk like this quote from a base newspaper:

Napalm and old-fashioned, high-drag, dumb 750-pound iron bombs are loaded on a pair of F-100Ds (nearer is 55-3548; further serial is unreadable) from the 481st TFS (USAF 95299)

RIGHT
Camouflaged F-100D (55-3577) banks into its bombing run to deliver finned napalm and 750-pound bombs against an enemy target. There's a smoke trail rising from the ground below, probably from the FAC's marking rockets (USAF 101733)

'Later, we strafed. I could see my 20 mm cannon fire inflicting heavy damage on the enemy positions. The debris was really flying.'

Fighter pilots speak good and colourful English. In the excitement of combat, it tends to get profane, slangy, and jammed with jargon. So the pilot quoted above might likely have said, when recalling the mission:

'Then we strafed, really shot the [expletive deleted] out of him, and the [expletive deleted] was flyin' all over the place.'

On the other hand, he might really have said, 'I could see my 20 mm cannon fire inflicting heavy damage . . .' But I'd bet he didn't.)

Journey of a Fighter Pilot

Pilots new to the theatre and to combat flew their first sorties on missions that were supposed to familiarize them with the country, the tactics, and the modes of weapons delivery. Broadly categorized as Theatre Indoctrination Training (you know what the acronym lovers called those missions), they generally began with back-seat rides in F-100Fs on in-country strikes.

Captain Don Schmenk, then with the 308th TFS, 31st TFW, at Tuy Hoa, was an experienced F-100 pilot, with a three-year tour on F-100s in England behind him. You can learn about one pilot's initial exposure to a shooting war from reading his PACAF Form 20, on which he recorded the pertinent data of each mission. Look at the first ten missions:

16 Oct (1969): 1.6 hr training flight, front seat of an F, practising instrument approaches.
17 Oct: 1.2 hr in an F, CAS (close air support), 'soft' load, finned napalm, LZP (landing zone preparation).
21 Oct: 1.3 hr in an F, CAS, 'hard' load, SEL (suspected enemy location)
24 Oct: 1.3 hr in a D, CAS, '1 rice (paddy), 3 fields'
25 Oct: 1.7 hr in a D, CAS, one hooch, one bunker
26 Oct: 1.1 hr in a D, CAS, TIT (theatre indoctrination training)
26 Oct: 1.2 hr in a D, CAS, TIT
27 Oct: 1.5 hr in a D, CAS, LZP and TIT
28 Oct: 1.3 hr in a D, CAS, KEL (known enemy location)
29 Oct: 1.1 hr in a D, CAS, KEL

In October 1969, 1st Lieutenant Joe Vincent joined the 309th TFS of the 31st TFW at Tuy Hoa. He was to spend much of his combat tour flying over Laos and up to the demilitarized zone (DMZ), mainly in the areas assigned to II and III Corps of the Army.

Tuy Hoa was on the coast, and had to be approached from over the water; just ten miles inland was a range of high mountains. The base had two runways—one concrete, one AM-2—that ran

HS
400
063
400

northwest-southwest. For six months after Vincent arrived, there was a constant 25-knot crosswind from northwest to southeast, which shifted at noon to a 25-kt wind crosswind from the southeast to the northwest. 'It really tested your landing skills,' he said. 'We lost two or three aircraft just to those crosswinds. And we watched one guy get caught in the "Sabre dance" (the pilot lets the airplane get behind the power curve, can't accelerate without losing altitude, but doesn't have any altitude to play with). It looked wild—he was blowing a big plume of sand, shedding his tanks and pylons, and then he had a stroke of luck. His tailhook was dragging in the sand, it caught a piece of old PSP and slammed him down on the ground in a belly landing. All the pilot got was friction burns from his shoulder harness.'

When Vincent arrived, it was the season for the autumnal tropical thunderstorms. From December through February there were constant monsoon rains; but as long as there were minimums, they'd fly. Then it was hot and muggy, with temperature inversions and haze for the next six months. And after that, it was time to start on the thunderstorms again.

'I spent the first few months going to the Mu Gia pass on the (Ho Chi Minh) trail in Laos,' said Vincent. 'They were interdiction missions, looking for truck parks to bomb, cutting roads, and that kind of stuff. It was about a two-and-one-half hour round trip, with a pre-strike refuelling. We worked with the Misty FACs; they said you could fly along the border, look north, and see trucks bumper-to-bumper "all parked at Alice's Restaurant" waiting for darkness. But we were forbidden to strike north.

'For those strikes, our ordnance load was "hard"; that meant low-drag 750-lb (340-kg) bombs—we usually called them "slicks"—fused to detonate below ground. We seldom strafed there, but sometimes we did use CBU-49 cluster bombs. For in-country strikes, we used a lot of "snake and nape", high-drag 750-lb (340-kg) Snakeye bombs and 750 lb cans of napalm, which we also called a "soft" load. We preferred 750s to 500-pound bombs; the 500-pounders seemed squirrelly, and didn't seem to have the accuracy of the heavier bombs.

Last thing before takeoff, munitions specialists meet the F-100s at the end of the runway, and arm the bombs and guns. Here, 1st Lt Ronald W Rubin waits, hands more or less in sight, while his guns are armed. Red streamers marked 'Remove before flight' are hanging from a loop on the specialist's trousers. After arming everything, he'll step back out of the way, show the streamers to the pilot, and the Huns will start to roll. Rubin is from the 612th TFS, 37th TFW, at Phu Cat, and his F-100D is one of the last built (56-3400). Squadron insigne, a bald eagle holding a bomb, dates back to 1955 when the 612th flew F-84 fighter-bombers. It's emblazoned on the nosewheel door, along with the plane number
(USAF 106494)

(Don Schmenk commented that he found the 750-lb bombs better than the 500-pounders on the basis of their horizontal blast effect, which seemed out of proportion to the weight difference between them. Schmenk also said that 'soft' and 'hard' loads had corresponding delivery methods; a 'soft' load was dropped from a low-angle, low-altitude pass, generally, and a 'hard' load from a high-angle, high-altitude pass).

'Occasionally', Vincent said, 'we carried CBUs in-country, and there we did strafe with 20-mm a lot.

'We'd go any time of day, either scrambled or on a pre-planned mission. There were very few pre-planned night attacks during the first half of my tour. Night alerts were different, though. The first few months of my tour, night alert duty was great; you hardly ever flew and you got the next day off. But when you did go, you might do two flights a night. They were low-enemy-threat missions; the biggest risk was takeoffs and landings, and especially the weapons delivery itself. The FACs used rockets to mark at night, hoping they'd start a fire for better spotting. The flight lead carried flares, and they would help. The FAC would mark, then lead would make a pass and drop a flare, the wing man would make the second pass and drop a weapon, then lead would make another pass with a flare, and the wingman repeat the weapon drop. Flares sometimes made things worse; some guys I knew flying A-1s and F-4s worked the Trail in total darkness.'

Then-Major Ron Standerfer, a New Jersey ANG

7 October 1969: today's target is near Tay Ninh city. This F-100D (56-3025) of the 352nd TFS, 35th TFW, is on the way from Phan Rang AB to deliver four 750-pound slicks. The glint on the forward fuselage shouldn't be there, if you believe in camouflage
(USAF K34897)

pilot with the 355th TFS and later the Misty FAC detachment, remembers night missions as two kinds: '. . . boring, and non-boring. Boring missions were Skyspot bombing runs (Skyspot was the AN/MSQ-77 radar system originally developed to score SAC bombing accuracy on training missions, but later worked in a reverse manner to direct bombing strikes by B-52s and tactical bombers like the F-100s).

'Non-boring missions were night gunnery, under flares that the "Spooky" gunships dropped, although even those non-boring missions got to be more nearly routine after you'd done some of them. You flew with a lot of attention to instruments. One time I flew off the alert pad to a target called in by a Marine FAC, who said that he'd have his ground guys fire an illumination flare for me when I was on base leg. Rog, I said, and proceeded to the target. I called in on base, and in a few seconds I saw this little ball of light brightening the ground around it for a few feet. And I was in absolute darkness, with at best a general idea of the terrain. So I dropped my napalm, set two big fires, and immediately improved the visibility 1,000 per cent. After that, I could see to do some strafing. That was a non-boring mission.'

'We flew a lot of missions "under the lights",' LTC Randall L Steffens former commander, 614 TFS, remembers. 'The C-47s were up there at about 5,000 ft (1676 m) dropping flares, and we worked from 4,500 ft (1371 m) and under. I had 50 missions like that, off the alert pads. We'd use a 15-degree dive angle for bombing, then strafe with the cannon. You

Charlie's out in the Mekong delta somewhere, and we're gonna go out and hit 'em with nape and dumb bombs. Who? The 'Crusaders', the 481st; see the visor on the helmet? Like the visor on a suit of armour. Our horses? Huns. This one's a D, 55-3569. We're ridin' out of Tan Son Nhut, and when we've killed the infidels, we'll go back to New Mexico and Cannon AFB
(USAF 95555)

On 22 February 1967, F-100D fighter-bombers strike ground targets in support of Operation Junction City. Streaking in at low altitude, this Hun has just dropped a finned napalm bomb
(PACAF/Pickett Collection)

Above the battle, the pilot begins the pullout in smoke shrouds rising from the blasted terrain below
(PACAF/Pickett Collection)

From a strike-camera pod mounted on the centreline, bomb explosions look like this. The outer ring is condensation of moisture, caused by the intense pressure wave generated by the blast. The inner ring is the blast itself. The pilot of the F-100 is beginning his pullout with a climbing right turn (PACAF/Pickett Collection)

always tried not to fire out your guns, to save a few rounds just in case. The cans for the two inboard guns held more rounds than the other four, and so when you got down to just two guns firing, it meant you had run out in the other four and you held fire.'

Routine for a Routine

What follows is a composite description of a typical mission, assembled from individual narratives furnished by pilots who were there.

It's two hours before takeoff, now, and the pilots on today's mission are gathering for briefings. First, the weather: forecasts for home base, the target area, and alternate fields for emergencies. Next, intelligence: the target and the purpose of the strike, previous strike experience in the area, known defences, and maybe a large-scale map of the area. Then the flight lead briefs: tactics and weapons, the parking place, when the crew bus leaves, how to cruise to the target area, how to contact the FAC. Much of that material was standardized, but each mission had at least one individual peculiarity.

A warrior, returning: F-100D 56-2953 taxis into the revetment area at Bien Hoa, pylons empty
(Pickett Collection)

About an hour before takeoff time, you put on G-suits and the Nomex flight coveralls, and then you 'sanitize' yourself, removing all personal possessions except for the Geneva Convention card and dog-tags. ('There's another bit of business in there,' said Standerfer. 'You load your .38 revolver, and you choose whether you're going to load with tracer or high-velocity ammo.') On the way to the bus, pick up your chute and two frozen flasks of water; the ice will melt by the time you leave the target and the cold water will be most welcome. One of the flasks goes in a G-suit pocket, the other in the map case. You ride the crew bus to your parked F-100D and pre-flight aircraft and armament.

Not exactly stable projectiles, are they? A salvo of 2.75-inch folding-fin air rockets (FFARs) blasts out of the starboard wing pod of F-100D 56-3415, headed for a ground target. It's April 1968, and the unknown pilot is part of the 31st TFW operating out of Tuy Hoa AB (PACAF/Pickett Collection)

(Ken Shealy, then a Lieutenant Colonel commanding the 612th TFS, 35th TFW at Phan Rang, and later at 37th TFW, Phu Cat, said that his squadron normally had between 15 and 19 aircraft on hand, with maybe nine or ten on the line and ready to go. Operations officers in the 612th counted on achieving an average of 1.1 sorties per day per aircraft assigned, which meant two sorties per available F-100).

TOP LEFT
Carrying four Snakeye high-drag bombs, this PACAF F-100D 55-2903 is going for an enemy base camp 30 miles southeast of Tay Ninh City the day after Christmas 1966. The strike force included nine F-100Ds and four Martin B-57A light bombers. Note the plane number—903—on the nose, and behind it the unfortunately illegible name of the pilot. Later, with empty pylons and no visible wounds (left), 903 heads home
(Pickett Collection)

ABOVE
The Hun's pilot has just pickled a pair of finned napalm bombs and almost simultaneously begun his pullout. The irony of war contrasts the productive fields below with the destructive weapons about to land in those fields. The aircraft is F-100D 55-3634
(Montgomery Collection)

'The crew chiefs were great,' said Vincent. 'They really kept those F-100s in great shape. You'd show up, and they had 'em ready to go. My crew chief was Sergeant John Edwards, and his name was on the canopy rail, too.'

So you climb in, crank up, contact lead, taxi out. At the end of the runway, ordnance specialists arm the weapons, and you're ready to roll. 'When you've got full internal fuel, full 335-gallon drop tanks, and four cans of napalm, and it's 95 degrees outside, you've got a real long takeoff roll coming. I've seen 7,,500-ft (2286-m) rolls on a 9,000-ft (2743-m) runway. And if you're number two, getting some warm exhaust from the leader, you might have a longer run than he does.'

You cruise to the target most of the time between 15,000 and 18,000 feet (4572–5486 m), because, with the usual armament load, you can't get much higher. Headed out, you're directed by one of the ABCCC aircraft, and they'll hand you off to the FAC. You hold 12,000 and 14,000 ft (3657–4267 m) above the terrain while working with ABCCC and the FAC; you never say your altitude over the radio in case you're being monitored, but refer to it as some height above a published base altitude.

You call the FAC, tell him your callsign, airplane type, altitude above base, weapons on board, and the loiter time you have to spare in the target area. FAC answers, 'Rog, I'm SNOOPY in OV-10, 50 miles on 180 radial off of 107 (numbered Tacan station) at base plus 600, and the target today is a suspected truck park.' Then he tells you the terrain elevation, either the forecast or known surface winds, the highest terrain in the area, the best place for bailout and the nearest base for a divert. And if there are friendlies in the area, he tells you that, and where they are.

In the target area, you see the FAC; by now, your

Empty pylons and a tight formation indicate that these F-100Ds are nearing base after a combat sortie
(Steffens Collection)

LEFT
In a 45-degree dive toward the tree canopy, the pilot of this F-100D (55-3572) has just released a 750-lb iron bomb. The outboard pylons are empty, and may have held napalm or some other weapon. The underside of the nose shows gun gas smears, recent or old
(Montgomery Collection)

flight has opened to a mile or two separation, and you're orbiting the FAC, still high, in a wheel with your lead, and any other flight waiting to strike. When the FAC starts marking, you break out of the wheel, one at a time, and let down to about 9,000 ft (2743 m) above the terrain. Then you start the roll-in to the target; ideally, you do this in a smooth curvilinear approach, no jinking, looking to establish speed and angle parameters during the turn. You want to find yourself headed toward the target at a 45-degree dive angle, and at the right speed, just about at the point you should release the weapon.

(Schmenk and Shealy reported that they used 30-degree dive angles in-country, and 45-degree for out-country strikes, but they emphasized that these dive angles were general numbers often modified by weather and other parameters of a particular strike. Standerfer pointed out that he and other squadron pilots had, on occasion, dropped 'slicks' (standard bombs) from near-level flight under a 2,000-ft (609-

m) overcast. The real challenge was to keep away from your own bomb blast under those circumstances.)

You use the gunsight presentation, depressed for dive-bombing, to put the pipper on the target. But even if the gunsight is inoperative, you still have the reliable TLAR system (That Looks About Right). Even with the gunsight working, you can tell how the pass is developing, and you know when it looks about right.

On the way in, you keep an eye on the FAC smoke markers, for what they can tell you about surface winds. Now, you're right at the release point. You roll level briefly, drop, and then break while jinking like mad. You try never to break the same way twice after a bombing pass.

The FAC calls in results, thanks you, and releases you to go home. The frozen water has melted, and it tastes so good. So you climb out, head for cruise altitude, and the easy ride back to base. You land, having logged somewhere between one and two hours of mission time.

What if enemy aircraft bounced you coming off the target? The F-100 could turn well, but it couldn't maintain its energy, so that you could only fight a downhill battle. Once you get to the surface, that's all. In the briefings, they tell you to avoid engagement, because any enemy aircraft can outfight you. If you're caught, clean the wings, light the burner, go zero-G to the deck and go supersonic on the deck if you can, because the MiG-21 can't. 'I never did see an enemy aircraft,' remembers Vincent, 'but I did hear some bandit calls at a distance.' (Schmenk agrees; 'I never saw any enemy air,' he said).

The arming wire on the port napalm bomb pulled free of the pylon, which means that the bomb is not armed. But not to worry; it will undoubtedly break open on impact, and its charge will be ignited anyway by the detonation of the bomb from the starboard wing
(Steffens Collection)

'We worked with a FAC whose callsign was JAKE,' said Schmenk. 'He could always manage to find something for you to strafe if you were coming home through his area with ammunition left.'

'I overhead two FACs talking after we'd left the target one day,' Vincent commented. 'One of them said he liked working with F-100s because they got right down there in the weeds. We did try to get close and hit the FAC's smoke. So we were amazed to learn that the F-4s were releasing their weapons 7,000 to 9,000 ft (2133–2743 m) above the terrain. The pipper covers a football field at that height. We called the Phantoms "Bombslingers",' Vincent added.

'I was asked by the FAC, one time,' remembers Standerfer, 'to drop 750-pound slicks within 50 metres of friendly troops. They'd been ambushed by

A late-model D, with nose-mounted threat-warning radar, and bombs and fuel tanks slung underneath, waits in the revetment for its next pilot to show. The Hun is assigned to the 309th TFS, 31st TFW
(Maene Collection)

the VC, guys had been wounded and killed, and they were pinned down. The ground commander specifically requested the close drop, because it was his only chance of getting out of the trap.

'Fifty metres was easier than the 40-metre accuracy you needed to qualify on ranges during training back home, but that was different. This was combat, with bad guys shooting at you, a real high-pressure situation. I was flight lead, and I remember my thoughts while I was coming down the chute that first time: you'll kill friendlies if you miss. Fortunately, we didn't, and the slicks went right in on target.'

Pilots often pressed home their attacks beyond normal handbook limits of performance, in order to ensure the accuracy of their drop, or more often, because fighter pilots tend to fixate on targets, determined to nail the one they are after at the moment. That tendency often created cruel and unusual punishment for the F-100s, but they seemed to be able to take almost anything a pilot could do to the rugged airframe.

'Let me give you one example of how rugged the F-100 was,' said Vincent. 'One of our pilots, Captain Mike Foley, had a really lucrative target he was working, and he flew repeated tighter patterns going downhill, got going a bit slower than he should have, and in his pullout he mushed through some trees. He came home with a six-inch tree trunk imbedded in the wing, and the right drop tank looked like you'd tried to tie it in a knot. There was wood in every crack and crevice of the wing.'

Not everybody was so lucky. It is widely believed that more F-100s were claimed by enemy trees than by enemy gunners. Ron Standerfer remembers the experience of a friend. 'He was up near An Khe, dropping napalm, and was in a 10-degree dive, doing about 450 knots, when he hit the trees. I talked to him in the hospital about two hours after he hit, and he said all he remembered was flames, and he thought he had pulled the ejection seat handles. In any event, the chute didn't fully deploy; it just streamed behind him and snagged the trees. Two Army helicopter guys got him out of the trees and back to the base.'

The Small Epic of Dak Seang

'In April 1970,' began Vincent, 'we supported the garrison at Dak Seang. They were hit by an NVA (North Vietnamese Army) division on its way north after being driven out of Cambodia. Dak Seang was a fire base camp ringed by mountains, like a little Dien Bien Phu, and for about a month, everything our wing had flew there for close air support missions. The sky was full of airplanes. The garrison was getting resupplied by air drops, two FACs were constantly working the area, and F-100s were there all the time.

'Some friends sitting night alert with a "hard" load got the word at daybreak to change to snake, nape and CBU. As soon as that was done, they launched, and got to the target just as the bad guys were overrunning the concertina wire around the fire base. When the F-100s pulled out, what was left of the bad guys was still in the wire, but not moving.

'Captain Johnny Coil and 1st Lieutenant Gary Newsome were the first pair to fly a mission to Dak Seang off the alert pad at Tuy Hoa. They said it was pretty exciting to know that what you were doing was definitely helping our guys on the ground.'

Interlude D: **Bombs, BLUs, and Bloops**

The ultimate fighter-bomber version of the Super Sabre, the F-100D, was equipped to carry 66 different types of non-nuclear external stores (see the

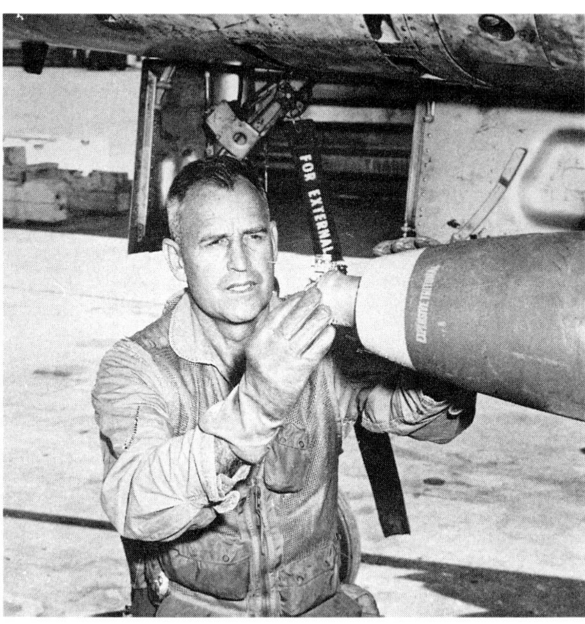

LEFT
This is Capt Arthur J Bergman, 510th TFS, 3rd TFW, at Bien Hoa, 31 years old, and he's just received notice of the award of the Distinguished Flying Cross. He's standing in front of an armed late model F-100D (56-3429), and he's holding a helmet clearly marked with the name Tomlinson
(USAF/Pickett Collection)

ABOVE
And this is Lt Col Robert E Erickson, graying and balding and older than 31, preflighting his Hun before climbing in. He's Bergman's boss; Erickson commands the 510th TFS. Before his war tour in Southeast Asia, he commanded a combat crew training squadron
(USAF/Pickett Collection)

RIGHT
At the time, charges and countercharges centred on bomb shortages in South Vietnam. So here's a PACAF Hun (F-100D 55-2856) being gestured out of her revetment at Bien Hoa by her tireless crew chief, and loaded with two 750 lb iron bombs. Her port outboard pylon is empty, which means the starboard one is also. Could the Hun carry more? You bet. Was there a shortage? You bet
(USAF/Pickett Collection)

0-52856
856

CE

listing below), three models of nuclear weapons (sometimes called 'bloops'), and five different types of drop tanks. Of the non-nuclear stores, 53 were weapons of destruction; the other 13 were flares, electronic countermeasures (ECM) pods, leaflet bombs, tow targets, and such. Additionally, each F-100 had 20-mm cannon: Four on the A, C, and D models, two on the F model.

To carry these external stores, C, D and F models had three hard points on each wing panel, at stations designated inboard, intermediate, and outboard, and a seventh hard point on the centreline of the fuselage belly. Seven different types of pylons could be fitted, with each assigned to specific stations. Thus, a Type I pylon could only be used on inboard stations, for example, and a Type VII only on the centreline.

With 74 stores, seven pylons, six wing stations and a fuselage station, there was ample potential for mistakes unless established procedures were followed carefully. Consequently, each of these weapons had to be loaded in compliance with voluminous technical orders, and each weapon imposed specific speed and G-load limitations on the aircraft.

Nuclear weapons could be carried only at the left wing intermediate, or the fuselage centreline, attachment points. Those special stores included the Mk 7, Mk 28 EX, Mk 28 RE, Mk 43, TX-43, and TX-43 X1, with yields ranging from a kiloton to something under ten megatons.

Because of the obvious risk inherent in the delivery of nuclear weapons, special techniques were developed to drop those bombs to minimize the chances of losing pilot and airplane to nuclear blast effects. Both the D and F models had LABS and LADD systems, and pilots were trained in those special delivery techniques.

The LABS (low-altitude bombing system) AN/AJB-1B for the D models, or the -5A for the F, was used with information from the A-4 gyro sight to provide aiming and release data for the automatic toss-bombing of nuclear weapons. The technique was simple; it used the energy of the airplane to sling the bomb well ahead of the flight path. Pilots of the F-100s approached low and fast, typically at 450 knots on the deck, pulled up at a steady 4G and, partway into what would become a half-loop, verified that the bomb had been automatically released. (Bombs for these training missions were practice shapes called 'Blue Boys', or the standard 25-lb (11.3-kg) bombs with spotting charges that were carried four to a rack under the wing.) They completed the half-loop, half-rolled out, unloaded the airplane aerodynamically, and headed for the deck again in afterburner, seeking to maximize the distance between bomb and bomber.

The practice bomb or, in the event being practiced for, the real thing, continued ahead in a ballistic trajectory that took it nearly out of sight. By the time it impacted, the aircraft would be miles away uprange. Accuracy was not very high, but '. . . close only counts in pitching horseshoes and hand grenades.'

The LADD (low-altitude drogue delivery) system took advantage of the fact that some nuclear weapons had been designed for delivery during a high speed run on the deck. To avoid vaporizing pilot and plane, those bombs were equipped with a drogue chute to retard their fall, and a timer, instead of a contact fuse, to detonate the bomb after a safe interval. The initial phase of the LADD lay-down was fast and low, followed by a pull-up to a somewhat-higher altitude where the bomb was automatically released. The pilot continued on his heading up and away.

Memories of the Job

Doug Henderson, now a botanist at the University of Idaho, was formerly a weapons mechanic, with Air Force Specialty Code (AFSC) 46250. Henderson was assigned to the 474th Fighter-Bomber (later Tactical Fighter) Wing at Clovis AFB (later Cannon AFB), New Mexico. His primary responsibility in Tactical Air Command was loading nuclear and thermonuclear weapons.

'Nearly everything about that job was classified,' he wrote, 'and, even though more than 25 years have passed since loading my last special weapon, I can still remember the name of the tests we performed and their sequence. I watched a SAC loading team just yesterday demonstrate loading a B-52G with a pylon of air-launched cruise missiles, and it was all strangely familiar: shouted instructions by the loading crew chief, plastic-covered check lists, and the hustle of crew members.

'With the F-100s, we erected a six-foot high wall of canvas around the loading area, and not even the Air Police were allowed to watch. The screens were not used, though, when we loaded the real weapons on alert pads at overseas deployment bases. There, we pulled duty in one-week increments on the alert pads,

TOP LEFT
One of the reasons for carrying high-drag bombs was to make low-altitude drops safer by providing an added margin of distance between the dropping aircraft and the bomb blast. But here, in this unusual shot, a formation of three F-100Ds (55-2889, 55-3710, and 55-2825) makes a level-flight simultaneous drop of six Snakeye high-drag weapons. It looks as if they dropped on a received signal, which may have come from a Skyspot radar used on occasion
(USAF/Pickett Collection)

LEFT
Just leaving the revetment at Bien Hoa AB, this F-100D (56-2920) is guided by a pilot from the 510th TFS, 3rd TFW. The warload is a quartet of Snakeye high-drag bombs
(USAF/Maene Collection)

USAF

Unfused 750-lb general-purpose bombs wait to receive tail fin assemblies and fuses, and then to be hung underneath the F-100s in the background. The two at the right are F-100F 56-4002 and F-100D 55-2912; the third is probably a D model. All are loaded with bomblet dispensers outboard, and fuel tanks on intermediate pylons, and all have empty inboard pylons where these bombs will fit. TAC badges on vertical tails, natural-metal finish, fuselage buzz numbers, and the fact that the base is Bien Hoa, all identify these Huns as early arrivals in Southeast Asia
(USAF/Pickett Collection)

LEFT
White smoke trails mark the flight path of an F-100C and the trajectory of a nuclear-weapon shape during a test of the low-altitude bombing system (LABS). Note that the aircraft leading-edge slats are extended fully, indicating a high-lift—and therefore high-G—pullout
(Smithsonian Institution Photo No 87–739)

with all activity inside a double barbed-wire fence under constant surveillance by guard-dog teams.'

Robert F Dorr, author of *McDonnell Douglas F-4 Phantom II*, *Vought A-7 Corsair*, *McDonnell F-101 Voodoo*, and *Grumman A-6 Intruder* in this series, and *Phantoms Forever* in the Osprey Colour Series, was an Airman Second Class stationed at Osan Air Base, Korea, in May 1959. F-100Ds also were there, six at a time standing nuclear alert with special stores under their left wings. Not wishing to advertise the presence of the weapons for both political and security reasons, the 'bloops' generally were covered by tarpaulins. But one day, the tarpaulins were missing and Dorr—ever the eager airplane spotter—climbed to the roof of the NCO Club across the street from the alert pad to photograph an airplane with The Bomb. (For the record, it was an F-100D-20, serial 55-3568, of the 36th TFS, 8th TFW.)

On the left, the loading team uses a self-propelled bomb hoist to lift a 750-lb bomb into place on the inboard pylon of this F-100. On the right, an armament specialist installs the nose fuse on the other 750-lb GP bomb. It's all at Bien Hoa, early in the war
(USAF/Pickett Collection)

Air Police quickly spotted the spotter, questioned him, exposed his film, and put in an unkind word with his first sergeant. 'We don't want anybody taking pictures,' he was told in very positive terms.

The F-100s assigned to Pacific Air Forces—and, presumably, those assigned to United States Air Forces Europe (USAFE)—were expected to be tactical nuclear fighter-bombers to the exclusion of almost any other mission. The *Aircrew Training Manual for F-100D/F*, PACAFM 51-6, stated explicitly that '. . . nuclear training will in every instance take precedence over non-nuclear familiarization and qualification. It is emphasized that conventional training will not be accomplished at the expense of the higher-priority nuclear training required by this manual. Non-MSF units will restrict conventional familiarization to the accomplishment of only one event per aircrew per year.'

The airplanes those aircrews flew carried the largest—450 US gallon (1704 lit)—drop tanks for long-range, probably one-way, missions, and they carried ECM pods for protection. But when the pilots were sent to a real, non-nuclear war in Vietnam, all the training and qualification required by PACAFM 51-6 were valueless. The drop tanks were too big and too draggy for that war and, to add insult to injury, the ECM pods couldn't jam North Vietnamese radars.

Hoses, Safety Pins, and 'Easy-Off'

'Our other responsibilities,' Henderson continued, 'centred on conventional weapons, the ejection seat and canopy remover, and armament electrical

Three Ds (56-3105, 56-3109, and 55-3750) flew weapons research and development tests. Distinctive yellow-and-black checkerboard decorations identify Fighter Weapons School aircraft. FW-105 carries a twin-Sidewinder launcher on both inboard mounts. FW-109 holds four 750-lb bombs on inboard and intermediate mounts. FW-750 slings six rocket pods from its inboard, intermediate, and outboard weapons stations
(Peter M Bowers/Maene Collection)

systems. A routine workday would involve armament preflights; we checked ejection seats (Hoses connected? Safety pins in?), all stores that were loaded (Safety pins? Underwing panels secured if no pylons?), the guns (Loaded? No round in six o'clock position in the drum?). If everything was OK, we signed off the armament preflight on the aircraft forms.

'We loaded all the ordnance, including the 20-mm ammo, limited to 200 rounds per gun although the cans held 250. But with 250 rounds, the guns could "cook off" rounds after about 200 had been fired in rapid succession. Sidewinders were a special love; they were light and so easy to load.

'Arming crews were stationed at the takeoff end of the active runway. Their job was to remove all safety pins, charge the 20-mm cannon, secure the rocket umbilicals after checking for stray voltage, and test the Sidewinders with flashlights (pilots would nod when they heard the characteristic rattle in the headsets, indicating that the Sidewinder seeker head was working).

'This was done only if the pilots held both hands out of the cockpit; we didn't want any accidents while working with live ordnance.

'Dearming crews cleared the guns after landing; it could be touchy with a jammed gun, because a stray half-volt somewhere could fire a round. And they'd re-install all the safety pins. The guns needed constant cleaning, and we used "Easy-Off" oven cleaner to clean the blast panels.

'During an Operational Readiness Inspection (ORI), we did all this on a round-the-clock basis with little or no sleep for days. Sometimes we passed, sometimes not. Maybe some pilots couldn't hit targets that time, or a munitions crew degraded a weapon's potential in loading. ORIs were exceptionally hard work, with unknown outcomes. The only certain thing was that the ORI alert was always called between midnight and 0400!

'As I recall these experiences, I have faith that today's training is even better than during my time. And there are some jobs that I know I still could do today, if I had to.'

Everything but the Kitchen Sink

The non-nuclear weapons and other stores available for the F-100D included:

A/A37U-15 tow-target system
AIM-9B/E/J Sidewinder missiles
B37K-1 practice bomb rack
BLU-1B fire bomb (also -1A/B, -1B/B, finned and unfinned)
BLU-1C/B fire bomb (finned and unfinned)
BLU-27/B fire bomb (also -27B/B, -27C/B, finned and unfinned)
BLU-32A/B fire bomb (also -32B/B, -32C/B, finned and unfinned)

U.S. AIR FORCE

BLU-52/B chemical bomb
CBU-1A/A dispenser
CBU-2A/A dispenser (also -2B/A, -2C/A)
CBU-3A/A dispenser
CBU-7/A dispenser
CBU-9A/A dispenser (also -9B/A)
CBU-12/A dispenser (also -12A/A)
CBU-24/B cluster dispenser (also -24A/B, -24B/B)
CBU-28/A bomblet dispenser
CBU-29/B cluster dispenser (also -29A/B, -29B/B)
CBU-30/A dispenser
CBU-34/A mine dispenser (also -34A/A)
CBU-37/A mine dispenser
CBU-42/A mine dispenser
CBU-46/A bomb dispenser
CBU-49/B cluster dispenser (also -49A/B, -49B/B)
CBU-52B/B dispenser
CBU-53/B cluster dispenser
CBU-54/B cluster dispenser
KMU-342/B guidance kit
LAU-3/A rocket launcher
LAU-32A/A rocket launcher (also 32B/A)
LAU-59A/A rocket launcher
LAU-68A/A rocket launcher
M117 GP bomb (also M117 with MAU-103A/B fin)
M117(R) bomb
M117(D) bomb
M117 GP bomb with 36-in M1A1 fuse extender ('Daisy-cutter')
M129 E1 leaflet bomb
MC-1 chemical bomb
MK-12, Mod 0 leaflet tank
MK-36 Mod 0 destructor
MK-81 GP bomb
MK-82 GP bomb
MK-82 GP bomb with 36-in M1A1 fuse extender
MK-82 Snakeye 1 GP bomb
MK-83 GP bomb
AN/ALQ-71 ECM pod
AN/ALQ-72 ECM pod
AN/ALQ-87 ECM pod
BDU-33 bomb
SUU-20/A practice dispenser (also -20/A(M), -20A/A, -20B/A)
SUU-21/A practice dispenser
SUU-25A/A flare dispenser (also -25B/A, -25C/A, -25E/A)

Six Mk 77 fire bombs (napalm) are mounted on this F-100D (56-3462), photographed at Seymour Johnson AFB
(USAF/Pickett Collection)

Chapter 7
Wild Weasel I
Interlude E: Misty FAC

24 July 1965: a flight of four Phantoms out of Ubon streaks northward on MIGCAP (MiG Combat Air Patrol), top cover for a strike force headed for targets near Hanoi. Ten minutes short of their destination, they get immediate action.

An urgent message from a Douglas EB-66C Elint (electronic intelligence) aircraft warns that enemy missile radars are on the air; launches can be expected west of Hanoi. Then a trio of missiles blasts upward. One scores, and an F-4C blows into a bright orange balloon of rolling flames. Two missiles detonate behind the flight; shrapnel hits the three remaining F-4s, causing damage but neither injuries nor loss.

It is the first US combat aircraft lost to an enemy missile in that war, and it spurs a quick reaction. The threat of enemy air defences has just multiplied.

The North Vietnamese air defence system then was growing and improving. Conceptually, it was a widespread and integrated radar network, tied to MiG-17 and MiG-21 interceptors and to radar- and optically-directed anti-aircraft artillery (AAA) of large and small calibres. By the spring of 1965, surface-to-air missile (SAM) batteries were deployed and ready, although in numbers well below their eventual strength.

On 5 April, a reconnaissance flight high over North Vietnam photographed an unusual installation 15 miles (24 km) southeast of Hanoi, quite unlike anything seen before in that region. But similar ones had been photographed on 29 August 1962, at locations in western Cuba, and detailed study confirmed it as an enemy SAM site, the first discovered in Vietnam. It was operational; several missiles, on their launchers, were deployed in revetments connected by a road network, with clustered radar huts and antennas parked nearby. Small- and medium-calibre anti-aircraft guns defended the site. By mid-July, five more SAM sites had been found by reconnaissance flights, and an EB-66C had monitored guidance signals from a sixth battery west of Hanoi. The missiles had been identified. All indications pointed to early introduction of a new threat.

The North Vietnamese were indeed ready to play their ace: the SA-2 surface-to-air missile (NATO name: *Guideline*). The SA-2 had been developed and deployed by the Russians, reported by intelligence sources, seen three years earlier in Cuba, and made history on 1 May 1960, when it reportedly shot down pilot Francis Gary Powers and his Lockheed U-2.

The SA-2 was a first-generation missile, designed to attack large formations of bombers flying at high altitudes. It never was intended to be manoeuvrable enough to catch tactical aircraft at low altitudes. It was a command-guided missile and, after launching, both missile and target were tracked by a single radar (NATO name: *Fan Song*). Tracking data were translated into computed steering commands transmitted to the missile. A proximity fuse detonated the warhead within lethal range of the target.

It was launched by a single solid-propellant booster rocket, and thrust on its flight path by a liquid-fuelled sustainer rocket trailing smoke by day

TOP RIGHT
Introducing the first of the Wild Weasel I breed, F-100F 58-1221, factory-fresh and posing at Palmdale. External differences are few and small: two antennae mounted under the inlet (only one shows as a black circle from this angle) and two more in a modified vertical tail housing. Internal changes include installation of the AN/APR-25 RHAW (radar homing and warning) system
(Fraizer Collection)

RIGHT
The arrow points to the twin nose antennae of the RHAW system on this F-100D, not a Wild Weasel bird. But the installation is identical to those used on Weasel birds, and this is the best available nose-on shot of those antennae
(Schwartz Collection)

The front cockpit of an F-100D (again, not a Wild Weasel aircraft) shows the typical installation of the APR-25 RHAW system, with scope at the upper left, and threat display to its right. The display categorizes the radar threat: anti-aircraft artillery, SAM, airborne intercept, launch
(Schwartz Collection)

and flame by night. Given the chance and some luck, the SA-2 could destroy any aircraft with the punch of a 220-lb (100-kg) high-explosive warhead.

The SA-2 reportedly had an effective slant range between 20 and 30 miles (32–48 km), and a lethal envelope extending from 1,500 to about 6,000 ft (457–1829 m). But the true performance was not that good; it accelerated slowly, and didn't reach its best speed of Mach 2.5 until it had climbed above 25,000 ft (7622 m). That characteristic later was used against the missile.

By today's standards, the SA-2 was unsophisticated. But there were dozens of them and, to anyone who was there then, they constituted a threat of awesome proportion. The risk of flying north had increased tremendously.

General Westmoreland wanted to strike the missile sites as soon as possible. He was prevented, he wrote later, by direct orders from the Secretary of Defense. An Administration official told him that the Russians sent the missiles just as a gesture of appeasement to Hanoi so, as a signal to the North Vietnamese, do not attack the sites. The North Vietnamese will understand our intentions and will not use the missiles. The General was not impressed with that theory, and the North Vietnamese, obviously, didn't buy it either. And so, on 24 July 1965, the USAF lost its first combat aircraft to an enemy missile in Vietnam.

Only then did the Administration permit a single special strike against SAM sites, and low-altitude photography of all of North Vietnam to locate occupied sites. Tight restrictions applied; no American aircraft was to violate three sanctuary areas: a 20-nautical mile diameter circle around Hanoi; an eight-nm circle around Haiphong; and a ten-nm circle around Phuc Yen, the main military airfield defending Hanoi. These, of course, were the very areas protected by heavy concentrations of defensive systems, including SAMs.

Further, said the Washington war managers, no SAM site could be struck unless and until it had been positively identified by photo-interpretation of low-altitude reconnaissance photographs. This also played into enemy hands, because SAM batteries—like all North Vietnamese anti-aircraft defences—were mobile. The enemy simply moved them from site to site, coordinating their redeployments to follow low-level reconnaissance runs.

Birth of the Wild Weasel

The situation demanded quick action. Brigadier General K C Dempster, Deputy for Operational Requirements and Development Plans in USAF Headquarters, was appointed to lead a task force to find an expedient way to counter the North Vietnamese air defence system. The Task Force, formed on 3 August 1965, immediately convened a seminar resulting in a requirement for a new kind of aircraft, a specialized hunter and killer aircraft that could detect, locate and destroy the enemy radars that guided the missiles.

Knocking out SAM sites in North Vietnam was expected to be risky, and to result in high losses until more effective methods could be developed and deployed. One temporary tactic for strike forces was to hug the ground. At low altitudes, the SAMs were accelerating to gain speed and manoeuvrability, and were sluggish in response to control inputs. But low altitudes put attackers within the effective range of North Vietnamese small-calibre AAA, so the attackers went back up to altitudes between 3,000 and 4,000 ft (914–1219 m), increased later to between 6,000 and 9,000 ft (1829–2743 m).

The next tactical idea was to stream the strike force into the target area in formations of four at timed intervals of one to three minutes. But there was little possibility for mutual support among the flights, once that procedure became standard. Further, when pilots took evasive action to avoid missiles, they jettisoned all ordnance before the manoeuvre to avoid over-stressing the airframe. Thus, the missile threat often broke the strike force, disrupting the bomb pattern or forcing the jettisoning of bombs before the target was reached.

But the missiles had a weakness: their guidance radars. Blind them, and an SA-2 was useless, because it depended on following the radar-generated signals between launch site and target. So the requirement for a new aircraft type began with the thought that the

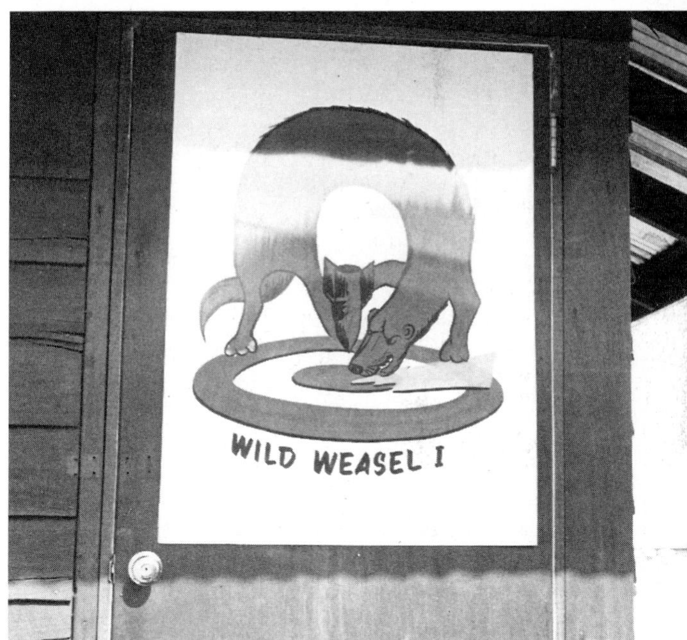

TOP
The second group of Wild Weasel I pilots arrives at Korat RTAFB, Thailand. The civilians are from North American and Applied Technology. Generally, new guys in foreground, old heads in background
(Ed White)

ABOVE
'Our unofficial emblem', said Ed White, first WWI pilot to land at Korat. 'We adopted it ourselves, and had patches made so we could have a unit identity. But we didn't wear them in combat because we didn't want to identify our mission for the enemy.' The door leads to the operations centre at Korat
(Ed White)

radars had to be destroyed; how mattered not. Further, the North Vietnamese radars were believed to be in shorter supply than the missiles and launchers. As former Weasel pilot Ed White (now Col, USAF) wrote, 'Our philosophy was simple: the best electronic countermeasure was a 2,000-lb (907-kg) bomb delivered on the radar antenna. Of course, we would take any disruption we could get elsewhere on the site.'

The Dempster task force recommended that radar homing and warning (RHAW) equipment be installed in a few F-100F-20 pathfinders. The two-place Hun was a known quantity, was available, and could be modified to test and prove the validity of the concept. North American, the USAF, suppliers and subcontractors swung into action. In one case, a contract was written on a blackboard. After it had been signed by both parties, it was photographed and became part of the official documentation.

(In a parallel effort, electronic countermeasures pods, crammed with jammers, were quickly developed, sent to Southeast Asia, and hung under the wings of aircraft headed north. They created loud and pervasive static that helped defeat enemy radars.)

Work to counter North Vietnamese defences had been under way for months, but was spurred by introduction of the SA-2 threat. Self-protection equipment was in production, but it was so expensive and massive that it was being installed only in large bombers, like the B-47, B-52 and the Navy's A-3. Fortunately, the age of the transistor had arrived; that meant that smaller, lighter, and less-expensive electronic countermeasure systems could be built for use by tactical aircraft. And one small company, Applied Technology Inc (ATI), was making a few of these compact, lightweight systems for the high-flying Lockheed U-2.

Dempster arranged demonstrations of the ATI RHAW equipment. Richard V Hartman, ATI Program Manager for the first system, remembers that, very soon after those demonstrations, ATI received a letter contract to build a radar warning receiver, a missile launch detector, and an IR-133 tuned radar intercept receiver, plus all the associated displays and control panels. The time allotted was 90 days; the price was $100,000.

'We worked around the clock on a seven-day week,' Hartman said, 'and delivered the first system to the North American Aviation special operations unit, at Long Beach (California), on time and within budget. It got a quick test on an F-100F (58-1231), and a subsequent telephone call from General Dempster turned on the production line. So then, naturally, the programme needed a code name, and mascot, and proper insignia.'

Ferret was out; that animal's name had been applied earlier in a different context. Mongoose also was rejected; there had been a clandestine operation during World War 2 with that designator. Finally, Air Force and ATI agreed on the weasel as the appropriate representative, because the weasel had a reputation of being fierce and fearless. The aircraft would go 'weaseling' into enemy territory at low altitude, sniffing out SAM sites, and marking them so that fighter-bombers could blast them. The 'wild' part was almost an afterthought, to describe the general atmosphere of the mission, and the probable personalities and attitudes of the crews. So the first phase of this long-term programme was named Wild Weasel I.

'The graphics department at ATI consisted of one artist who had never seen a live weasel or a good picture of one,' said Hartman. 'His first tries produced creatures looking like skinny, friendly dogs. But with some practice, he devoloped a fierce-looking weasel, and we had our insignia.'

The Well-Dressed Weasel

The equipment, modified from units developed for the U-2, was hand-built for the Wild Weasel I programme and installed by NAA's Los Angeles Division in four F-100Fs: 58-1221, -1226 (later to be referred to by Weasel crews as 'too, too sick' because it had continuing maintenance problems. When it was flown back home at the end of the Wild Weasel I tour, it sported a large Band-Aid painted on its side), -1227 (which survived the war and, as *Excalibur 4*, flown by Colonel Charles F Blair, made the first single-engine jet fighter flight across the North Pole, August 1959), and -1231. The new equipment had three basic functions. First, it warned aircrews that their aircraft were being illuminated by *Fan Song*, *Firecan* and other anti-aircraft and airborne interception radars. Second, it warned that a missile was about to be launched against the aircraft; it did this by sensing a power change in the L-band *Fan Song* command guidance radar. Third, it furnished automatic direction-finding of the SAM radar signals, which allowed Weasels to home in on the threat with good accuracy.

Those installations of Wild Weasel I equipment included:

AN/APR-25 (originally designated Vector IV) radar homing and warning receiver, to detect S-band signals emitted by the SA-2 fire-control radar and AAA radar. Aditionally, the APR-25 detected C-band signals from upgraded SA-2 systems, and the X-band signals from enemy airborne intercept (AI) and ground-based AAA radar. Cockpit displays were a threat panel and a three-inch diameter cathode-ray tube (CRT) to show the bearing of the threat signal.

AN/APR-26 (originally WR-300) tuned crystal receiver to monitor the L-band to detect missile guidance launch signals. The cockpit display was a red launch-warning signal light.

IR-133 panoramic receiver, with greater sensi-

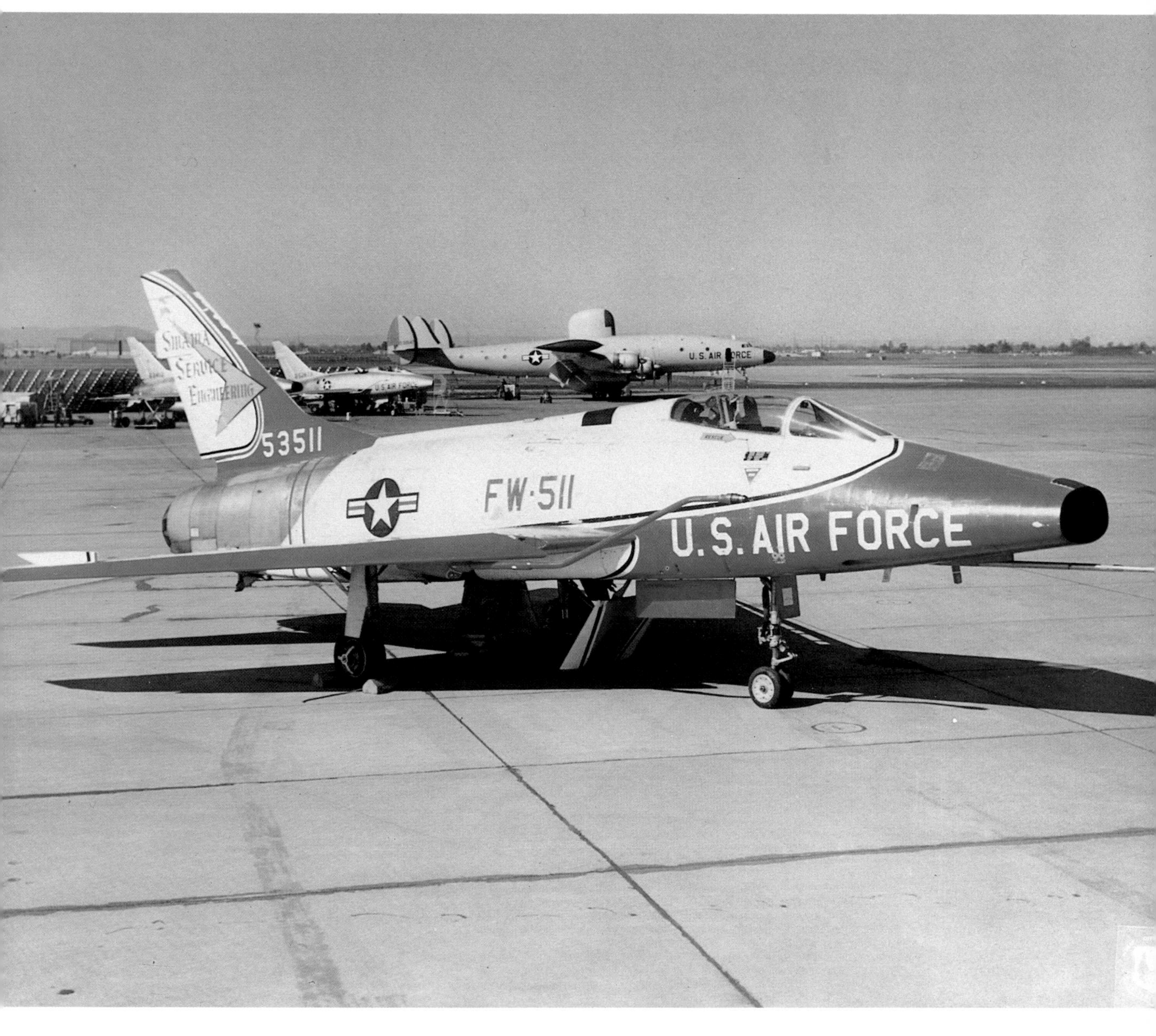

This entry in the 'Most Colourful F-100' sweepstakes flew flight-test duties at the Sacramento (Calif.) Air Material Area (SMAMA), the logistics support centre responsible for F-100s. It's an F-100D, 55-3511
(USAF/SMAMA)

TOP
Armed Forces Day, 1958, at Cannon AFB brought out this F-100F (56-3902) of the 312th F-BW, complete with dummy Mk 7 ('Blue Boy') nuclear weapon
(Doug Henderson)

ABOVE
The black and yellow chevrons identify F-100Ds 56-3112 and -3101 of the 429th F-BW, deployed at McChord AFB, Washington. Notice the triple rocket launchers under the wings
(Doug Henderson)

TOP
This white and gold F-100D (civil registration N100X) was owned and operated by Flight Test Research, Inc, Long Beach, California
(Dave Musikoff)

ABOVE
SM 263 (serial 56-3263) stands on the Tuy Hoa ramp, in the 308th TFS area. RHAW antennas under the nose and high on the vertical fin; a command radio antenna rises behind the cockpit, and an IFF blade antenna protrudes just above the nose inlet. SM 263 had a Doppler navigation system; the giveaway is the inlet on the leading edge of the fin
(R D Jones)

It's a May, 1968, open house at Dijon, city of mustard and fine food, and the citizenry inspect F-100D 11-EA of Escadre *11. Her serial (54-2187) identifies an early model D*
(Magendie/Musikoff Collection)

RIGHT
A tight formation of a trio of F-100Ds from the 474th F-BW
(Doug Henderson)

63186
U.S. AIR FORC

TOP

The tail says this almost pristine F-100D standing in its revetment is SM 903 (serial 55-2903) with the 308th TFS, 35th TFW, at Tuy Hoa. Note the RHAW gear in the vertical fin housing

(R D Jones)

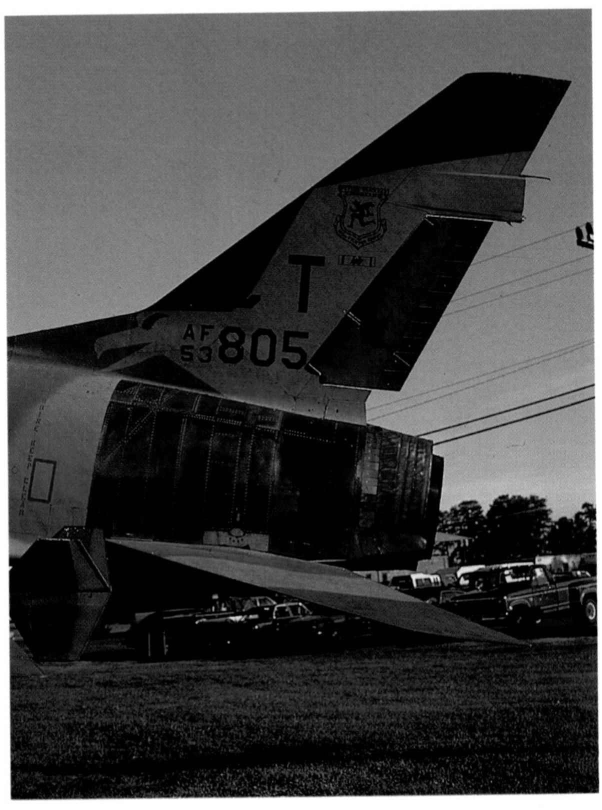

RIGHT

F-100D 55-3805 is a gate guardian for the 103rd TFG, Connecticut ANG, at Bradley International Airport. The standard camouflage finish was varied to form a stylized eagle on the vertical tail of the unit's F-100s

(David A Anderton)

Thunderbird F-100C (55-2724) at an unknown location in late 1962
(Mike McLain/Musikoff Collection)

TOP
Yellow-orange trim enlivens F-100F (56-3880) of the Iowa Air National Guard
(Iowa ANG)

ABOVE
Late afternoon sun at McChord AFB, near Tacoma, Washington, lights the side of F-100D 56-3065 from the 312th F-BW, deployed from Cannon AFB
(Doug Henderson)

tivity, to detect S-band signals at greater range than possible with the APR-25, and to indicate the type of threat by signal analysis.

KA-60 panoramic camera, to record physical details of sites, strikes, and missile launches or attacks.

Dual-track tape recorder, a common item of equipment aboard many tactical aircraft, to record enemy radar signals for later identification and training.

The pilots were selected from volunteers in Tactical Air Command, averaging two from the F-100 wings at England, Homestead, Luke, and Myrtle Beach AFBs, and from the Fighter Weapons Wing at Nellis AFB. They were asked to volunteer for combat missions, but did not find out the nature of those missions until the official formation of the Wild Weasel I unit. The EWOs (Electronic Warfare Officers) were transferred out of similar assignments in SAC B-52 and TAC B-66 crews.

Training began in a trailer at North American's Los Angeles plant, and continued at Eglin AFB for flight testing of the system. That began on 4 September 1965, with four aircraft, five aircrews (10 officers), and 40 supporting personnel, plus a number of civilian system specialists.

(Sidelight: for the record, the first five Wild Weasel I crews were Captains Allen T Lamb, Jr, pilot, and John E Donovan, EWO; Edward B White and Edward E Sandelius; John J Pitchford and Robert D Trier; George H Kerr and Donald J Madden, and Maurice G Fricke and Truman W Lifsey. Their commander was Major Garry A Willard, and Major Robert Swartz was operations officer.)

While at Eglin, Weasel crews flew training missions that imitated the North Vietnam combat environment by simulating the SAM radar. But one ex-Weasel pilot said that they flew against the genuine article, a Russian *Fan Song* radar system that was '. . . stolen from somewhere.'

In late September 1965, when Wild Weasel I activity was accelerating, the US government imposed new restrictions. Attacks on all SAM sites within a 30-nm radius—not diameter—of Hanoi were prohibited. Within two months, just as the first Wild Weasel was arriving in the theatre, that ludicrous limit was lifted, but with a proviso: missile sites had to be observed firing at US aircraft before they could be attacked.

The first crews completed testing and deployed from Eglin on 23 November, and the advance party—White and Sandelius—touched down at Korat RTAFB on Thanksgiving Day, 1965, on a TDY assignment. Their recently-formed unit was the 6234th Tactical Fighter Wing (PACAF), assigned to operational control of the 388th TFW. The remaining three F-100F Weasel birds arrived soon after. Orientation training flights began on 28 November, and the first combat mission was flown on 3 December, teaming a pair of Wild Weasel I aircraft and their crews (Willard and Lifsey, White and Sandelius) with a flight of F-105Ds.

These special flights were called Iron Hand, and they combined, typically, one F-100F Wild Weasel I with four F-105s. In addition to a full load of 1,200 rounds of 20-mm ammunition for their cannon, the Weasels carried a pair of LAU-3 canisters loaded with 24 rockets which served a dual function as markers and effective weapons that could demolish a radar antenna or van with direct hits. They also carried drop tanks, and later added napalm to the arsenal.

The Thuds bombed on the markers, or added the weight of their bombs to the rocket fire of the Weasels. A single RF-101 sometimes accompanied the Iron Hand flights to get pictures of the missile sites before and after the attacks. An RF-4, equipped also with a gun pod, went along on later missions to give the flight some measure of air-to-air protection. A combat photographer flew in the RF-4 back seat to take strike photos.

Ways to Go Weaseling

'Iron Hand flights required the top pilots in the command,' wrote General W W Momyer, who commanded the 7th Air Force at the time. 'They had the most demanding job and the most hazardous, for these flights were the first into the target area and the last out. It was their task to attract any active SAM site that was a threat to the strike force.'

The attack procedure began as the Wild Weasel back-seaters listened for signals. They had learned the importance of auditory training back in the United States, listening repeatedly to the sounds of enemy radars and mentally filing them away for future use. They learned that early warning radars groaned, and missile guidance radars sounded like angered rattlesnakes. When the enemy radars came on the air, and were detected and identified by their sound patterns, the back-seater quickly tried to determine the approximate position of the signal source from instrument indications.

The small CRT indicator among the front-seat instrumentation showed the pilot the bearing of the missile site with an accuracy of perhaps 15° or 20°. But the back-seater's IR-133 receiver was able to pinpoint the site within a bearing error of only one or two degrees, so that the pilot was directed more precisely to the target by his back-seater. The fighter-bombers loosely trailed the Weasel as it proceeded toward the target radar. Then came the hard part.

The Weasels had to fly deliberately toward the radar signals in order to confirm the identification that the RHAW gear had made. If they got close enough without being fired upon, they dove in on the missile site, firing rockets. The F-105s also attacked the target with iron bombs.

By a risky, empirical procedure, Wild Weasel and

LEFT
The long runway and taxiway mark Korat Royal Thai Air Base, photographed from an F-100F Wild Weasel during a local test flight in December 1965. White ramp area in the centre is parking area for Weasels and F-105s. At lower right is Camp Friendship, an Army installation
(Ed White)

BELOW
Weasel 58-1221, first of the few, takes on JP-4 jet fuel from a KC-135 tanker modified with probe-and-drogue system. This profile view clearly shows the extent of modification to the vertical tail housing that holds the paired antennae for the RHAW gear
(Ed White)

RIGHT
The Weasel operations centre was clearly marked by this sign. White doesn't remember whether replacement F-100F WWI crews erected it, or if it came with the later F-105 WWII crews
(Ed White)

BOTTOM RIGHT
In early December 1965, most of the first Wild Weasel group posed by one of their birds for a photo. Left to right, front line: Capts Walt Lifsey, Shep Kerr, Ed Sandelius, Ed White, unit commander Maj Garry Willard, Capts Jack Donovan, Al Lamb, Jack Pitchford, Maurry Fricke, unk. maintenance supervisor, operations officer Maj Bob Swartz
(Ed White Collection)

Thud pilots from Korat had evolved an effective evasive manoeuvre to use against the missiles. It required first seeing the missile at launching or a split-second later. When the flash of the booster signalled liftoff, the attacking pilots shoved throttles outboard into full afterburner while visually tracking the missile. At one point in its flight, it seemed to accelerate suddenly—probably after booster burnout and its immediate jettisoning—and that was the critical moment. Then the pilots broke toward the missile in a tight diving turn, a move that every reflex fought against, and which seemed suicidal at first. But that plunging spiral, followed by a rolling pullup, worked. The SA-2 guidance system lost target lock-on, couldn't respond fast enough to pick it up again, and whizzed past to explode or crash (a large percentage were duds, and caused substantial damage inside enemy lines that was blamed on the 'Yankee air pirates').

In practice, time often elapsed between detection and marking of the site, and the incoming strike; the missile crews could anticipate the attack. They often were able to fire a missile, or at least to alert the anti-aircraft batteries that defended the missile sites. Further, the backseaters in the Weasels had come from positions as EWOs in bombers that generally flew fairly straight and level. They had not been trained to concentrate during the kind of flying that fighter pilots call 'yankin' and bankin''. It was very difficult to read and interpret instruments inside the hurtling, manoeuvring, gut-straining Weasel. And what was worse, the tactics—which essentially were those of forward air controllers in a very-high risk environment—laid the Weasels open for killing.

Wild Weasels were part of the lead flight on all deep-strike fighter-bomber missions headed North. There was little time for learning the ropes. New

crews on their first mission could find themselves leading a 24-aircraft fighter-bomber strike to Hanoi, with the heavy responsibility of protecting those two dozen Thuds from being clobbered by missiles. Post-mission briefings showed that Weasel crews were exposed to missile fire for as long as 24 minutes and seldom for less than 15 minutes. In the crucible of combat, those times are eternities.

First Wild Weasel Loss

On 20 December, less than three weeks after the Wild Weasels began operations, the first F-100F crew was shot down. Pitchford and Trier, in -1231, call-sign APPLE 01, were flying with four Thuds on an Iron Hand strike north of Haiphong. Trier heard the rattle in his headset and began working the signal to determine its bearing and distance. Guided by Trier, Pitchford began trolling for SAMs.

Anti-aircraft artillery was positioned to defend the sites. As Pitchford and Trier neared the SAMs, they came under heavy ground fire, and a single 37-mm anti-aircraft shell exploded in the aft fuselage of the F-100F. Pitchford had been able to fire his marker rockets to pinpoint the SAM site for the Thuds; they rocketed the target, then followed the F-100F with the intent of observing the damage, helping with communications, and—if necessary—staying to protect the crew after they ejected.

The Weasel bird was in bad shape; Pitchford headed for the Gulf of Tonkin, but never made it. With hydraulics out, the F-100F was uncontrollable; it pitched, then dove toward the ground. Trier ejected first, as routine, and Pitchford followed. He was immediately surrounded and captured by North Vietnamese militia; Trier, landing some distance away, was later listed as missing in action but had been killed resisting capture (his remains were returned to the United States late in 1982).

The marking rockets and napalm soon were replaced by iron bombs, giving the Weasels additional, heavier weapons. 'The savest way to attack,' said Major Donald L 'Buns' Fraizer, 'was what you'd expect: fast and low. Low meant anything between about 500 feet and the deck, and the lower, the better. You went as fast as it would go, and you'd tap the burner every time you made a turn.' Unfortunately, by the time the F-100Fs refuelled for the trip up north, and because of the extra weight they were carrying in back-seater and equipment, they were just too heavy and sluggish to be outstanding fighter-bombers. That made them more vulnerable, also.

Nevertheless, on 22 December, the Weasels hit back successfully. Lamb and Donovan, flying -1226, made the first kill of a SAM radar system during a Rolling Thunder strike against railroad yards at Yen Bai, northwest of Hanoi.

The basic evasive manoeuvres to shake off the SAMs had been working well. During the five months of 1965 that the SAM's were in service, 180 were fired, averaging just over one each day. They destroyed 11 attacking aircraft during approximately 19,000 sorties flown against the North during the same time frame. That equates to 0.58 aircraft lost for every 1,000 sorties, hardly a crippling rate. But the missile's kill probability—11 hits for 180 rounds fired—calculated to almost exactly six per cent, too high to be acceptable. Suppose, the questions kept coming, suppose they can stockpile them and fire them in salvoes?

Teaming a Shrike with a Weasel

Three more F-100F Wild Weasel I aircraft (including 58-1212 and -1232) and more crews began arriving in the theatre in February. By spring, the first shipments of AGM-45A Shrike missiles had begun to arrive. Shrike had been developed in 1961 specifically as a counter to Soviet radar systems. The missile's passive homing system directed it to ride an enemy radar beam back to its source, to hit and destroy the transmitting antenna and the associated nearby equipment and crew.

With these weapons under their wings, the Wild Weasels were sent out to attack the radars with a new-technology missile with built-in smarts. Fraizer—by then a Major commanding the second detachment of Weasels that had relieved the first—and his EWO, Marshall Goldberg, fired the first Shrike in combat, on his first mission in the theatre on 18 April 1966. Major Garry Willard, former Wild Weasel I commander, and Lieutenants Howard and Richter, all three flying F-105Ds, accompanied Fraizer and Goldberg in their F-100F.

Goldberg detected a *Fire Can* radar signal (*Fire Can* was a towed, trailer-mounted tracking radar used with 57- and 85-mm AAA) and began directing Fraizer toward the target. When the Weasel receiver indicated that the site was 20° down from the flight path, Fraizer armed and launched the Shrike. The sky was very hazy, and the Shrike's trail was soon lost, so the flight broke to the left and departed the area. Some black smoke was spotted in the general direction of the radar site, but there was no confirmation. Willard later asked Fraizer why he hadn't followed the missile to see if it had been effective, and Fraizer responded that he had learned in Korea not to go nose-to-nose with guns, and breaking was instinctive at that time.

A few days later, the Fraizer/Goldberg team, their F-100F armed with another Shrike, was hunting at the southwest end of the Red River Valley. They detected radar signals, manoeuvred into position, and fired the Shrike. This time Fraizer did follow the smoke trail and, as he said, '. . . followed and followed and followed. A grand tour of North Vietnam was in progress. I surely passed where the missile had landed, but I didn't see the site, and then the F-105s called that they had lost me. Then Goldberg shouted,

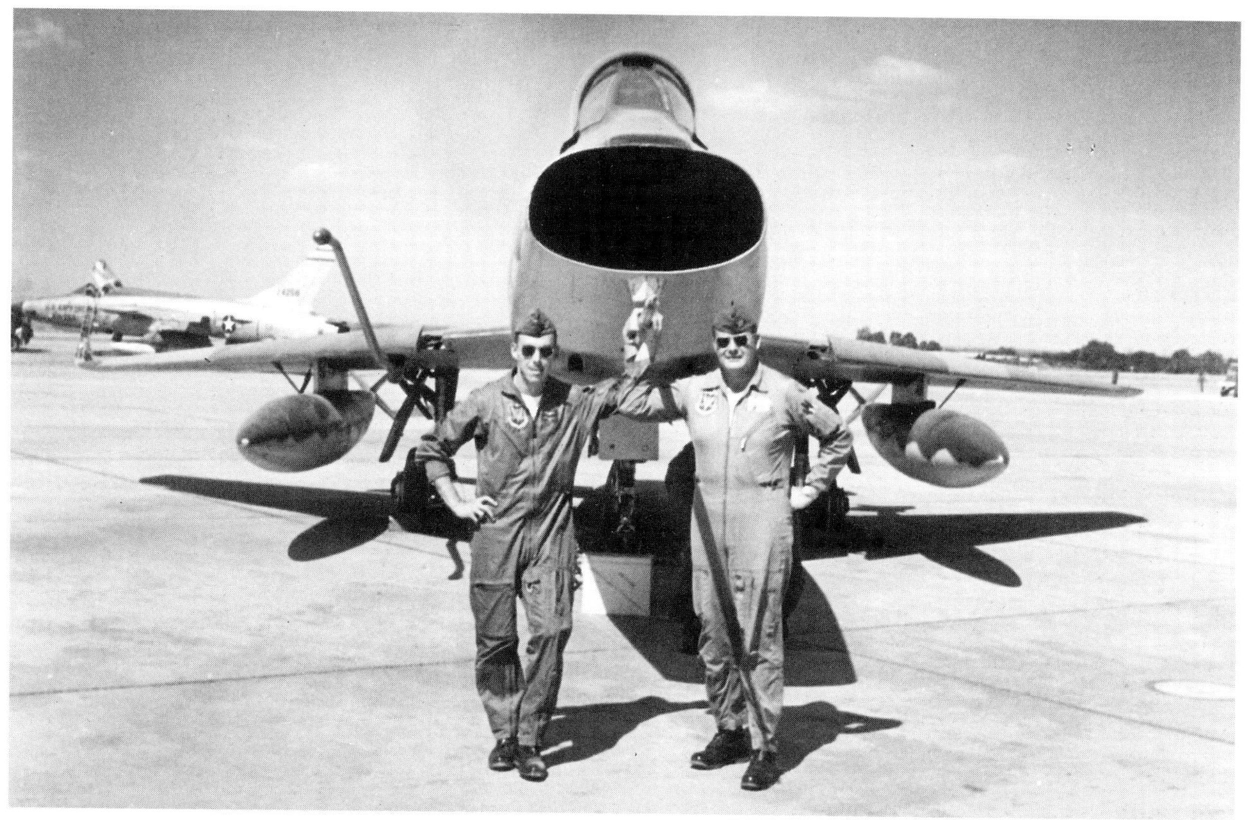

Ed White had flown this airplane (F-100F 58-1227) while serving with the 416th TFS at Misawa AB, Japan, so he was delighted to see it again as his Weasel bird. That's Capt White on the left, with his EWO, Capt Ed Sandelius, on the ramp at Korat. In the background is a Republic F-105D
(White Collection)

"My God, we're over the Red River!" and I accomplished a quick exit stage left and headed for home.'

'There were targets all through what we called the Holy Land, the forbidden areas around Hanoi,' said Fraizer, 'and we weren't supposed to hit them. There was one missile site in particular that was giving our fighters hell, so we wanted to take it out. You didn't just go and do it, because every single target had to be approved in Washington before we could hit it. So I put in a request to go after that one site, and it got bucked up the chain of command, and one night in July I got called to Headquarters for an urgent telephone call.

'On the other end of that line was LBJ (President Johnson) himself, the commander-in-chief of everything, and he personally gave us permission to hit that missile site. He also told me very emphatically to try not to hit any civilians while I was doing it. Well, there were civilians all around those missile sites, and it looked like it was going to be impossible to follow LBJ's suggestion. But we went up there anyway and hit it, and I don't think we hit any civilians.'

The arrival of the Shrike marked the beginning of the end for these pioneering crews. The aircraft were due for replacement; the perils of combat and the corrosive atmosphere of Vietnam were proving too much for the hastily installed systems. Of the four that were ferried back to the US, only two had acceptable electronics.

Because of their specialized gear, with its ability to detect a number of different enemy radars, the Wild Weasels also were assigned to other missions. They flew about once a day, routinely, chasing radar targets, but they also often flew night cover for strikes against targets in Route Pack 1 and 2. One time they also attacked missile sites in RP 2, which had been assigned to Navy control. The Navy complained, and the Wild Weasels thereafter stayed in their assigned areas.

The Wild Weasel I aircraft were stop-gaps, not ideally suited to the mission. So early in January 1966, General Dempster briefed the Air Council on the experience with the F-100F, and recommended quick conversion and deployment of the F-105 Wild Weasel III, and F-4 Wild Weasel IV. On 16 January, the first F-105G Wild Weasel conversion flew. (That story has been told earlier in *Republic F-105 Thunderchief*, another volume in this Osprey Air Combat series).

So, while the first batch of seven Wild Weasel I F-100Fs was proving the concept, the Air Force and Republic had begun modifying the two-seat F-105F to take over the Weasel missions. When the first

The enemy radar is on that hill, just a hundred yards or so above the bomb crater, and boring in on it is 'Buns' Fraizer and his EWO, Marshall Goldberg
(Fraizer Collection)

Fraizer triggers off a salvo of FFARs (arrows) from port and starboard pods
(Fraizer Collection)

Clusters of white dots (arrow) are the visible flames of the rocket motors, still burning as they race to the target ahead of the speeding Weasel bird
(Fraizer Collection)

The FFAR motors have burned out but the rockets are still on course (arrow), made visible by smoke trails
(Fraizer Collection)

'Gotcha!' was Fraizer's succinct caption to this photo. The rockets are right on target, and that radar, at least, will be off the air for some time
(Fraizer Collection)

Carrying finned napalm inboard and slicks outboard, this pair of F-100Ds is out hunting
(Steffens Collection)

modified Thuds arrived in the theatre, their crews at Korat flew their first missions in the company of an F-100F Wild Weasel in orientation training. According to one Wild Weasel I pilot, the Korat-based F-105Fs and Gs had a '. . . lot lower loss rate than the guys out of Takhli because of that F-100F training.'

The experiment had proved that properly equipped and armed aircraft could detect and destroy enemy defence radars. That had, of course, been proved twice before in two earlier wars. Specifically, the F-100F Wild Weasel I programme accounted for nine confirmed SAM radar kills, and an uncounted number of radars forced off the air, a result as effective, at least temporarily, as destroying the radar.

The cost to the unit was four officers—Clark, Dawson, Pitchford and Trier—listed then as missing in action. Pitchford came home as a liberated prisoner of war; Trier's remains were returned; Clark and Dawson were killed in the crash of their aircraft.

Interlude E: **Misty FAC**

Air war consists of finding the target, fixing its position, and destroying it. Behind that simple statement is a complex network of gathering intelligence, planning the mission, specifying ordnance loads, readying aircraft, and—after all that has been done—launching the aircraft, their pilots heading for some predetermined point to deliver weapons.

A key factor in the Vietnam air war equation was the FAC (forward air controller), an airborne strike boss who marked targets, directed strikes, corrected weapons deliveries, and reported results. In Vietnam by mid-1966, FACs flying piston-engined planes with light-plane performance were at such risk from enemy anti-aircraft that they had been withdrawn from their familiar operating territory just north of the demilitarized zone. There, they had been a major source of information about enemy forces and deployment.

The dive is about 30 degrees, the pickled load is two finned napalm bombs, and the target is somewhere down in that jungle. The pilot is from the 614th TFS, 35th TFW, and his home base is Phan Rang
(Steffens Collection)

General William W Momyer, then commanding 7th Air Force, credits 7th AF with conceiving the idea of putting the FAC in the back seat of a fast jet fighter, an F-100F or F-4. Another source credits the idea to Major George E 'Bud' Day, later to command briefly the first fast FAC unit. Regardless of whose idea it was, the purpose was to improve the survivability of the FAC, but not reduce the quality of information and the effectiveness of the strike control that only a FAC could produce.

To do that, 7th AF organized a skilled and specialized force to use eyeballs and cameras in a systematic checkout of potential ground target areas. Flying at low altitude and high speed, they would report target information to an Airborne Battlefield Command and Control Centre (ABCCC aircraft, an EC-130 with the callsign HILLSBORO). It was the job of the ABCCC team to divert and direct strike-fighters to the FAC, who would mark the targets and control the strike in the usual way.

In 1967, the mission was properly organized, formally coded Commando Sabre, and assigned to the 612th Tactical Fighter Squadron's Detachment 1, attached to the 37th Tactical Fighter Wing at Phu Cat. Later, the 612th became, in effect, a headquarters squadron, attached to the 31st TFW at Tuy Hoa, and flying F-100Fs belonging to other squadrons at that base.

Because they were FACs, and FACs needed an individual callsign, and because 'Bud' Day was the first unit commander, and he and his wife liked Errol Garner's song, 'Misty', its title was adopted as the callsign.

Momyer wrote that a '... shortage of F-4s led to the first combat test of a high-speed FAC taking place in an F-100F in Route Package I (Route Packages were seven designated areas of North Vietnam—I through V, VI A and VI B—assigned to Air Force or Navy as 'exclusive' target areas). After a number of trial missions, the high-speed FAC became standard where there were SAMs, AAA, and the threat of MiGs.'

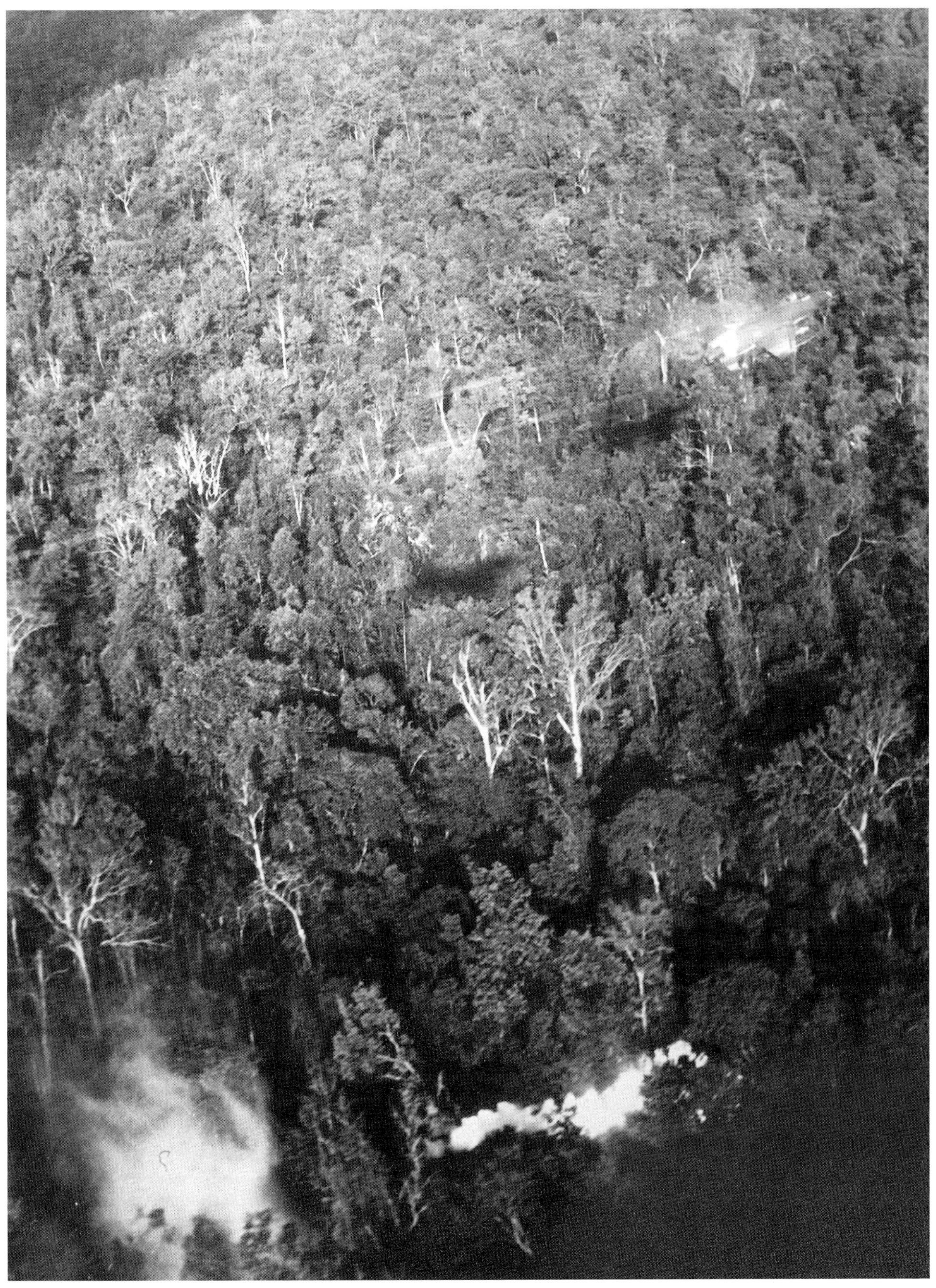

On 26 August, Day's F-100F (58-3954) was hit by ground fire during a Misty FAC mission over North Vietnam, and Day ejected, to be captured and tortured. He escaped, was recaptured and tortured again, and finally returned with other prisoners of war on 14 March 1973. For his conduct during imprisonment, Day received the Medal of Honor.

Misty FAC missions soon standardized on individual F-100Fs, with equally qualified pilots alternating front and rear seats between missions. The guy in front concentrated on flying; the guy in back was the observer, operating a belly-mounted panoramic strike camera and a hand-held camera with a wide-angle lens. But, because the missions lasted for several hours, pilots developed a cooperative workload arrangement.

The usual mission was pre-planned. 'When we were working in Laos on Steel Tiger, we'd go out with two Mistys at the same time,' remembers Ron Standerfer, who flew Misty FAC missions on TDY with the 612th. 'One would cover the north end of an area, for example, and the other the south. The typical routine for each Misty was that the guy in front made the takeoff, flew to the target area, and flew the road recce for 30 to 45 minutes. As soon as he pulled up from his recce run to head for the tanker, the guy in back took over, flew to the tanker, made the refuelling, and flew back to the target area. Then the guy in front would take over and fly another recce run.

'The guy in back had all the maps, took pictures with a hand-held strike camera, communicated with HILLSBORO, and vectored in the fighters to the target area. But when they arrived, the guy in front took over, fired the markers and directed the strike. Then maybe he'd fly out to the tanker and do the refuelling, while the guy in back relaxed, or maybe flew it back, and then the guy in front would do another road recce.

'We did two rounds of road recce and two refuellings most of the time, then we'd go back and do one more road recce, just in case we missed something. Then the guy in back would fly it home and land it. The standard mission lasted about three and one-half hours, and we refuelled twice. Missions were scheduled to give dawn to dusk coverage. The first takeoff was before dawn, so that we'd be over the assigned area at sunrise.

It's May 1967, and the Hun beginning pullout above the tree canopy is part of the air strike force supporting Operation Manhattan. The napalm dropped on this pass has detonated and, if that's the FAC's smoke marker just to the left of it, it was a near miss. Notice the two shadows of Hun and photo plane, and the condensation trails marking the lift increase at pullout. The target is described as a POL (petroleum, oil, lubricants) storage area 15 miles southeast of Tan Ninh City
(Pickett Collection)

'The way you flew these recce runs,' Standerfer continued, 'was with constant rolling left and right 90 degrees, and every time it got up on the wing, you'd both look out and down to see what you could. The unwritten rules were that you never got below 1,000 feet (305 m), because of small-arms fire, and you never went slower than 400 knots (741 km/h).

'If we saw anything suspicious, we kept right on going, playing dumb, out of sight, over the horizon. Then we'd swing way around and come in on the same spot from another angle, fast as she'd go, to make it difficult for gunners. Then when we came over the spot where we'd seen something, we'd half-roll, and the guy flying would stand on the rudder while the guy in back ran the cameras. Then we'd get out, and call in the coordinates to the ABCCC.'

The ABCCC was on station around the clock, and its airborne controllers directed armed fighter-bombers to rendezvous with the Misty FAC at a Delta point—a suitable area that covered a region of enemy-held territory—the FAC had designated.

'When the strike came in, they'd call when they saw us, and we'd start being a FAC. We had rocket pods with Willy Peter (white phosphorus) warheads for smoke markers, and we'd rocket the site to show the Thuds or the Phantoms where to drop. We got real good at firing marker rockets; our standard firing pass was almost straight down. We'd split-S right over the target, fire the rockets, and pull out maybe 6,500 ft (1981 m) above the terrain.

'Most of the time, we were looking for truck parks, always hoping to find someplace where they'd stashed them for the day. They ran at night; by 1969, we'd driven the trucks off the Trail during the day. We did try a different idea in April 1969, I think it was. We took off late in the afternoon with one Misty and two F-100Ds flying in trail, and they were loaded with hi-drag and cluster bombs. We were planning to make one sweep, thinking we might catch some trucks on the Trail just starting an early-evening run. But we didn't.

'The bad guys were good gunners, though, and brave. They'd keep those ZPUs and 37-mm guns going even after we'd dusted them with 750-pounders. And I remember once flying along the usual road in the usual way and suddenly being hosed by a lot of flak. It was almost like an ambush, and we thought maybe they had a crude warning system; they'd telephoned from down the road somewhere that we were coming, and alerted the gunners.

'I was FAC for the battleship *New Jersey* once up in Pack I, and I have to report that their accuracy was awful. They didn't get closer than one kilometre to the target. There were just too many variables for the kind of accuracy needed for the targets we worked.'

Standerfer and others were part of a small group of Misty FACs—only 142 pilots total during the war—who volunteered for the mission. (Dick Rutan, who with Jeana Yeager recently flew non-stop around the world in the Voyager, was also a Misty FAC).

63063

TOP LEFT
Festooned with 'Snake and nape', this Hun rolls in on a bombing run. The wing slats have popped out in response to the need for more lift in the tight turn
(USAF/Maene Collection)

LEFT
In a 45-degree dive, the pilot of this uncamouflaged Hun (F-100D 56-3063) pickles two 750-lb iron bombs. He's one of the 'Crusaders' from the 481st TFS, 3rd TFW, at Tan Son Nhut
(USAF/Maene Collection)

ABOVE
Coming home with the racks empty, this pilot (531st TFS, 3rd TFW) begins a slow descending turn that will put him in the pattern at Bien Hoa. His F-100D (56-2910) has an APR-25 threat-warning antenna under the inlet and a command radio antenna on the dorsal spine
(USAF/Maene Collection)

Standerfer said that volunteering for Misty FAC gave the '. . . drivers down south a chance to take a little walk on the wild side. It really was. I watched that operation from May '68 to the following winter, and I just couldn't stand it any more and volunteered to do it. The guys in the squadron said, you're out of your gourd, and my crew chief said, "Come on, Major, you're gonna go home in two months. You mess around, you're gonna get shot down." What did he know? Well, it happened, of course.'

And it did. Standerfer, riding the rear seat, and his pilot, were shot down on April Fool's Day 1969, in a known high-threat area, in marginal weather. They had marked the target, and the F-4s on the strike had asked for another marker. The Misty crew rolled in flat and long, pulled off the target amidst heavy ZPU fire, and the warning lights came on. Eventually the engine quit, and the two ejected, to be picked up by the Jolly Green Giants of the Air Rescue Service. Standerfer, having landed in a tree and fallen to the ground, was pulled to the chopper by a jungle penetrator through more trees, and was severely battered in both processes. On his next Misty FAC mission three days later, he lost sensation in his right leg and lower back after a couple of hours in the air. That was repeated on the next mission and, after a detailed examination by the flight surgeon, he was returned to the strike unit where he flew shorter combat missions which did not produce the same problems.

When the Misty FAC operation ended after the summer of 1970, the aircrews had logged more than 21,000 hr of combat time. The Misty FAC mission was copied by other high-speed FAC operations: Wolf FAC, with F-4Ds from the 8th TFW, Ubon, Thailand; Stormy FAC, F-4Ds from the 366th TFW, Da Nang, RVN; and Tiger FAC, F-4Es of the 388th TFW, Korat, Thailand. The Marines had a similar operation, using TA-4 two-seaters.

Momyer summed up: 'Theirs was a tough mission; these high-speed FACs . . . were among the most courageous pilots of the war.'

Chapter 8
Super Sabres in the Guard
Interlude F: Keeping the Huns in the Air

The five best F-100 units in Vietnam combat were Air National Guard squadrons. So said General George S Brown, testifying before Congress during 1973 hearings that led to his confirmation as USAF Chief of Staff. Brown had commanded the 7th Air Force during a part of the war in Vietnam, and had the first-hand opportunity to observe the comparative fighting performance of Guard and regular F-100 squadrons.

The five units Brown praised were the 120th Tactical Fighter Squadron, Colorado ANG; the 136th, New York ANG; the 174th, Iowa ANG; the 188th, New Mexico ANG; and the 355th, nominally an Air Force unit, but manned predominantly by ANG personnel.

Eight ANG tactical fighter and three tactical reconnaissance groups had been recalled to active duty on 26 January 1968, by Lyndon B Johnson's Presidential Executive Order that followed the seizure of the USS *Pueblo* by North Korean naval units on 23 January. But, following the initial US reaction that included mobilization, the *Pueblo* incident didn't escalate into a widening of the war, as anticipated, and so the ANG units were, in effect, all dressed up with no place to go.

Three months later, they did have a place to go: war in Vietnam. That conflict had been raging for several years, and the light that had been frequently observed at the end of the tunnel was getting neither brighter nor closer. So the Administration decided to send half of the mobilized ANG fighter units, with their F-100s, to combat in Vietnam. Two other F-100 Guard units were deployed to Korea. The remaining two moved to Myrtle Beach AFB, South Carolina, to train regular USAF pilots who would rotate to Southeast Asia to fly the Super Sabres.

Before the Guard units arrived, 13 regular USAF F-100 squadrons were attached to four tactical fighter wings in South Vietnam. The number of F-100s assigned to those wings varied between approximately 280 and 380, depending on attrition, aircraft in maintenance, and other factors. The Guard squadrons increased the Super Sabre force in Southeast Asia by 88 aircraft, a major gain in total F-100 strength.

First to arrive in the war zone was the 120th TFS from Buckley ANG Base, Denver, Colorado. The squadron's advance detachment left Denver on 28 April. The squadron pilots flew their 20 F-100Cs all the way, with overnight stops at Hickam AFB, Hawaii, and Andersen AFB, Guam. The flight time totalled more than 22 hr, and involved between 11 and 13 air refuellings. The unit touched down at Phan Rang AB, South Vietnam, on 3 May. By 8 May, its pilots had begun flying operations with instructor pilots from the 35th TFW. By 1 June, all had completed their in-theatre check rides and were flying combat as qualified flight leaders.

That pattern was duplicated by the other three ANG F-100 squadrons. With an absolute minimum of fuss, only four delayed aircraft arriving a day later, and with no accidents, this ready reserve force deployed efficiently from bases in the United States to a combat theatre, and were ready to fight within a few days after arrival. It was unprecedented in Air Force annals; there had been earlier Guard deployments in force, but at a great loss in readiness and a quickly apparent lack of capabilities. And these ANG units had been recalled with only 24-hr notice, instead of the usual 30-day alert period that eases the transition from civilian employment and obligations to military duty.

Between May 1968 and April 1969, the Air Guard pilots in Vietnam logged more than 38,000 combat hours on more than 24,000 sorties. Seven pilots and one intelligence officer were killed, and 14 aircraft destroyed by enemy action. None of the five squadrons had a single reportable accident due to pilot, materiel, or maintenance failure.

Explanation of this level of performance, unrea-

The mountain lion on the nosewheel door identifies an F-100C (54-1836) of the 120th TFS, Colorado Air National Guard, attached to the 35th TFW at Phan Rang AB. On this fine afternoon of 22 June 1968, the pilot is about to drive his Hun out of the revetment and to the end of the active runway. There, the red streamers now dangling from safety pins on the 750-lb Snakeye bombs will be removed, and the guns will be cocked
(USAF K35323)

ched by regular Air Force units, was also in Brown's testimony. 'The aircrews were a little older, but they were more experienced,' he said, 'and the maintenance people were also more experienced than the regular units. They had done the same work on the same weapons system for years, and they had stability that a regular unit doesn't have.

'We had a different breed of cats when we got the Guard over here,' Brown had said. 'We can turn them loose. They can go on because they can understand how to fly . . . Their average pilot time in the F-100 is 1,000 hours. In my squadrons here, my average time in the F-100 is 150 hours.'

The Guard had come a long way from its 'flying club' status of the late 1940s. In two solid decades of rethinking and relearning, it had grown to be a major component of the nation's military strength. Its performance in Vietnam underscored the value of the continuing experience in the same equipment that was shared by ground crews and aircrews alike. And the use of that equipment—the Super Sabre—began early in the Guard.

Early Users, Early Mobilization

With unseemling haste, the Air Force unloaded its first batches of F-100As as rapidly as possible, passing them along to the Air National Guard. The 188th TFS, New Mexico ANG, was first to receive its As, beginning in April 1958. C models were brought into Guard units during fiscal year (FY) 1960. The first ANG F-100Ds went to the 174th TFS, of the Iowa Guard, during FY 1974. F-100F aircraft also were assigned to ANG units during the early 1960s.

So the Guard experience with the F-100 covered 21 years, an exceptionally long time to operate a single type of fighter aircraft. But it led to an extremely high efficiency of operation. Guard pilots knew every quirk of the Super Sabre. Guard maintenance specialists could have drawn its structure and systems from memory, and repaired them in the dark ('Only a slight exaggeration,' said one Guardsman).

F-100s equipped a total of 23 tactical fighter or interceptor ANG squadrons—the early As were classed as air defence interceptors—and when the

723

A thirsty New Jersey ANG F-100C (54-2114) tops off on JP-4 delivered by a Tennessee ANG KC-97. Note that the Hun is hanging on its opened slats at a fairly high angle of attack to generate the lift needed to stay down at the cruising speed of the clunky tanker. This refuelling occurred during the May 1967 deployment to Elmendorf AFB
(Maene Collection)

LEFT
The first New Jersey ANG F-100C-10-NA (55-2723) arrives at Elmendorf AFB, Alaska, for a joint exercise during May 1967, and there to park it is John Maene, Jr
(Maene Collection)

final phaseout began in 1979, ten squadrons were still flying the venerable, reliable, and much-loved Super Sabre.

Less than three years after the Guard first began receiving its Super Sabres, the Berlin crisis broke. By Presidential Executive Order, John F Kennedy mobilized the Guard on 1 October 1961. Fighter-bomber squadrons, flying F-84s, were deployed to Europe to augment NATO air forces. But three fighter squadrons, equipped with newly received F-100Cs, stayed in the United States: the 120th TFS; the 121st TFS, Washington, DC, ANG; and the 136th TFS. All three were demobilized during August 1962.

The performance of the Guard during the Berlin crisis was first praised; but as later studies indicated, there were problems of readiness and operational capabilities, once readied. In August 1965, after getting involved in the Vietnam war, the Department of Defense began the Selected Reserve Force programme, planned to build and maintain a strategic reserve in the United States as a backup to the active units in combat in Vietnam.

Designated *Beef Broth* (later, *Combat Beef*), the programme included nine tactical fighter groups from the Air Guard, equipped with a total of 225 F-100s, plus four tactical reconnaissance groups with RF-84Fs, and a tactical control group. When the whistle blew, those units would be prepared to deploy overseas within 24 hr of their mobilization.

It took only a year to accomplish; by August 1966, all the Air National Guard *Beef Broth* units were considered combat-ready.

U.S. AIR FORCE
U.S. AIR FORCE

Then Came the Big One

On 25 January 1968, President Johnson mobilized a major portion of the Selected Reserve Force, which included eight Air National Guard squadrons equipped with F-100C fighters. The recalled units were alerted to prepare for deployment within 72 hours. During the time between recall and the actual deployment about 60 days later, all aircrews were sent TDY to Homestead AFB, Florida, to attend the Southeast Asia Survival Course. With that out of the way, the aircrews next went TDY to Cannon AFB, NM, for *Top Off* training, special instruction in weapons delivery techniques, including heavy load sorties. *Top Off* lasted about a month, from the end of March to the end of April, 1968. Each of the mobilized units sent six of its F-100C aircraft, aircrew and supporting personnel. The training programme had barely been completed when the units began leaving for combat.

The 120th TFS deployed to Phan Rang AB, and attachment to the 35th TFW of the regular Air Force. The 174th TFS went to Phu Cat AB, and the administrative control of the 37th TFW. The 136th and 188th TFS both joined the 31st TFW at Tuy Hoa AB.

The midwesterners—the 127th TFS, from the Kansas Guard, and the 166th, from Ohio—were deployed with their F-100Cs to Kunsan AB, in Korea, and, with some augmentation of air and ground personnel, became the 354th TFW of the regular Air Force.

The easterners—the 119th TFS, of New Jersey, and the 121st, of Washington, DC—moved from their home bases to Myrtle Beach AFB to establish a USAF tactical fighter rotational training unit, teaching USAF pilots how to fly the F-100.

Moving South from Jersey

The 119th move was typical. After call-up, the unit continued to operate and train out of the National Aviation Facilities Experimental Center (NAFEC) airfield at Pomona, NJ. Like other Guard units called to active duty, it also waited for the other shoe to drop. When it did, early in May 1968, the 119th was ready.

On the morning of 6 May, the first four F-100Cs were taxied out to the long runway at NAFEC by Major Harry White and Captains David Wolfe, William Charney, and Donald Miller. At 10:30 am, they began their takeoffs; airborne, the quartet formed and roared back over the field in a farewell

A mix of aluminium-lacquered and camouflaged Huns from the New Jersey ANG share the ramp at Elmendorf AFB, Alaska. These are all C models, and the nearest is, as you can read, 54-1803
(Maene Collection)

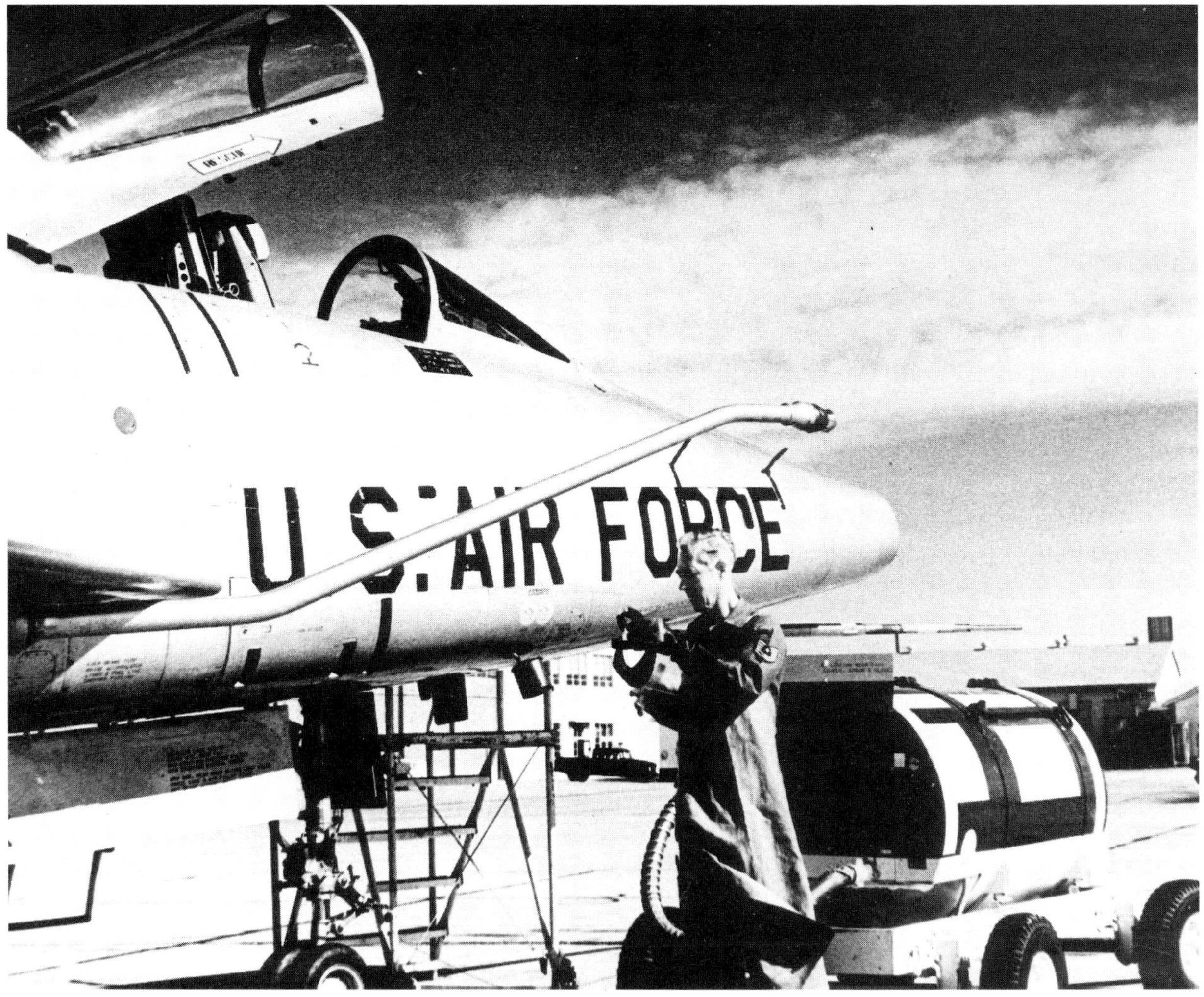

salute. Plane after plane took off to follow them in the flight to Myrtle Beach AFB.

Three Lockheed C-130s from Langley AFB, Virginia, arrived during the first day of the move, scheduled to transport the half-million pounds of equipment and the non-flying personnel. It required about 20 trips by the cargo carriers before everybody and everything had been off-loaded on the ramp at Myrtle Beach.

In all, 522 officers and men of the 119th TFS made the move; about 350 were left behind and within a month had received orders transferring them to other bases. About half of the pilots from the 119th, along with a number from the 121st, were assigned to the 355th TFW, at Tuy Hoa, and made up 85 per cent of the strength of that regular USAF unit. (Among the pilots from the 119th who went to the 355th was Major Ronald G Standerfer, whom we have met as a Misty FAC in Interlude E.)

The Iowa Guard had similar experiences. After activation, giant C-141 transports waddled into the base at Sioux City, loaded support equipment, and took off, headed West. On 14 May, the 174th TFS departed with 22 F-100s for Vietnam, with intermediate stops in Hawaii and Guam. They landed at Phu Cat Air Base, 12,000 miles (19,308 km) away, after 22 air hours and a dozen inflight refuellings.

Combat Performance by the Colorado Guard

The 120th, commanded by Lieutenant Colonel Robert Cherry, included 21 airline pilots on its roster. When they were first recalled to active duty in January, 1968, they began a programme of accelerated training at their home base, then continued specialized training in survival and ordnance delivery.

Orders to begin the move arrived 22 April, and six days later the advance party of one officer and nine enlisted men left for Phan Rang. The complete move totalled 31 officers and 345 enlisted men, the first ANG unit to deploy to a combat zone since World War 2.

The standard roster for a USAF Tactical Fighter Squadron then required 152 men, so the remaining 224 members of the 120th TFS were absorbed in the 35th TFW's support units.

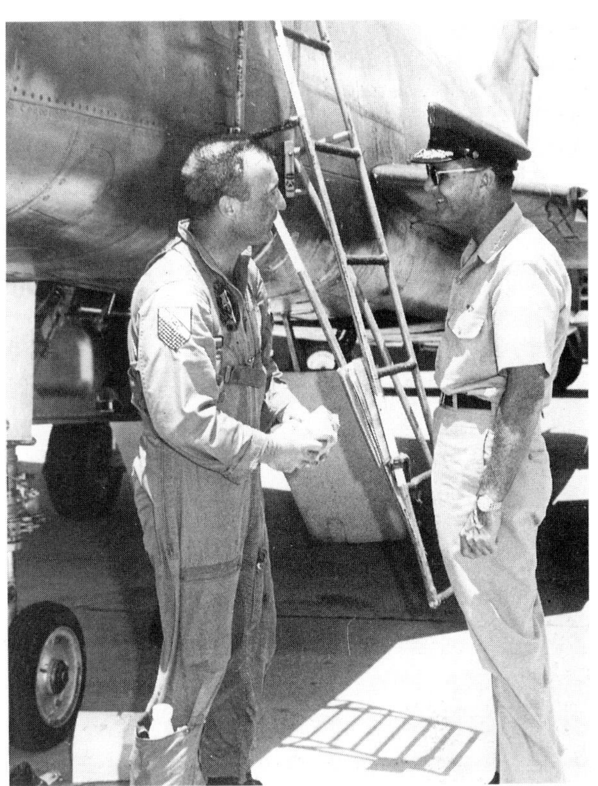

LEFT
One of the innovations brought to squadrons by the F-100 was its liquid oxygen life-support system. Here, TSgt Green, 120th Consolidated Aircraft Maintenance Squadron, Colorado ANG, gets ready to charge the LO_2 system on a Guard F-100C at Buckley ANG Base, near Denver. Face shield, apron, and gloves were required protection gear for this job
(Ulrich Collection)

RIGHT
The first ANG unit to arrive in Southeast Asia was the 120th TFS from Colorado. Capt William J Wilson, of the 120th, is welcomed to the war by Gen William M Momyer, commander of the 7th Air Force
(Ulrich Collection)

BELOW
Maj Jack Wilhite, 120th TFS, buckles into his F-100C (54-1780) at Phan Rang. Note the cougar emblem of the Colorado ANG on the nosewheel door, and the opened saddleback on the Hun's spine
(Ulrich Collection)

A competitive attitude, born of years of enduring the jibes of regular forces, has always been characteristic of Air National Guard squadrons. Their actions in combat underscored that attitude. After less than eight weeks in action, the Colorado Guard aircrews were flying more than 24 missions each day, and delivering more ordnance than any other unit of the 35th TFW. According to one source, the squadron's munitions and release reliability exceeded 99.5 per cent. (That figure was important for two reasons: first, the 120th was not wasting expensive ordnance on non-targets; second, the enemy searched for, and salvaged, unexploded bombs as well as other ordnance to convert them for their own use.)

The only problem that affected squadron operations was outside the control of the 120th or, in fact, of any other F-100 unit in South Vietnam. Beginning in November 1968, the 120th began sending its aircraft—typically, three to four at a time—to Taiwan for replacement of the wing centre section structure assembly, a modification that took the aircraft out of action for three weeks. But when they came back, their new wing centre sections permitted increasing the maximum limits in pullouts from 6 to 7.33G. Before the modification programme, the squadron was averaging 24 combat sorties a day, a rate of about 1.1 sortie/aircraft, somewhat higher than the wing average. But during the modification programme, a typical day would see the 120th flying ten pre-planned missions and four from the alert pad, for a total of 14.

The 120th flew its last missions on 8 April 1969, completing an enviable record. The unit had flown 6,127 sorties, of which 5,905 were combat missions. It had an 86.9 per cent Operationally Ready Rate, a

RIGHT
A sky full of Cs from the Air Guard, 16 of them, sleek shapes streaking sunward
(Steffens Collection)

BOTTOM LEFT
While pilots were sleeping, briefing, lounging, or whatever, a bunch of talented and overlooked airmen were busting their tails keeping airplanes fixed and ready to go. Here, two Colorado ANG specialists at Phan Rang AB work over F-100C 54-1950, readying it for a strike. Bombs hang on the inboard pylons, safety pins and streamers in place
(Ulrich Collection)

0.5 per cent Abort Rate, and a 98.8 per cent Munitions Reliability Rate, all three the best figures in the 35th TFW. The 120th had delivered more than 14.3 million pounds of bombs, 5.6 million pounds of napalm, 423,000 rockets, 227,070 pounds of cluster bombs, and 1.8 million rounds of 20-mm ammunition.

The cost was one pilot killed in action, and the intelligence officer missing in action. Four enlisted men were wounded during the many enemy attacks on the base.

On 11 April 1969, the 120th began redeployment to Buckley ANGB, and everyone was home again by 16 April.

Sioux City Air Guard Experience

The 174th, out of Sioux City, Iowa, was commanded by Lieutenant Colonel Gordon Young. It had 11 airline pilots on its roster, commuting to Sioux City from as far distant as Seattle and New York City. Operating out of Phu Cat, nearest of the bases to the demilitarized zone dividing North from South Vietnam, the 17th flew most of its missions out of country, into the North. They were tougher missions, because of the greater exposure to enemy fire, and in their first 30 days, the pilots flew 563 combat missions averaging about 1.5 hr duration.

For those whom statistics enchant, this is the record of the 174th TFS during about a year of flying combat missions out of Phu Cat: 1,864,801 rounds of 20-mm ammunition fired; 12.9 million pounds of bombs dropped; 3.0 million pounds of napalm delivered; 154 tons of rockets fired; 512,000 pounds of cluster bombs released. The squadron's pilots flew 6,359 missions, logged 11,399 combat hours.

Three aircraft were lost in combat, one pilot was killed in action, and a ground accident caused a fatality.

The squadron redeployed home with its 19 remaining airplanes, and arrived in Sioux City, Iowa, on 14 May. The lineup of camouflaged, war-worn Super Sabres wore their white HA tail codes. On their noses, the names: *Karen*, *Carol's Crisis*, *Corrine's Corruptor*, *Loyal Linda*, *Darling D*, *Patty's Pumpkin*.

The Roadrunners Go to War

The 188th TFS of the New Mexico Air National Guard left Albuquerque on 4 June 1968, headed for Tuy Hoa AB and attachment to the 31st TFW. The squadron—364 officers and men, and 22 F-100Ds, plus support equipment—made the three-day trip as if they had been doing that kind of travel year in and year out. Actually, it was the very first overseas deployment for the 188th TFS.

In common with other ANG units, pilots of the 'Enchilada Air Force' had logged many hours on the F-100s; average time on type in the 188th exceeded 1,100 hours. So they required an absolute minimum of briefings on theatre tactics and weapons delivery, and they were ready to fight.

Nearly 200 experienced technicians were transferred out of the 188th to supervisory positions with the wing. The NMANG non-commissioned officers were placed in charge of major shops and sections, reflecting their long experience with the Super Sabre, and the unusually high standards established by ANG units equipped with the F-100.

In August, the 188th flew 701 combat sorties, nearly 23 a day. And during the ten-month combat tour, the 188th averaged 18 combat sorties each day.

They gained a reputation for accurate delivery of ordnance, often under harrowing conditions of weather and enemy ground fire. Letters of praise came from Army officers whose troops had lived to fight again because of close support from the NMANG pilots. One wrote: '. . . your pilots delivered their ordnance effectively and accurately even though the target was immersed in darkness . . . had it not been for . . . your pilots, the camp would have been lost before morning.'

And another letter described a difficult task: '. . . the pilots [had] to run in below the surrounding [mountainous] terrain, twisting in and out along a river bed to deliver their ordnance on target. Tracking time was so short that the FAC was completely amazed that ordnance could be delivered anywhere near the target. All ordnance was delivered within ten metres of the point requested. This is . . . almost unbelievable under these conditions. It is

A gaggle of five F-100Ds of the Connecticut Air National Guard refuels on a deployment. Nearest is F-100D 56-3022, with CT tailcode, the 'Running Pilgrim' insigne on the fin and an Outstanding Unit Award just below it (CtANG)

CT
AF
63 022

always a pleasure to work with pilots of the calibre of Taco 01 and 02.'

Every regular Air Force officer in contact with any of the Guard squadrons deployed to Vietnam had something good to say about them. They brought clean and mechanically perfect airplanes, said one. Fantastic bombing accuracy, said another. Best flying next to the Thunderbirds, said a third. All they had to learn when they got here were the rules of engagement.

And an article in the *Air Reservist* said that the Air Guard units were '. . . flying more combat missions than other squadrons at their bases, and in-commission rates, bomb damage assessment, and other criteria by which tactical fighter units are judged, rate higher than other F-100 squadrons in the zone.'

Further North, a Different Story

The hard-luck side of the 1968 deployment was shared by the two ANG squadrons that went to Kunsan AB in Korea. The problems surfaced when the 127th TFS and 166th TFS were augmented by personnel from Air Force Reserve units and from other ANG units, and reorganized to form the 354th Tactical Fighter Wing. The forced reorganization was perceived as a slap in the face of the Guard units, aside from the time it wasted in reassigning personnel and jobs. Consequently, the 354th took longer than it should have to become operational. Further, its primary assigned mission was air defence of Korea, a task made difficult by the simple fact that the F-100Cs equipping the squadron had no all-weather air-to-air weapons, and besides that, couldn't climb to altitude very rapidly.

Worse, there were no spare parts for the F-100Cs in stock in the Far East, and the units in Vietnam had the priority of receipt of whatever spares came through the pipeline to the region. As a result, aircraft availability went down and readiness dropped below Air Force minimums. Aircraft were lost in accidents, a pilot was killed, the Wing failed an operational readiness inspection (ORI), and finally the combat readiness rating was downgraded to marginal.

In fairness to the Guard squadrons, the mess was not of their doing. No unit, however sharp, can operate without spares. All units need an identity; morale drops when units are absorbed, reorganized, broken into new sections. In spite of all, the 127th and 166th worked to remedy the deficiencies, and by the

The paint on the tailcone has burned off enough to reveal that this F-100D (56-3093) of the 118th TFS, 103rd TFG, Connecticut ANG, once was Thunderbird One. The Connecticut Guard first was equipped with F-100As from October 1959 through December 1965, then flew Convair F-102s, and then converted to F-100D models in April 1971, keeping them until the summer of 1979 (CtANG)

Over the fence at Bradley International Airport, Windsor Locks, Connecticut, comes F-100F 56-3769 of the CtANG, flaring for a landing
(CtANG)

time they were released to go home again, they had passed a second ORI and were again rated as combat-ready.

Similarly, the Colorado guardsmen found disappointment in Korea. On 22 July 1968, about 140 officers and airmen from the Colorado ANG were sent to South Korea from South Vietnam, most of them going to Osan Air base which was Headquarters for Air Forces Korea. They were assigned as individuals, replacing regular USAF personnel. It was a disappointment to be broken out of their tightly integrated and experienced units in the ANG, but their experience was badly needed. They became key personnel immediately.

In addition to trying to cope with the chronic shortages of everything, not just spare parts for the F-100Cs, they had to live in tents, many of which were rotting. That shortage of housing lasted for most of the tour, and some airmen were still living in tents when they were ordered home in April 1969.

Last Days for the Super Sabre

In 1979, the last Air National Guard squadrons flying the F-100 began the final phaseout. For the last time, pilots in Missouri and Ohio, Indiana and Connecticut, Georgia and Massachusetts, Texas and Arkansas, strapped into an F-100D or F-100F, barrelled down the runway for the last time, climbed, came back around in a screaming low-level pass in salute to the base and the Guardsmen assembled, and headed for Davis-Monthan AFB, in Arizona, and the Military Aircraft Storage and Disposition Centre (MASDC). There, many of the F-100s became candidates for conversion into pilotless drones, targets for younger sisters (Chapter 10).

In a tribute to the unit's F-100s, an anonymous author in the 174th TFS wrote: 'So now it's time for most of us to go that big retirement home in Arizona. In the 16 years that my sisters and I served with the 185th (TFG), we've probably flown over 42,500,000 miles. Figure an average of 5,000 flying hours per year for 15 years at an average speed of 500 mph. Then add 11,399 combat hours at an average speed of 450 mph for Vietnam. And in all those miles there were seventeen aircraft accidents, including three in Vietnam, with four fatalities, including one KIA (killed in action). Would you believe that in the same period of time, nine 185th personnel were killed in traffic accidents?

'On 17 May 77, the last three Ds flew to Arizona. But, while my sisters retire, I'll still be on guard. When the front gate is relocated, I'll be put on a pedestal . . .'

The experience of Iowa ANG pilots was probably typical. The pilot roster accompanying the story quoted above shows two pilots with more than 3,000 hours, seven with more than 2,000, and 14 with more than 1,000 hours logged in the F-100. But those numbers seem almost minuscule compared to those logged by members of Arizona's 152nd TFS.

That squadron was given the F-100 training mission for both the Guard and Tactical Air Command, beginning in mid-September 1969. The 152nd flew C, D and F models until mid-1976, when the unit began the transition to A-7Ds. As a result, there are pilots in the Arizona ANG whose logbooks show more than 5,000 hours in F-100s. Willie Wilson, a pilot in both USAF and ANG, has 5,200 hours on type. The high-time F-100 pilot is Dick Salazar, who has logged more than 5,600 hours on F-100s. His logbook entries span 20 years in the Super Sabre.

The very last ever operational mission of an F-100 was flown by Guard pilot 1st Lieutenant William D Layne of the 113th TFS, 181st TFG, Terra Haute, Indiana. On 10 November 1979, Layne walked out to his F-100D (56-2979) parked on the ramp at Hulman Field, and signed the forms proferred by his crew chief, TSgt Ryan O Funkhauser. Layne climbed in; Funkhauser checked harness and hoses, wished him a good flight, and took away the ladder to begin the start procedures. Soon after, Layne lifted off the runway, writing 'finis' to the Hun's story.

The last pilot to strap on an F-100 was Brigadier General Frank L Hettlinger, commanding the 122nd TFW of the Indiana ANG. Soon after Layne's final operational mission in the Hun, Hettlinger ferried 979 from Terra Haute to MASDC. Said Hettlinger, 'The aircraft handled as perfectly as if it had just come from the factory . . . a memorable trip.' F-100D 979 was 23 years old, had logged more than 5,000 hours in the air, and—like many Guard F-100s—was a veteran of the war in Vietnam.

TOP
This F-100D (55-2895) has just been modified at these Taiwan facilities to strengthen its wings after a series of accidents imposed limits on the loads pilots could pull in flight
(Robert Breckel)

LEFT
An unusual and unsymmetric ordnance load hangs under the wings of F-100C-1-NA (53-1752) of the 188th TFS, New Mexico ANG. Left to right, they look like a laser seeker unit, a napalm bomb, a 500-lb GP bomb, a 750-lb GP bomb, a rocket pod, and another pod-mounted laser seeker unit. The scene: Kirtland AFB, near Albuquerque, NM
(Pickett Collection)

It was the end of the Super Sabre, and of an era for the Air National Guard. For the first time, that organization would be getting new fighter aircraft, instead of second-hand or castoff equipment from the Air Force. Now, Guard units fly and deploy in F-15s, F-16s, A-10s, as well as the ubiquitous F-4s, although they, too, are phasing out.

But there are times when the hangar flying gets loud and prolonged, and the arguements start about this fighter or that. There will always be Guardsmen who remember the F-100 fondly, and start with, 'Let me tell you about a real airplane!'

In my own case, the hangar flying began on a visit to the Connecticut Air National Guard's 103rd Tactical Fighter Group, and with a description of the F-100's flying and handling qualities by past Hun drivers Lieutenant Colonel John C (JC) Seymour and Major Al Hillman. Their collected comments went like this:

'Most fun of any airplane I ever flew . . . nothing since ever felt as good. I flew it by the numbers, the way the instructor pilots did, and I'm a better pilot now because I flew the F-100. It was an honest airplane. It had no fancy avionics, just basic instruments and a 1950 gunsight. You had to plan ahead and keep ahead; but it flew well cross-country, and in bad weather, and in formation. In the Guard, the airplanes were so well maintained, and were in such beautiful mechanical condition that the only weak link was how well you felt the day you flew.

'We flew four-ship air-refuelling night flights in bad weather, groping for the tanker, and they worked fine. If you had faith in the lead, there was no problem. It was a stable instrument airplane, right down to the landing.

'I had a basic 1 v 1 (one-against-one practice in air combat) with another pilot which I will remember forever. We met at 15,000 ft (4572 m) and finally terminated the fight over the commanding officer's farm. I was going straight down, in afterburner, at 250 knots (463 km/h) and 3,000 ft (914 m) when we decided to knock it off. I was young and strong and so was the F-100, and we made it, obviously.

'If you really worked on it, you could prove you were an aviator, not just an airplane driver. You always wanted to look good around home base, and look your sharpest in the pattern. It wasn't easy to look sharp on final; the F-100 made men in the final turn. You learned how to land and stop; how to get the chute out in the flare just before touchdown, hoping the guy in the RSU (Runway Supervisory Unit) wouldn't notice.'

In a later communication, Hillman elaborated on the landing technique: 'There were two schools of thought on how to fly the F-100 *after* touchdown. One I will refer to as "get the nosewheel on the runway fast"; the other I'll call the "thinking-pilot" method. I'm of the latter persuasion, as were most of the instructor pilots at the last USAF F-100 training wing at Cannon AFB. They proved beyond question that aerodynamic braking (keeping the nose high after touchdown and the nosewheel above the runway) was safe, though obviously not in severe cross-winds because of the weathervaning effect of the drag chute. It would slow the aircraft down more rapidly, and would preclude almost all barrier engagements if the chute failed.

'The former method was adopted years ago, allegedly because there was more directional control with the nosewheel on the runway. That was true, but it was at enormous cost in stopping ability. The F-

Looking like elongated Easter eggs, the colourful wing tanks on Brig Gen Boyd Hubbard's F-100F-10-NA (56-3846) have the only unusual markings on this basic bird. The shot was taken at Luke AFB, and Hubbard was undoubtedly a wing commander, there or elsewhere. During World War 2, Hubbard was a younger pilot flying a B-29 named Fleet Admiral Nimitz, *and was a participant in the last raid on Japan, on the night of 14–15 August 1945* (Pickett Collection)

100 rudder was very effective even at runway speeds as low as 100–120 knots (185–222 km/h).'

And Colonel Donald Joy, 103rd Group Commander, remembered his reaction to the F-100: 'It really was my favourite airplane; it was more challenging, and a lot more fun to fly than anything before or since. But you had to work harder at it, and so you appreciated it more when everything went right. That led to a sense of pride that you could do these things in that airplane, and you build squadrons on individual pride.'

Interlude F: **Keeping the Huns in the Air**

'The "lead sled", our terminology for the F-100, was not an overly difficult plane to maintain,' wrote Wallace Little, Lieutenant Colonel, USAF (ret), then a newly promoted Major and line maintenance officer of the 416th TFS in Misawa, Japan. 'But it took willing personnel, motivated to do the work properly. That is what we had to develop.'

Little had received a tough assignment, sent as a trouble-shooter to the 416th to straighten out some major problems in its maintenance operation, aggravated by poor morale. The 416th had lost four pilots in the fatal crashes of two F-100Fs, and the investigations blamed sub-standard maintenance. The NCOs were walking on eggshells because the previous maintenance officer threatened to court-martial anyone who made a mistake, thus the troops were without effective leadership. 'Our situation was that we supported six aircraft on the alert pads in Korea, with nuclear weapons aboard,' Little continued, 'and with 22 maintenance personnel who had to be five-level (Air Force proficiency measure) or higher. We had a total of just under 100 maintenance people, so with the rest of the troops, many at the one and three levels, we had to support a flying programme of 800 to 1,000 hours a month at the home base.'

Little had stepped into a demoralized organization, on a downhill slide; even the crew chief system wasn't working right for lack of enough skilled personnel. So

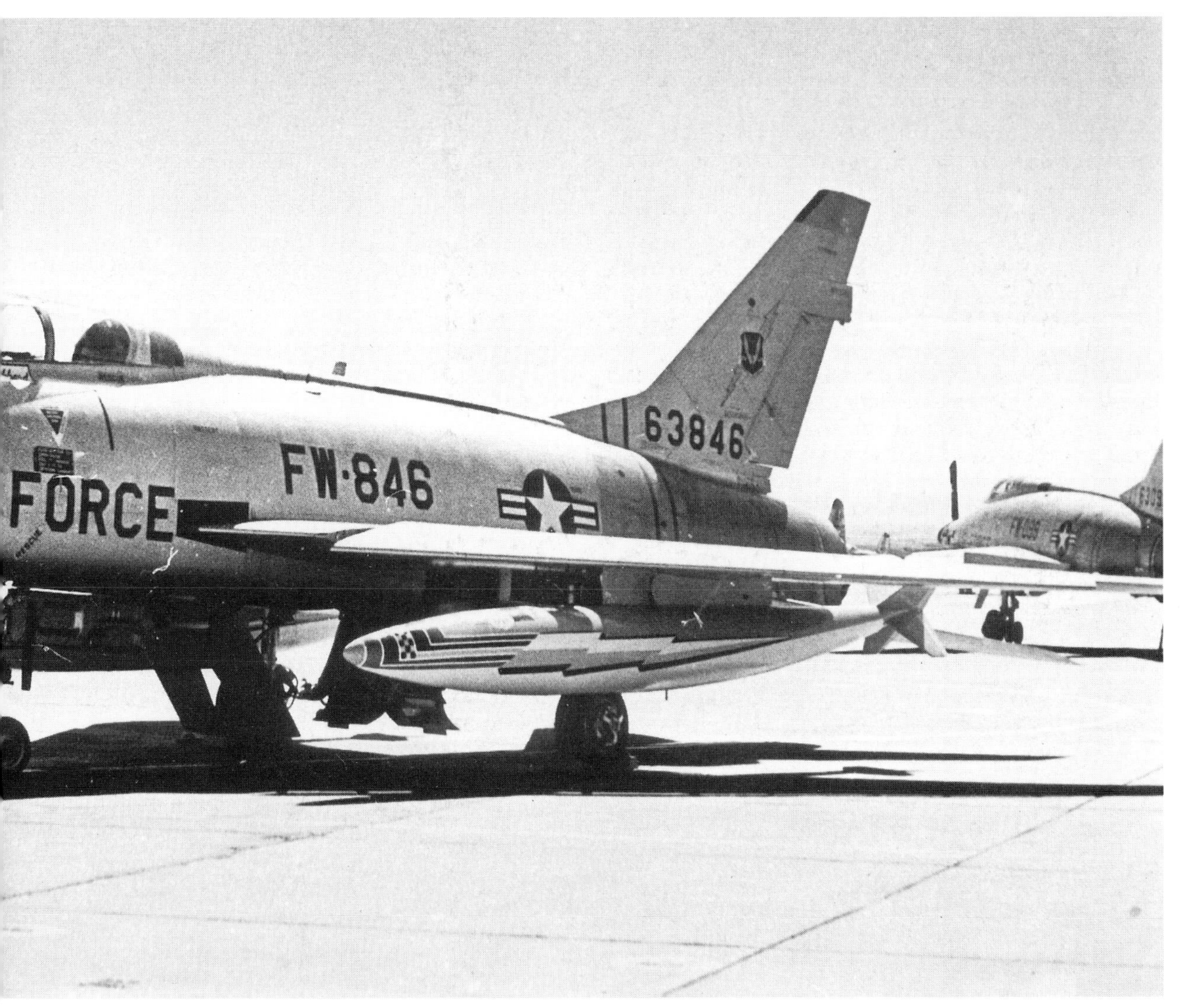

his first step was to assign the lesser-skilled personnel to 'gas and oil' work; their responsibilities were limited to getting the pilots off and receiving them after flight, and turning around the in-commission planes. Their maintenance limits: wheel changes and servicing the aircraft.

'When the birds returned from the last flight of the day, they were received by a post-flight crew, who then performed their work at night, in a lighted hangar, exactly according to the work cards, with no deviations permitted. At midnight, that crew was relieved promptly by a preflight crew, who inspected the aircraft, again according to the work cards. When the airplanes were ready for flight, they were turned over to the "gas and oil" crews.

'We also established a heavy maintenance crew which took responsibility for any aircraft needing more than minor maintenance. And finally, there was a special inspection crew that chose one airplane each day, and peeled it open like a banana to identify and fix problems before they became major ones.

'Within six months, we virtually eliminated overtime, and went from the lowest to one of the highest readiness ratings in PACAF; on a final Operational Readiness Inspection (ORI) just before I rotated to the US, we met our commitment with a 98 per cent rating.'

Little's accomplishment, although pre-Vietnam, was the kind of approach that was needed to solve some of the maintenance problems that had plagued the F-100s in earlier operational service. But whether the individuals were ram-rodding maintenance officers like Little (who had been a fighter pilot in China during World War 2 with the Tiger Sharks of the 23rd Fighter Group, and had flown fighters until he was grounded with Meniere's Syndrome), or efficient and accomplished wrench-turners among the non-commissioned officers, their presence was the key to the operational availability of the F-100.

Maintenance crews kept the airplanes available for service. There was real danger in that work; in Vietnam, enemy raids struck airfields and occasionally penetrated the totally inadequate perimeter protection. Then, technicians became riflemen, grabbing M-16s instead of a familiar box of socket wrenches.

But most often, the enemy was weather, cold, hot, dry, or wet; it always seemed to be the kind of weather that made things stop working. Take the environment of Vietnam, for example.

Heat, Humidity, Monsoon Rains

Moisture and electronics are, basically, incompatible. In Vietnam, there was ever-present moisture ranging from high humidity to drenching monsoon rains.

'I worked on instrument systems only at the time,' wrote Bruce F Hanke, formerly an Airman First Class in the 31st Armament and Electronics Maintenance Squadron, 31st TFW. 'The most troublesome was the fuel quantity indicating system. It was extremely sensitive to moisture, especially in the wiring and the probe connections.

'One particularly troublesome aircraft was constantly plagued by fuel-quantity indicator problems. One of our supervisors decided that drastic measures were needed if we were to get the airplane off "hangar queen" status. Two of us were asked to volunteer to work on it around the clock until it was fixed, in exchange for three days of non-chargeable R&R in Hong Kong. So Sergeant John Slaughter and I "volunteered"; we disconnected, cleaned, and dried every wire and probe on that airplane, stopping only to eat or cat-nap, and I recall that it took us about three days to free that bird of fuel-quantity indicator malfunctions. Once the airplane worked again, that promise of R&R was conveniently forgotten.

'The fuel-quantity indicator problem was typical of a lot of airplanes, and because we had about 100 F-100s on base from June 1968 through May 1969, we worked! Around the clock, seven days a week, sometimes two shifts, sometimes three, if we had the people. Usually we had one day off a week, but sometimes not. And never more than one day off.

'Periodically an aircraft would abort a takeoff because of no indication of airspeed. The aluminium tubing from the pitot tube to the cockpit had been damaged by vibration and shock of gunfire from the cannon which were right next to the tubes. On landing, the weakened line broke, not to be discovered until the next takeoff. Our only solution was to perform a pitot-static leak check every morning on all aircraft scheduled for the day. Since the 31st usually flew 50 to 60 or more sorties each day, a lot of work went into those checks of the system. But as a result, a large number of potential aborts were averted.

'Least troublesome systems were the MM-3 Remote Attitude Indicator and the J-4 Compass System. When they did break, we usually replaced a component and solved the problem. We had a standard joke in the squadron that the autopilot guys might as well go home, because whenever they got a discrepancy, they simply pulled the circuit breaker on the system and let the airplane fly as is. I seem to remember that, at any given time, half the aircraft were flying with inoperative autopilots.

'My pet hate was engine calibration checks, which involved checking the exhaust gas temperature (EGT) indicators. To do that, you had to crawl into the exhaust nozzle to place heater probes over the thermocouples, and often the engine wasn't completely cooled down when we did that. The already warm environment didn't help any. We probably did one or two of those checks nearly every day, and it seemed as though I got my turn once every three or four days.'

Chapter 9
The Hun Abroad
Interlude G: Super Sabre Thunderbirds

Four foreign countries operated Super Sabres: Nationalist China (F-100A, RF-100A, F-100A Rehab), Denmark (F-100D/F), France (F-100D/F), and Turkey (F-100C/D/F), all supplied under the US Military Assistance Program (MAP). The Danes, French, and Turks received at least 203 out of the 1,274 F-100D models built, or 16 per cent of the fleet, as part of measures taken to modernize and strengthen the tactical air forces available to the North Atlantic Treaty Organization (NATO).

The transferred F-100Ds were modified by installing the AN/ARN-21 navigation equipment standardized by the NATO allies; it cost, in those early years of the 1960s, $17,755 per airplane. A further modification, installing equipment and pylons necessary to arm the F-100Ds with early Sidewinder (GAR-8) missiles, was approved for only 150 of the aircraft, at a unit cost of $13,333.

F-100s in *l'Armée de l'Air*

France was the first foreign country to receive Super Sabres; the first F-100F arrived on 1 May 1958, and the first D, 18 May. Eventually, *l'Armée de l'Air* included 85 F-100Ds and 15 F-100Fs, assigned to two *Escadres* (approximate equivalent of a USAF wing) attached to the NATO 4th Allied Tactical Air Force (4 ATAF) and stationed at forward bases in Germany.

It is not widely known that France, while a member of NATO, assigned its mission of tactical bombardment, with both conventional and nuclear weapons, to the F-100 force. It also is not widely known that the nuclear weapons they would have carried—and for which they trained—were US Mk 43 one-megaton bombs.

Escadre 3, based first at Reims and then moved forward to Lahr, Germany, had two active *Escadrons* (approximate equivalent of a squadron, with 24 aircraft assigned to each *Escadron*): I/3 *Navarre* and II/3 *Champagne*. These units flew their F-100Ds until 1966, then transferred the remaining aircraft on strength to the second F-100 operational unit, *Escadre* 11.

At the time of its original equipping with F-100Ds, *Esc* 11 also had two active squadrons: *Escadron* I/11 *Roussillon*, and II/11 *Vosges*. First stationed at Luxeuil, and then in Bremgarten, Germany, *Esc* 11 was destined to operate Huns until the last day of 1978.

When President Charles De Gaulle pulled France out of NATO in 1967, US Air Forces in Europe were forced to move from their French bases and out of the country. The bases were promptly re-occupied by French units; *Escadre* 3 moved to Nancy-Ochey, and *Escadre* 11 to Toul-Rosieres (which had been an American field during World War 1). *Escadre* 3 sent its F-100Ds to *Escadre* 11, and that unit operated them for the remainder of their service life with the French.

Even after leaving NATO and 4 ATAF, the French continued to keep and operate the F-100s as a major component of their air strength, but changed the missions. In Europe, they were tasked for air defence, air base protection, and army close support. In the framework of the Berlin Accords, the principal mission was ground attack, the secondary was air defence. For overseas missions, *Escadre* 11 was part of France's CAFI (*Composante Air des Forces d'Intervention*), and participated in plans to reinforce, in times of trouble, '. . . a certain number of French-speaking territories in Africa.'

One of those French-speaking territories was, of course, Algeria. And during the strife that racked that country, French airmen introduced the F-100 to its first combat, flying strikes from bases within France against targets within Algeria.

To cope with the increased number of F-100s, *Escadre* 11 established a fourth squadron—III/11 *Corse*—at the end of October 1967. During 1972 and

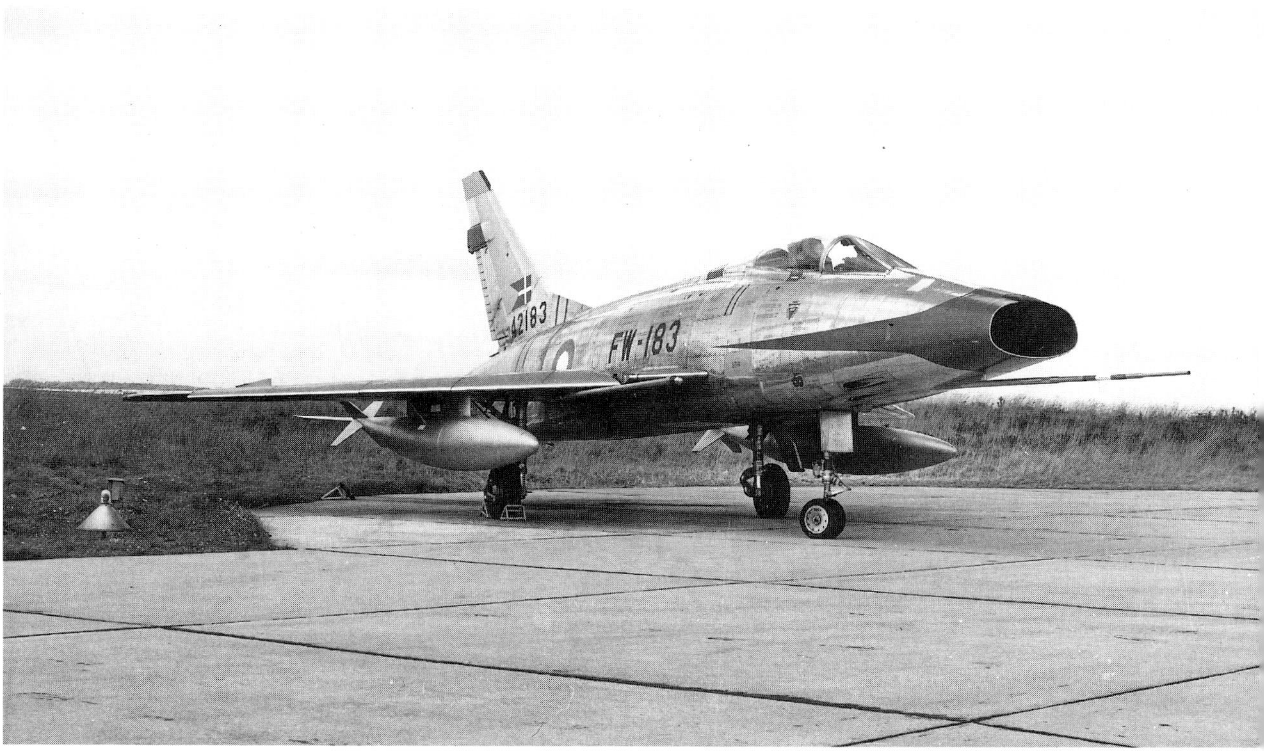
42183
FW-183

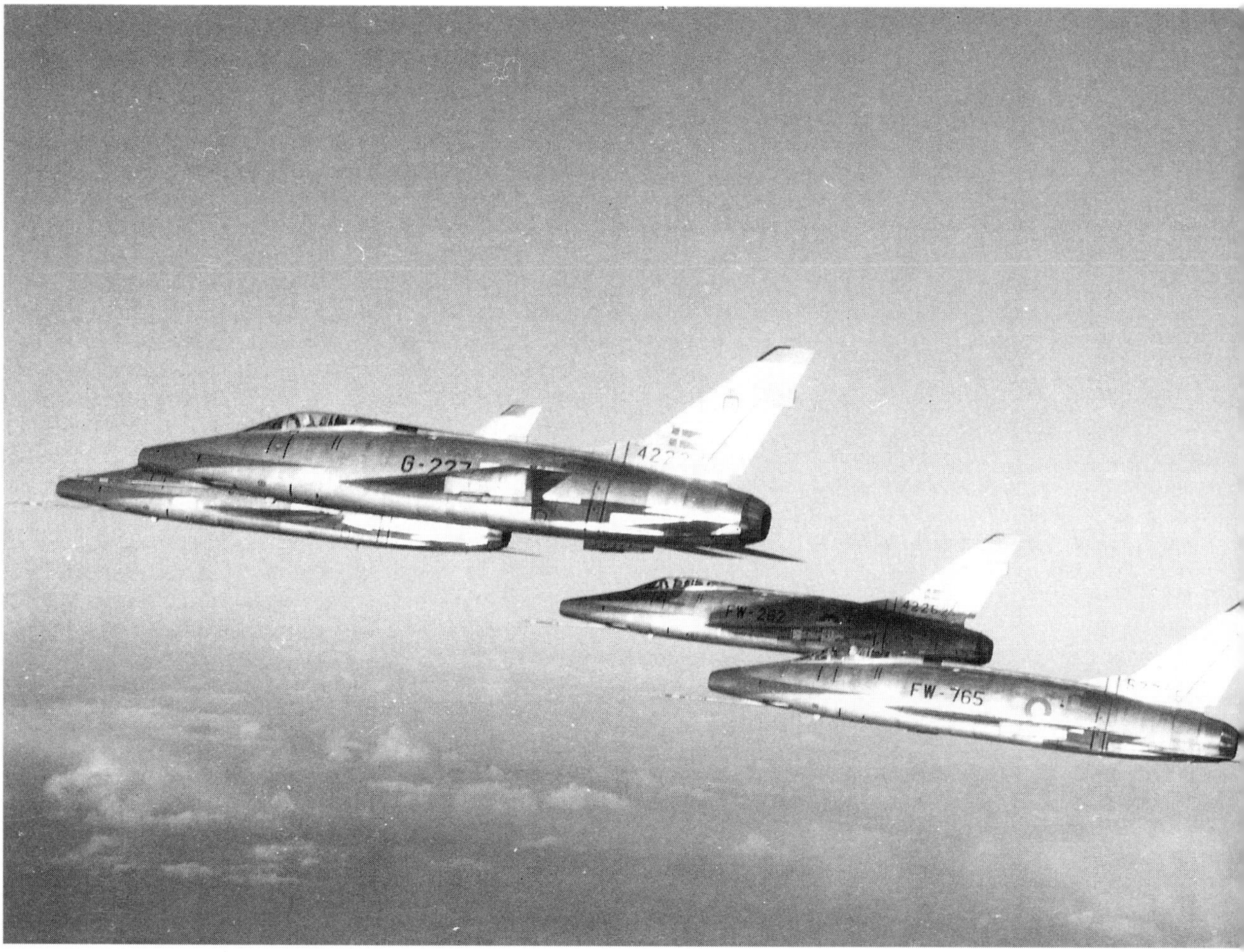
FW-282
FW-765

TOP LEFT
About a third of the way through the first production batch of F-100D models, this one (54-2183) was selected for the Royal Danish Air Force. The red nose decoration adds to the streamlined beauty of the sleek Super Sabre
(RDAF)

LEFT
In tight formation, these four Royal Danish Air Force F-100Ds seem more like a school of predatory fish than the graceful birds all designers try to create. But the Super Sabres were born to fight, and this quartet looks ready, willing, and able
(RDAF)

ABOVE
*Ex-*Armée de l'Air *F-100D fighter-bombers lined up at RAF Sculthorpe, Norfolk, in August 1977 following their return to US control.* Escadron *II/11* Vosges *gave up these aircraft after converting to the SEPECAT Jaguar strike aircraft. Serials are (left to right): 42239, 42157, 42163 and 42223*
(H J van Broekuizen)

1973, its aircraft were camouflaged with the same basic scheme used by other NATO fighters. Then, in 1975, *Escadron* II/11 re-equipped with the Jaguar fighter-bomber, and sent its remaining F-100s to another new squadron, IV/11 *Jura*, which had been formed at Djibouti early in 1973.

The transfer had been rehearsed in November 1971, when three F-100Ds from III/11 went to Djibouti on temporary deployment for a three-month operational evaluation. In June 1973, the first F-100Ds were transferred permanently to IV/11, eight of them replacing ageing Douglas AD-4s. In June 1974, five more Huns were transferred to IV/11.

In January 1975, the French air force began a modification programme at Chateauroux, eventually raising the life of 30 to 40 F-100s to 5,000 hr. When the programme began, their high-time F-100 had logged 4,200 hours.

The two last units flying the Hun were II/11 *Vosges* at Toul-Rosieres, which retired its last F-100D on 26 June 1977, and IV/11 *Jura* at Djibouti, which hung on to its Super Sabres until 31 December 1978.

As they were replaced by Jaguars, the F-100s finally were returned to US control. They were ferried by French pilots to Great Britain and the Royal Air Force base at Sculthorpe, Norfolk, for storage and scrapping. A total of about 40 remained of the 100 originally sent to France.

L'Armée de l'Air had operated F-100Ds and Fs for just over two decades, first as tactical bombers and then as (what might now be called) swing fighters. They served well and faithfully, and there are French pilots today who look back nostalgically on the days when they operated the only deep-strike, air-refuellable aircraft the French could muster.

F-100s in *Det Kongelige Danske Flyvevaben* (DKDF)

Deliveries of MAP F-100s to Denmark's air force began in mid-July 1959, with three factory fresh F-100Fs and 17 F-100Ds drawn from USAF inventory. Further deliveries followed in early 1961, when seven additional F-100Fs and 31 F-100Ds arrived, for a total of ten F models and 48 D models.

They were operated by *Eskadrille* 725, based at Karup, and *Eskadrilles* 727 and 730, based at Skrydstrup, both locations near the centre of the Jutland peninsula. All three units were assigned to the *Flyvertaktish Kommando*, equivalent in concept, if not in strength, to the USAF Tactical Air Command. As replacements for Republic F-84G fighter-bombers, the Danish F-100s took over the same basic missions: close air support as primary, and maritime attack and air defence as secondary.

The F-100 everywhere had a bad safety record during its early life, and the Danish operators suffered as much as any. Problems with the P&W J57 engine grounded the fleet more than once. Wing fatigue cracks limited the planes to manoeuvres imposing less than a 4G normal load, a difficulty fixed eventually by the installation of thicker wing undersurface skins. Eight of the first ten F-100Fs were lost in crashes; 27 of the 48 F-100Ds suffered the same fate. The worst years were 1962 and 1963, when four and five D models were lost; by 1968, a third of the fleet had been destroyed.

The safety record also had an impact on the operational capability of the DKDF. During 1967 and 1968, it was the only type in the inventory that remained consistently below the 70-per cent availability rate established by NATO as a norm for its aircraft. In an attempt to maintain combat-ready strength, the Danes went looking for additional Super Sabres to replace those lost to attrition. The USAF turned them down; its entire stock was needed for the war in Vietnam. The Danes made an approach to the French, but didn't reach the negotiation stage.

All three squadrons were then well below normal strength of 20 assigned aircraft plus a few held as reserves. Beginning in September 1970, *Esk* 725 re-equipped with Saab J35 *Draken* fighters, turning its remaining F-100s over to *Esks* 727 and 730, which continued to operate the F-100 for the remainder of its service with the DKDF.

In 1974, DKDF organized an operational conversion unit (OCU) to teach pilots how to fly the Super Sabre. The OCU was equipped with an additional 14 F-100F two-seaters, six that came out of long-term storage at the Military Aircraft Storage and Disposal Center (MASDC), Arizona, and eight

In low-visibility markings and overall dark green camouflage, this RDAF F-100D typifies the hulking Hun. Look at the background: a dense stand of evergreens. In that grove, a dark-green Super Sabre would become invisible from just a few metres distant
(RDAF)

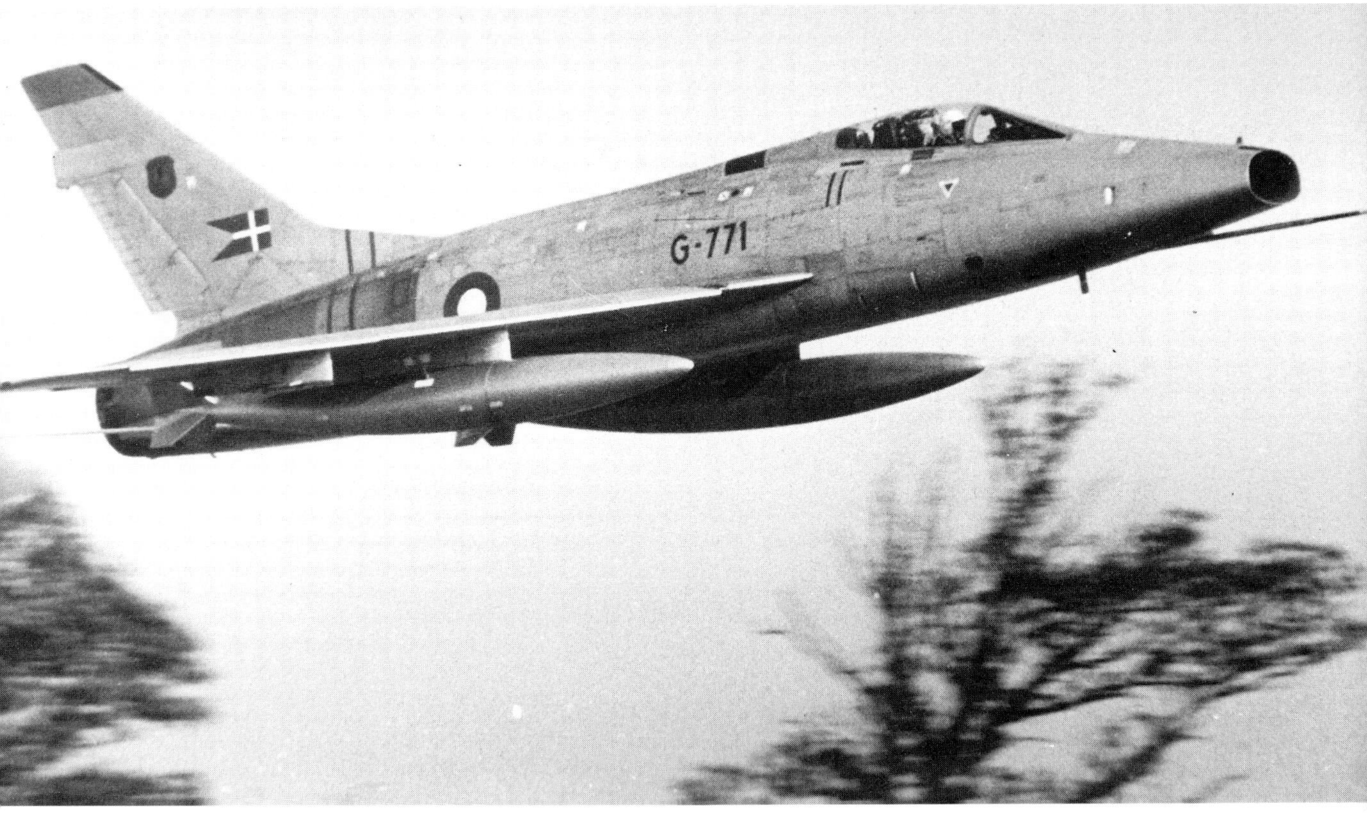

An RDAF F-100D streaks by the photographer at low level
(Robert F Dorr)

from the inventory of the Air National Guard. They were modified to DKDF requirements at Karup, making them somewhat different from the original batch of F-100F aircraft, and so were redesignated TF-100F.

For two years, the fleet was accident-free. And then, in 1976, three F-100Ds, two F-100Fs, and two TF-100Fs crashed; two more Ds and an F were lost the following year, and the F-100 was again grounded while the accidents were investigated. There was no discernible pattern; but DKDF tightened its maintenance and servicing procedures, made some modifications, and installed new afterburners. The F-100s began flying again in mid-October 1977, and achieved two more accident-free years.

By then, the F-100s had two decades of active Danish service behind them. *Esks* 727 and 730, both at Skrydstrup, were operating a combined inventory of 22 D models and 14 of a mix of F-100F and TF-100F types. Both units were scheduled to re-equip with the General Dynamics F-16A, and so began to retire the F-100s, splitting the squadrons into sections that flew a single type. *Esk* 730-100, the Super Sabre section of that squadron, continued to operate its eight F-100s until 11 August 1982. Eventually, some of the fleet were reportedly transferred to Turkey, four TF-100Fs were bought by Flight Systems, Inc, to tow targets for USAFE fighter gunnery training under contract, and those that were left were ferried to RAF Sculthorpe and—probably—the scrap pile.

In 1985, three remained in Denmark. A pair of TF-100Fs (56-3870 and 56-3908) are gate guardians at Skrydstrup. The third (56-3927) has been kept for a Danish musuem.

F-100s in the *Turk Hava Kuvvetleri* (THK)

In the late 1950s, Turkey received an initial batch of 87 F-100 aircraft, mixed C, D and F models. The first, an F-100F, arrived on 16 October 1958; the first Turkish F-100D came five days later. Published reports suggest that the final total of F-100s received was 206; some of these came from USAF surplus inventory, and a few from the Danes. Turkish pilots were trained in their own country on the type by USAF pilots.

The Super Sabres were operated by at least five THK *Filo* (equivalent to a squadron): *Filo* 111, at Eskisehir, 131 and 132 at Konya, 171 and 172 at Erhac-Malatya. It has been reported that they saw extensive action with the Turkish forces during the 1974 conflict with the Greeks over Cyprus.

F-100s on Taiwan

The Chinese Nationalist Air Force (CNAF), based on the island of Taiwan, operated early Super Sabres, and was the only air force outside of the United States to include F-100A models in its strength. The first aircraft to arrive was, typically, an F-100F, delivered 1 October 1958. In mid-1959, the first batch of 15 F-100A aircraft was transferred to the CNAF, followed in 1960 by an additional 65. In late 1961, four 'Slick Chick' versions, the unarmed RF-100A, were delivered. Attrition losses were balanced by 38 more A models, repossessed from Air National Guard inventory, raising total strength to 118 F-100A and four RF-100A aircraft.

In the decades of the fifties and sixties, the US and the Peoples' Republic of China (PRC) were cold-war enemies. The CNAF flew missions to gather intelligence about PRC defences, and often passed that information along to US agencies. Such missions were risky; there are reports that the CNAF suffered several losses to PRC defences.

To improve crew survivability on such missions, many—perhaps all—of the F-100As were modified in two major ways: they received the vertical tail surface of the F-100D models, with its AN/APS-54 tail-warning radar, and were equipped to carry and fire Sidewinder missiles for defence against enemy fighters.

In that modified form, the aircraft were designated as the F-100A Rehab. One F-100A Rehab, unidentified by serial number, was evaluated at the Air Force Flight Test Center during October 1959 by project pilot USAF Captain William F Knight. The purpose was to determine changes in stability and control characteristics caused by the new tail, and to study the effects of the Sidewinder installation on performance, stability and control.

A black panther of Filo *111: before they received a NATO-standard coat of tactical camouflage, Turkish Super Sabres were highly colourful birds. The pilot is either waiting for the technician to finish a turn-around task or helping him to diagnose a fault. Whatever, he is unlikely to take off soon*
(Stephen P Peltz)

RIGHT
The 'skull and crossbones' motif of Filo *171 on the leader's machine has obviously weathered better than the flash, and his aircraft also lacks the nose ring carried by the others. Turkish Super Sabres were a mixed bag, but these F-100Ds would have come from USAF stocks*
(Stephen P Peltz)

Interlude G: **Super Sabre Thunderbirds**

During 1953, the Air Force formed the 3600th Air Demonstration Flight at Luke AFB, Arizona. Later, there would be other official organizational designations; but the unit became known around the world as the 'Thunderbirds', a magical name, describing an elite team of accomplished pilots and exceptional support crews. They routinely showed their mastery of high-speed jet aircraft in public, in aerial manoeuvres that were daring, crowd-pleasing, beautiful, and precise.

'When we convinced our generals that we should change aircraft,' said Jack Broughton recently, but then a Major commanding the flight, 'the F-100A was in service at Nellis and the first C models had yet to be delivered. So we went to Nellis to give the A a try.

'It was a new airplane, and the people there were skeptical that we could harness the monster into an air show routine, and even if we could, it would take months of practice. The first morning (1 May 1956) we each got a quick cockpit check, strapped on an F-100A and launched. After about 30 minutes, I rendezvoused with my slot man and dearest friend, "Lucky" (Captain Edwin D) Palmgren, and we had a ball pulling our guts out in formation.

'That afternoon, I got four aircraft for another ride. "Lucky", (Captain) Billy Ellis, right wing, (1st Lieutenant Robert D) Bob Anderson, left wing, and I joined up in a diamond as soon as we were out of sight of the field. After a half-hour's work, I brought the diamond back over the base, did a few loops, rolls and wifferdills before pitching up for landing. The Nellis guys were real nice after that.

TOP LEFT
FW-967, a Turkish F-100F, rotates at the start of a training mission. The Turks are fine pilots, but they knew that the aircraft's handling characteristics, particularly on finals, made it essential for Hun driver's to convert from the two-seater
(Stephen P Peltz)

LEFT
Camouflaged F-100D, serial 56-2919, rolls out at the end of its landing run at an airfield 'somewhere in Turkey'
(Stephen P Peltz)

ABOVE
An F-100A Rehab of the Chinese Nationalist Air Force (CNAF), tail number 31627, at the end of a mission from the beleagered island of Taiwan. CNAF aircraft and their operations are shrouded in secrecy
(via Phil Chinnery)

'We were scheduled to get the first six F-100Cs off the Los Angeles production line, and to do our first show with them in one month. But since our birds were still being built, none of us had flown a C model yet. And about two weeks before show time, we really hit a snag. Our birds made it through production and acceptance flight tests in record time, but still needed to be painted with the Thunderbird scheme. I was told I couldn't have the aircraft for at least a week. At my request, the North American executive staff

ABOVE
Pardon the intrusion; this is not a Thunderbird, but one of USAFE's Skyblazer team from the 36th TFW at Furstenfeldbruck, Germany. The impressive colour scheme for F-100C (54-1980): nose and tank stripes are red, white, and blue, front to rear. The tail fin is blue, with white stars. The rudder is white with red stripes. The USAFE insigne is on the right side under the cockpit. Note the smoke pipe hooked toward the exhaust nozzle exit (Peter M Boyers/Maene Collection)

LEFT
The problem with all the spectacular shots of Thunderbird demonstrations is that you seldom know where and when, and therefore who. That's the case here. All we can ascertain is that these are F-100D models (Smithsonian Institution Photo No 87–742)

One of the more spectacular Thunderbird routines is this knife-edge pass, with two solo performers, each rolled 45 degrees left and headed straight down one side of the runway. They're going to miss, of course, but from the side it surely looks like a death-defying feat (USAF/Pickett Collection)

RIGHT
Thunderbirds above Lake Tahoe, one of the landmarks often seen in photos of the USAF demonstration team (USAF/Maene Collection)

assembled and listened while I said that I had to call Washington and cancel the first show because North American wasn't able to deliver.

'I don't know what happened during the next few hours, but the very next morning we strapped on six gleaming red, white, and blue F-100Cs and launched for Nellis.

'We learned a lot in the next two weeks as we shook the bugs out of the new machines. Problems with the new anti-skid brake system showed up on my bird. I pitched for landing, the rest of the diamond spaced behind me, and made a smooth touchdown on my side of the runway. A few hundred feet into the landing roll, my brakes locked, full on. In a couple of seconds, two loud bangs told me the tyres had blown; I was sliding down the runway. So I engaged nosewheel steering, kicked full rudder, and slid sideways, slowing a bit and then reversing the action to stay on the runway. It was like making a series of check turns in skiing. At the last thousand-foot marker I held full left rudder and hung on. The nose turned 180° and when I released the rudder, she slid straight backwards till the tailpipe was hanging over the end of the runway, and she stopped. I got out fast; the bottom halves of the wheels were ground flat, and the tops were molten.

USAF
USAF
USAF

TOP
Thunderbird One, Maj Jack Broughton's aircraft (F-100C 55-2723), shows a dozen flags under the windshield, signifying the number of countries where the team displayed its flying skills
(Peter M Bowers/Maene Collection)

ABOVE
Broughton leading in Thunderbird One (F-100C 55-2723), the four-man team lines up for takeoff. Left wingman's plane is almost completely hidden. Right wing is 55-2729, and the slot man is 55-2726
(Peter M Bowers/Maene Collection)

RIGHT
And a few years later, when the team had visited 45 countries, the pilots posed with Thunderbird Three, a shining F-100D. From top to bottom: commander and leader Maj Neil Eddins, Capt Mack Angel, Maj Stan Musser, Capt Jack Dickey, Capt Tony McPeak, and Capt Mike Miller. McPeak's bailout after structural failure of his D is related in these pages
(USAF/Pickett Collection)

AIR FORCE
THREE
3

'I couldn't believe it—and sly glances indicated suspicion of heavy feet on the brakes—when the system checked out OK. So next day on final I called, "Thunderbird Lead, gear down and checked, feet on the floor." And the same thing happened all over again. From then on, our landing call was amended to include, "Anti-skid off."'

'We made our first show 30 June (1956); it wasn't our greatest, but we were on our way. We never cancelled a show due to aircraft problems.'

Super Sabres equipped the Thunderbirds from 1956 until 1969, longest of any model aircraft flown by the team. In 1964, the Thunderbirds converted to D models, and in 1967, on 21 October, Captain Merrill A McPeak participated in an unusual bit of drama that added to the thrills of the show.

McPeak, now USAF Deputy Chief of Staff/Programs and Resources, was flying one of two solo aircraft in a Thunderbirds demonstration at Laughlin AFB, Texas. He roared past the crowd in a low-level pass, and pulled up to begin a series of aileron rolls. But at about a 20° pitch angle, things happened rapidly.

McPeak reminisced about the incident recently. 'I heard an explosion and instinctively relaxed my pull on the stick—something we did routinely for compressor stalls—and then I thought, that ain't no stall, podner. The wings folded. When the centre box failed, it dumped fuel from the forward fuselage tank into the engine and it exploded. The intake was blown off—the first six feet of the airplane—and it blew the nose gear down and the drag chute out. Then it started pumping fire through the cockpit pressurization system, and I had to eject. It was a rather high-speed ejection, but I'd been to the Army's jump school, and I tucked myself into a good body position for chute deployment. I remember thinking: I wish the guys at Fort Benning could see me now.

'I landed fairly close to the crowd, about 2,000 ft left of the show centre. We were wearing white showsuits that day, but mine had been blackened by the fire in the cockpit after the engine blew. When I ejected, the wind blast tore off my helmet, and there was some blood from that. Then, there was about a 30-knot wind blowing, and my chute dragged me around some after I hit the ground. So I looked awful; soot, blood, green grass and brown earth stains all over my formerly nice white show-suit.'

McPeak's airplane (F-100D 55-3520) was carefully studied. There were at least 40 cracks in the wing from fatigue loads, and it was determined by analysis that the wing broke at about 6.5G. The Thunderbirds were temporarily grounded, while the accident was investigated and fixes determined. But the Super Sabres then in combat in Vietnam were cleared to fly with a 4G limit. There had been a number of losses in action during the pulloffs from bomb drops, and it was possible that some of them had the same problem McPeak had.

The fatigue cracks propagated from bolt holes just inboard of the main landing gear mounts on the lower wings. The temporary fix was a relatively simple reinforcement: spanwise metal strips attached across the bolt holes. It cost less than $900 to fix each airplane and, for the moment, it solved the problem. But later studies resulted in a complete modification to the wing structural box; that fix was considerably more expensive, and took the F-100s out of service for major rebuilding.

After the fixes, the Thunderbirds were operational again with modified D models. McPeak was making his first flight in the beefed-up bird, and was practicing for the first time the difficult inverted-to-inverted manoeuvre. Luckily, he was high—at about 500 ft—when he tried it. The canopy promptly blew off '. . . with a hell of a bang, and I thought, oh, no, not again. When I got my heart restarted I slowed down and rolled back upright.' It was a unique incident; the ejection seat had been removed during the wing modification and, when it was reinstalled, the seat handles had not been seated properly. 'I put a little negative G load on the seat when I rolled, and it moved the ejection seat handles enough to fire the canopy.

'But the Hun was a tremendous airplane, and I was comfortable in it. It didn't slow down or accelerate well, compared to modern fighters, and its visibility was a bit limited. It wasn't an easy airplane to fly well, and each successive model was a little harder than the previous one.

'Once we flew all the way from Paris to Colorado Springs. It was a 14 hr 25 min flight, with seven air refuellings, and we hand-flew those birds all the way. You just could not trim them for hands-off flight.'

Chapter 10
What Else Can You Do with the Hun?
Interlude H: Takeoffs from World's Shortest Runway

Any aircraft progamme produces a number of 'cats and dogs', models or modifications out of the mainstream of development. In the Super Sabre programme, those outsiders included the F-100B interceptor that became the F-107A fighter-bomber, the RF-100A 'Slick Chick' tactical reconnaissance aircraft, QF-100 drones, and specialized chase and research aircraft.

Genesis of the F-107A

Much has been written about the F-107A, not all of it consistent. The material that follows was taken from NAA internal documentation; direct quotations are from those documents or from project personnel.

The Air Force told North American that an improved F-100A should be the company's next effort. On 4 March 1953, NAA management asked for an estimate of engineering requirements for a proposal for the F-100B. Planning established Engineering Study Order (ESO) 7130 on 11 March, estimating that F-100B design would require 7,500 engineer-hr, an amount later raised to 18,800.

Specification No NA 53-389, dated 22 May 1953, defined the F-100B as '. . . an evolution of the F-100A that can be realistically placed into production by 1955.' The goal: a faster F-100A day fighter, following a programme of drag and weight reduction to attain maximum performance from the basic airframe and the J57 engine.

First layout retained the planform of the original F-100A wings, but used a 5 per cent wing t/c ratio rather than the 7 per cent t/c of F-100As. Designers area-ruled the fuselage, increased its fineness ratio. The upgraded J57 engine, fed by a variable-area inlet duct, had a convergent-divergent nozzle, and produced 16,000 lb (7257 kg) of thrust. The 1,160 US-gallon (4391 lit) fuel load was carried in integral wing tanks; there were no external tanks. Dual landing-gear wheels promised operations from unprepared fields. The F-100B was expected to be essentially the same size and weight as the F-100A.

Estimates showed a speed potential of Mach 1.80, nearly double that of F-100As, an ambitious goal. At that velocity the F-100B would be '. . . approaching the region of significant aerodynamic heating problems.'

To make the F-100B more useful, NAA studied it also as an all-weather interceptor (sometimes designated F-100I, sometimes F-100BI), described in Specification No NA 53-425, of 3 June 1953. The interceptor was the F-100B, except for a modified cockpit, and the addition of a radome, rocket armament, heated leading edges, and provisions for external wing tanks. The forward fuselage was redesigned with an undernose variable-area inlet. In short, the F-100BI was another updated F-86D.

The F-100B was designated NA-212 on 20 October 1953, in an internal order starting production engineering and design, and limiting Engineering to a budgeted expenditure of $78,000 (which, then, bought a lot of engineering time and effort). The engineers began wind-tunnel studies to evaluate performance of the new variable-area inlet. The experimental shop built a detailed cockpit mockup, because that was a critical aspect of the new design, and began an airplane mockup.

Hardly a month later, NAA management elected to include fighter-bomber capabilities in the design. Specification NA 53-1098 of 18 November presented 11 configurations to show adaptability of the F-100B air-superiority fighter aircraft to fighter-bomber missions. Engineers added six hard points to the wing, changing wing structure, controls, and cockpit design appropriately. They retained the design load factor of 7.33 for the fighter, but the fighter-bomber load factor would be lower, dependent on which stores and tanks were selected. Other changes were made: single-point refuelling was added; radio equipment was upgraded; cockpit, windshield and

The converted auxiliary fuel tank under the left wing of F-100D 55-3505 contains an optical area-correlation tracker developed by Martin Orlando. Tested at Eglin AFB, the tracker probably was a part of the Bullpup air-to-surface missile programme, or of a development of that optically guided weapon
(Martin C3881)

RIGHT
NAA engineering test pilot Bob Baker readies himself and the F-107A for first flight. The clear panel aft of the cockpit is an obvious recent change
(Baker Collection)

canopy were revised to improve the pilot's view; a retractable tail skid was installed; and the flight-control system was upgraded by the addition of pitch and yaw dampers.

On 15 January 1954, the anticipated programme was drastically cut back at the request of NAA President Lee Atwood. A 21 January memo summarized '. . . the new engineering plan . . . concerning the F-100B and F-100 Interceptor.

'. . . a change from a full production engineering release schedule to a Phase I type comprehensive engineering study would be more desirable for the next few months . . .

'A mockup of each airplane will be constructed as originally planned; however, the completion dates have been re-scheduled to 1 May 1954, for the F-100B and 29 May 1954 for the F-100 Interceptor.'

Then, on April 16, NAA decided to '. . . revise the general configuration of the F-100B to embody the general aerodynamic and thermodynamic configuration that has been developed for the F-100 Interceptor.'

WARNING
EJECTION
SEAT
DANGER
DANGER
9-7-56
212-0-2

Six days later, North American learned the USAF was interested in the F-100B as a fighter-bomber with an 8.67 load factor. Company engineers bent to their task of further modification, analysis, and redesign. On 15 May, NAA's Dayton, Ohio, representative telegraphed Atwood that the USAF was mailing a directive to procure long lead-time items for 33 F-100Bs, as '. . . an all-out fighter bomber version with an 8.67 load factor and carrying all available fighter bomber equipment, in regards to navigation, radar, etc. Present planning is that production rates will be held to a maximum of 3 per month for 24 months.'

The next day, the word was passed to Engineering: stop all work on the F-100B; the ground rules have just changed. But telling that to engineers can convince some to keep on working even harder. Before May was out, they made an exciting discovery: aerodynamic studies showed that low-speed handling could be improved, and landing speeds lowered by about 25 knots, if an inboard blown flap were used for boundary-layer control. (Bear in mind that the F-100 had been designed without wing flaps, and that the high landing speeds and handling qualities at landing were continuing concerns to the USAF).

The list of additional features, developed to make the F-100B primarily a fighter bomber, included the change from a 7.33 to an 8.67 load factor; installations of a manoeuvring autopilot, an AN/APW-11A radar beacon, the LABS (low-altitude bombing system) 'B' unit, an AN/ALF-2 chaff dispenser, an AN/APS-54 radar warning system, a plotting board and a computer in the cockpit; a change to larger and heavier wheels and brakes; and electrical fuzing of external stores.

Dated 11 June 1954, Air Force letter contract AF33(600)-27787 authorized design, mockup and procurement of long lead-time raw materials for 33 F-100B fighter-bombers to Specification NA 53-1172 of 1 June 1954. On 8 July came an official notice that the aircraft was designated F-107A, appropriate to a production aircraft.

Late in 1954, the Air Force issued General Operational Requirement 68, calling for a tactical fighter-bomber and an air-superiority day and night fighter. North American responded; confirming documents are not available, but—given the frenetic pace of design change during gestation—it's reasonable to assume that continued study and analysis produced the major airframe changes that characterized the final layout of the F-107A.

Meantime, Pratt & Whitney had developed the

Liftoff! The F-107A rotates and rises almost immediately as Baker applies back pressure on the controls. Notice the semi-submerged store shape half in and half out of the belly, an innovation being rediscovered 30 years later and this time called 'conformal storage'
(Baker Collection)

U.S. AIR FORCE
55118
F-107A
9-7-56
212-0-2AA

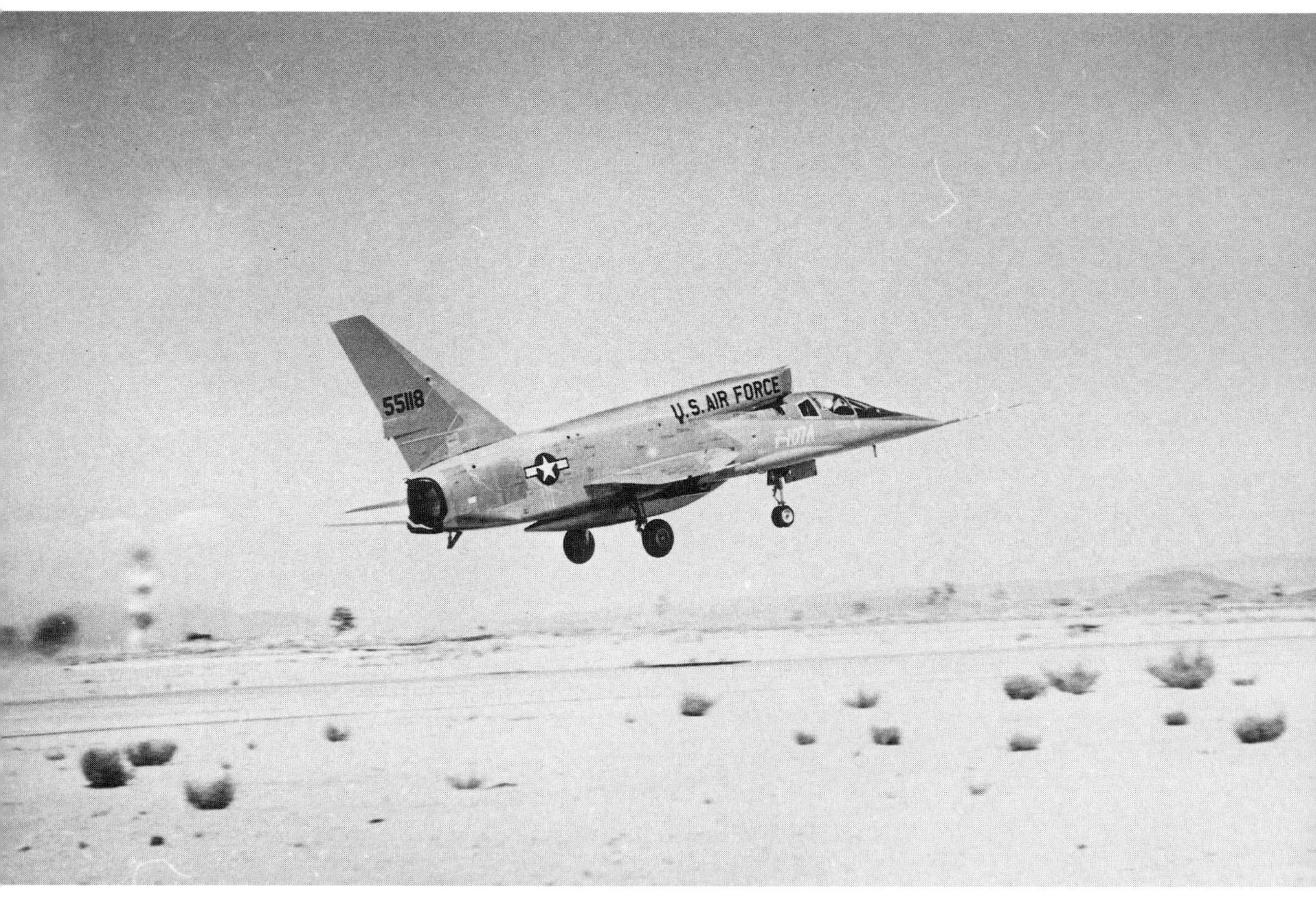

The decorative red paint accents have not disappeared, but they have been made less prominent by a filter over the camera's lens. It's still the F-107A, and Baker is still the pilot, and the desert and the lakebed and the weeds and the everlasting dry heat are still the same
(Baker Collection)

newer and more-powerful J75 engine, and was ready to apply it to aircraft. Both NAA and Republic designers seized upon the new powerplant as the answer to their needs.

NAA engineers redesigned the vertical tail as a single-piece slab, like the horizontal surface. A complex spoiler-slot-deflector system gave lateral control. A stability-augmentation system was installed. The major weapon—a nuclear store—was to be semi-submerged in the fuselage belly on the centreline, as an alternate stowage system to a closed bomb-bay with its tough design problems and structural requirements. Because of that stowage position, NAA commissioned a series of wind-tunnel tests to check release and separation of the weapons. The results showed some problems, caused by flow interference from the nose radome and chin inlet. Engineers did the logical thing to solve the problems; they avoided them by moving the inlet to the top of the fuselage, giving the F-107A its characteristic appearance.

(Later in the programme, NAA's Al White flew a series of tests to check weapons release, separation, and drop of the standard TX-28 nuclear store and a special nuclear-weapon shape developed by Sandia. The tests showed that the unusual semi-submerged weapons storage system worked successfully).

The first F-107A (AF55-5118) first flew 10 September 1956, from the runway at Edwards AFB, California, with NAA chief pilot Bob Baker at the controls. Baker remembers: 'On the first flight, the oil pump pressure light came on near the top of the climb just prior to reaching supersonic speed. The preflight brief said to return and land within five minutes, so I reported and requested ground to confirm the briefing. I dropped the nose from Mach 0.92 climb to level flight and went supersonic with military power, then chopped to idle and was on base leg at 20,000 ft (6098 m) over Rosemont before the ground said to land.

'I had lowered the gear, and found that full flaps resulted in too-sensitive lateral control, so I retracted them about halfway to control the roll to plus or minus ten degrees. I didn't have time to check the minimum controllable airspeed, so I added ten knots indicated to the tabulated data, interpolated between flaps up and flaps down, and turned final.'

On landing, the drag chute malfunctioned, and the F-107A rolled rapidly along the runway toward the dry lake bed. Baker elected not to use hard braking to stop the airplane; 'We did not have 200-knot tyres in those days', he said, 'and I had five miles of smooth lake bed after using three miles of concrete runway.' But erosion on the lake had created enough of a ditch to collapse the nose gear. The F-107A slid about 500 yards; damage was not severe, but the main landing gear tyres were worn smooth down to the cord. The airplane flew again three days later.

Baker completed the first few flights, and was then sent to Washington to brief a long list of Air Force and NACA people. In his absence, NAA pilot J O Roberts took over the project and, says Baker, '... did a really fine job. I got one or two flights in later, but J O Roberts did the bulk of the engineering flight test work on that bird.'

NAA test pilot Albert W Blackburn took over a portion of the test flying on 28 March 1957, to evaluate the variable air inlet duct (VAID) that was built into the third prototype (55-5120) and the stability augmentation system, and to make maximum performance climbs. On the latter, Blackburn remembers: 'I tried all the well-known ways, steady climbs at subsonic and supersonic speeds, and zoom climbs from maximum Mach at 35,000 feet (10,670 m). Nothing I did ever got the airplane above 51,000 feet (15,549 m). But in defence of both the VAID and the J75 engine, neither was fully developed at the time.'

When Blackburn was testing the VAID, he was asked to check a phenomenon known as 'duct buzz'. It usually developed in flight as a result of instability of the flow at the inlet, and was a common occurrence in the earlier years of the jet age. One one of his last flights with the airplane, Blackburn levelled the F-107A at 35,000 feet (10,670 m) and accelerated to Mach 1.8. Then, following the instructions on the flight-test card, he reduced power to minimum afterburner setting and closed the engine bleed-air doors.

Said Blackburn, 'It buzzed, for sure, and it scared the hell out of me. It was a horrendously loud noise, like a small cannon firing behind my head, banging away at something like 15 cycles per second, swallowing and expelling the shock wave at the inlet. The flight-test boom on the nose of the airplane was vibrating through a two-foot arc, and I decided to get back on the lake. I turned, slowed down, and the noise stopped.'

The F-107 was in direct competition with the Republic F-105, an aircraft with periodic and continuing problems, being built by a company with periodic and continuing problems. The Air Force planned a competitive evaluation before the end of 1956, but rescheduled it to the spring of 1957 when it became apparent the F-105 wouldn't be ready in time. Rumours flew: the F-105 couldn't reach Mach 2; the F-107 would be built by Republic on Long Island. The final decision, without the comparative fly-off, favoured the F-105; the North American design became one subject in this chapter, rather than the title of a book.

The first and third F-107As were turned over to NACA. The first reached NACA's High-Speed Flight Station at Edwards AFB on 6 November 1957, and entered a flight-research programme. Three major features of the YF-107A interested NACA engineers: the unusual VAID system, the ALCS (augmented longitudinal control system, later used in the A3J-1 *Vigilante*) system, and the all-moving vertical tail surface (also used in the A3J).

The first F-107A was so mechanically unreliable that NACA grounded it after four flights, making it a spare-parts depot for the remaining aircraft. The grounding also ended flight progammes on the inlet system, because of its mechanical problems. Eventually, the inlet of the other F-107A was fixed in a position limiting top speed to Mach 1.2.

NACA added a sidestick controller to the third F-107A (AF55-5120) for evaluation. Although the plane was delivered on 10 February 1958, it did not fly until October. It made 40 flights, eventually, during 1958 and 1959. On the basis of these tests, NAA refined the design of its sidestick system going into the X-15, and NASA pilots John McKay, Forrest Petersen, and Bob White, who had been designated to fly the research plane, gained experience with the sidestick system in the F-107A before getting into the X-15.

It was damaged beyond economical repair on 1 September 1959, when Scott Crossfield, then North American's project pilot on the North American X-15, aborted a takeoff because of control problems with the F-107A. Both tyres blew, and the left brake burst into flames. The resulting damage ended the F-107A's career as a NACA test aircraft, and the Air Force junked it.

The first aircraft is in the Pima Air Museum, Tucson, Arizona, repainted in its original colours; the second (AF55-5119) survives in the Air Force Museum, Wright-Patterson AFB, Ohio.

Reconnaissance RF-100As: 'Slick Chick'

The early 1950s were the years of the Cold War on many fronts, and the Korean war on a Far Eastern front. The Communist countries were re-arming with some haste and in great secrecy, and intelligence information was needed, the kind of intelligence that concerned itself with the makeup of Russian and East German armoured divisions or Czechoslovakian motorized infantry units. And the best way to get that kind of data, it seemed, was to make some high-speed dashes along or across the borders of Soviet-bloc countries while taking some pictures.

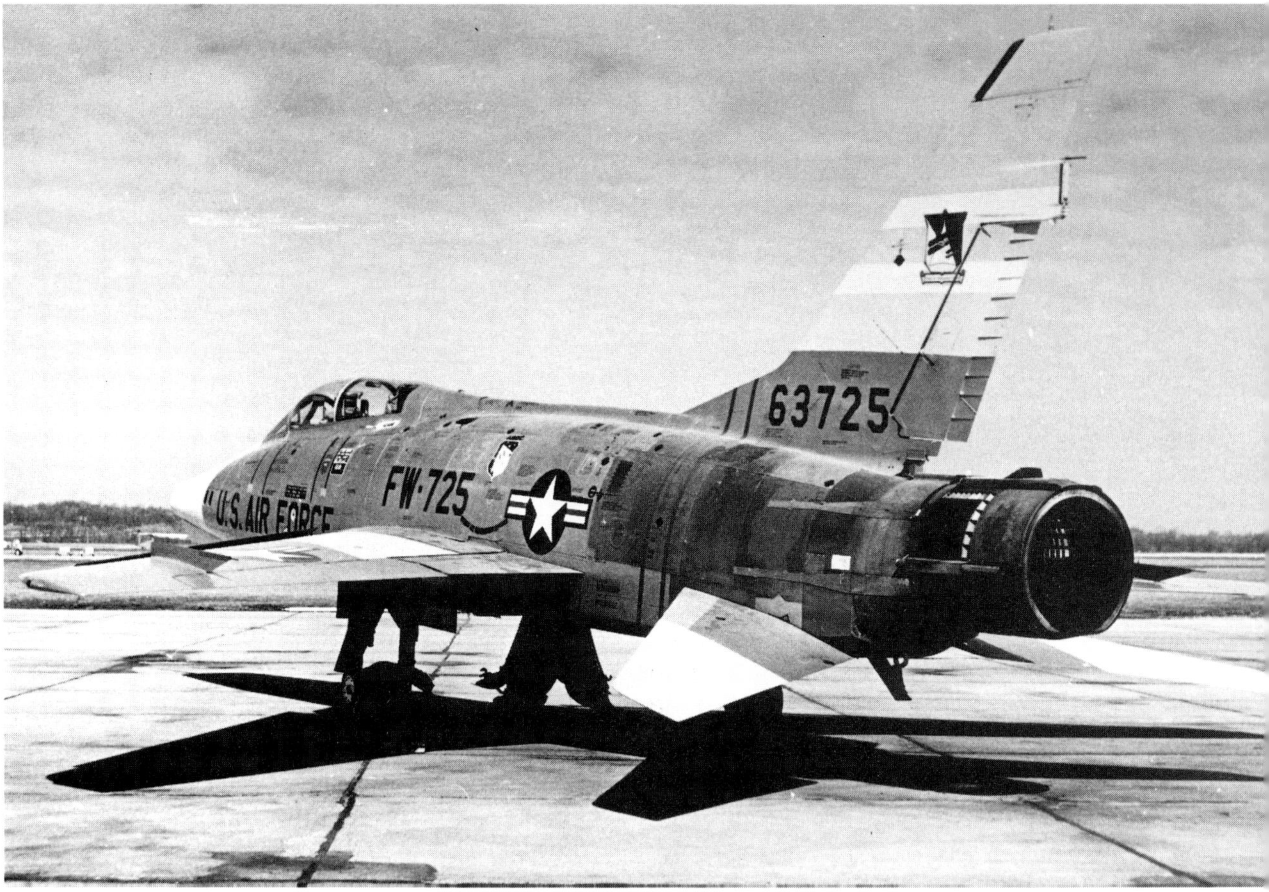
63725
FW-725
U.S. AIR FORCE

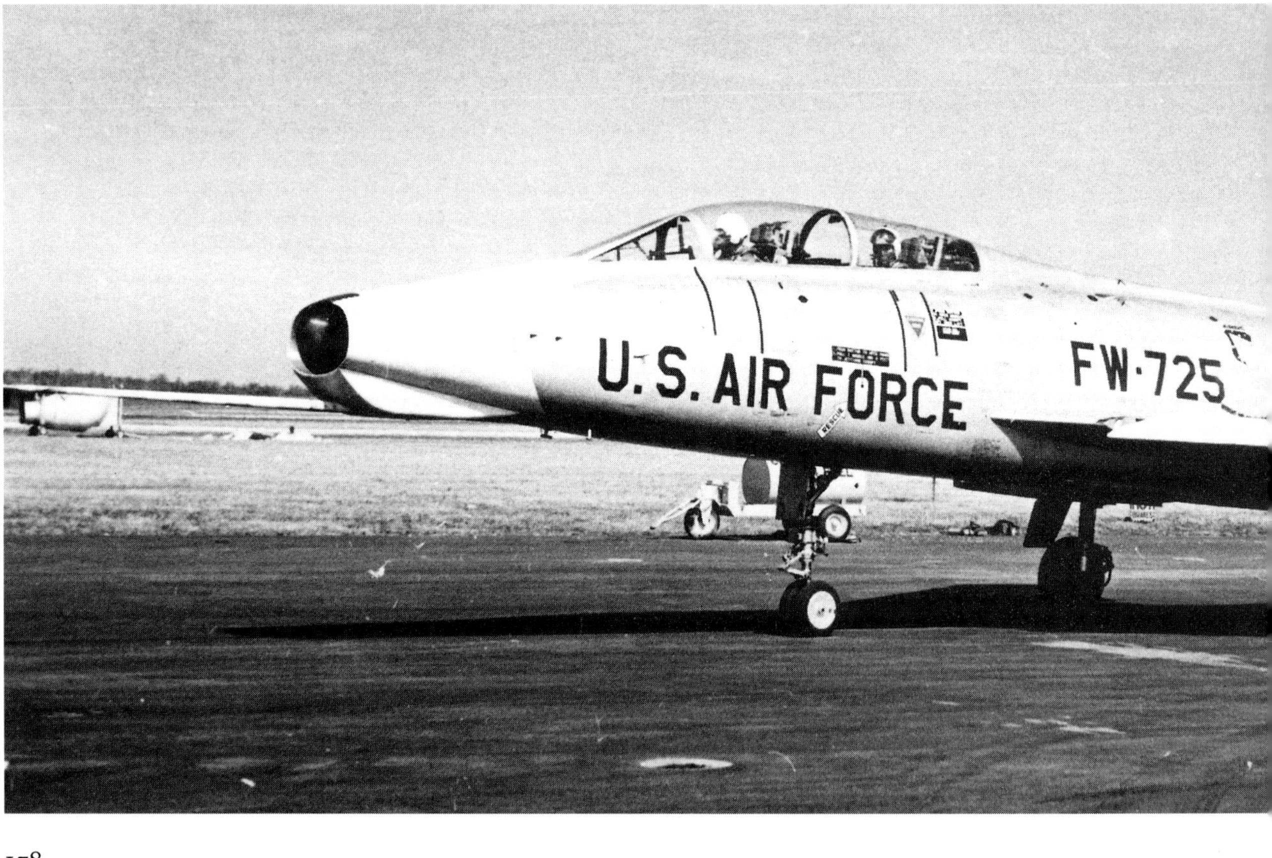
U.S. AIR FORCE
FW-725

TOP LEFT
One of the drag-inducing add-ons to F-100F 56-3725 was a cascade-type thrust reverser. Heavy external straps reinforce the tail section, and multiple vanes direct the thrust outward instead of aft. The Wright Air Development Center insigne is on the vertical tail; the Air Research and Development Command insigne is on the fuselage between buzz number and national insigne
(Peter M Bowers/Maene Collection)

LEFT
Ready to roll, F-100F 56-3725 holds briefly at the end of the Wright-Patterson AFB main runway waiting tower clearance for takeoff. The fairing under the inlet holds test instrumentation to monitor and measure the steep-approach tests flown in the first F-100F (56-3725). The strange device that appears to be mounted on the pitot beam actually is parked a hundred feet distant, and looks like a mobile engine sound suppressor
(Peter M Bowers/Maene Collection)

ABOVE
Apologies; this copy of a copy of a copy makes a poor print. But it's a good one of a very rare RF-100A (53-1546, a genuine serial number). The cameras are mounted in the 'canoe' fairing underneath the cockpit
(via Robert F Dorr)

63725
USAF
37

So NAA modified a half-dozen F-100As to a tactical reconnaissance configuration during March and April 1955. For the record, they were NAA F-100A Nos 40–43 (AF53-1545/-1548), 46 (-1551) and 49 (-1554). The 20-mm nose cannon, ammunition boxes, chutes and feed mechanisms, were removed from the nose and the resulting volume was filled with five reconnaissance camera systems that looked ahead and to each side of the airplane.

Soon dubbed 'Slick Chick', the RF-100A didn't particularly deserve that name. The camera systems wouldn't fit inside the fuselage contour, and were covered in part by external fairings on the outboard edges of the fuselage belly, extending from below the windshield to nearly the trailing edge of the wing. It was an obvious recognition feature. The RF-100As carried four droppable fuel tanks, because the flight profile called for a lot of afterburner use, and there was no provision for aerial refuelling.

The first RF-100A, after some delays, was ready to fly its final check flight on a Saturday. Project pilot Jim Brooks had just married Martha Tilton, former vocalist with the Benny Goodman band, and so Bob Baker offered to make the flight, scheduled to ferry the plane from Palmdale to Sacramento for final installation of Government-furnished equipment.

Baker wrote, 'I took off from Palmdale and went through 35,000 ft (10,670 m) in a hurry; the afterburner was turned up and tuned for over 50,000 ft (15,244 m). I felt the nose dropping as Mach number increased through .92 to .93, and the stick would not come back any further. The Mach started to increase rapidly to .95, and George Smith's recent bailout at supersonic speed crossed my mind.

'I also was familiar with a pitch control reversal just below Mach one, and I didn't want that. So I chopped the power, opened the speed brake and, as the Mach number decreased, the nose came back up. As I descended, I was able to reduce the minimum indicated airspeed from 250 down to 200 knots and, with the stick all the way back, I touched down at 190 knots on what is now the orbiter (NASA space shuttle) runway.

'Nobody went home that night; the whole engineering team came up from Los Angeles. By noon Sunday, the problem was still unsolved. Then I reminded "Stormy" (Harrison Storms) that I'd been pressurized when the problem occurred. So we set up for an engine run, and I pressurized the cockpit, and the stick would not go all the way back.

'There was a bell crank on the right side of the cockpit in the control linkage that goes from the stick to the stabilizer actuator. A special piece of equipment, unique to "Slick Chick" bulged into the cockpit and its cover plate jammed the bell crank when the airplane was pressurized. The fix was the classic aircraft industry fix, made with a hammer. One of our guys crawled into the cockpit with a hammer, dented the cover plate in the tight spot, and the bell crank was free to move again. We delivered the aircraft that way.'

One of the pilots who flew 'Slick Chick' missions remembers a typical one: 'We'd take off from Hahn or one of the other German bases near the border, get to altitude, go full burner, accelerate until we were going as fast as we could, and then zip over the border on a straight supersonic dash. The cameras were turned on, and started shooting. You stayed straight to stay supersonic, because turns really ate up your speed.

'We'd go out to some predetermined point, start a climbing turn, gain altitude, and start to dive, still in the turn. We'd be supersonic when we headed into the return run. The flight paths looked a little like a keyhole pattern, so we called them "keyhole" flights.

'Sometimes we'd see them scrambling MiGs, but they never got near us. I think I got shot at a few times by flak, but the gunners weren't that good then. They sharpened up later.'

Four of the 'Slick Chicks' were later rehabilitated and updated according to letter contract AF-04(606) 7099, issued 8 October 1958. These may have been the aircraft sent to Taiwan. Among the 'Slick Chicks' that operated in the Far East was one photographed over Japan, with the spurious tail number 32600 that had been assigned to a Northrop F-89D (AF53-2600).

X-15 and Dyna-Soar research

As research and development programmes to explore space gained momentum, so did efforts to understand and anticipate some of their problems, such as the steep approach characteristic of aircraft returning from space. Eventually, lifting-body research aircraft were built and flown to investigate that characteristic and others of aircraft that operated in space. But briefly, a Super Sabre was pressed into service.

The first F-100F built (AF56-3725) was modified by the USAF Systems Command's Aeronautical Systems Division to fly very steep approaches and very fast landings. To get an ordinary F-100F to do that required building in an additional and large drag increment that could be added or removed as simply as by using a speed brake.

The drag chute and afterburner were replaced by a thrust reverser that could be opdrated in flight. The standard belly speed brake, measuring about 12

The first F-100F (56-3725) was tested in the full-scale 40- × 80-ft wind tunnel at the Ames Research Center, Sunnyvale, California. This airplane was modified to study handling characteristics during steep approaches to landings, such as were planned for the USAF Dyna-Soar programme and became typical for the space shuttle. Note the refaired fuselage tail section around the stabilizer attachments
(NASA A24789)

square feet (1.1 m^2) in area, was replaced by a perforated drag brake measuring 33 sq ft (3.1 m^2) in area.

The landing profile began conventionally. At 6,000 feet (1829 m), the pilot deployed the thrust reverser and popped the speed brake. The flight path almost instantly steepened to between 20 and 30 degrees. The F-100F came down the slide, flared, and touched down at a blistering 230 mph (370 km/h) instead of the usual 155 mph (249 km/h).

Support of the growing space programme was routine for the F-100. They had frequently flown chase for the X-1 series of research aircraft. They also provided data to advance space flight technology. Neil A Armstong, NACA research pilot later to achieve immortality as the first human to step on the Moon's surface, began planning to fly the X-1B in November 1957. As preparation, he flew one of NACA's F-100A Super Sabres to gain familiarity with the planned flight profiles of the X-1B. A high-speed run, followed by a zoom, positioned the F-100 on an approximation of the X-1B trajectory and its position over the lakebed.

An available production airplane which, like the F-100, could fly at sustained supersonic speeds for significant lengths of time, reduced the need for specialized research aircraft whose performance was not much greater. In fact, the availability of the F-100 actually made the Bell X-1C research aircraft superfluous. That airplane had been ordered; but soon after, the order was cancelled, and no hardware ever went to the USAF.

F-100s for NACA/NASA Research

NACA received an early F-100A (52-5778) to evaluate in support of the Air Force programme. As specialists in stability and control, NACA engineers began their flight research to measure parameters of those two characteristics. But they shifted priority to detailed studies of directional stability and inertial roll coupling, after the former had been implicated in Welch's accident, and the latter in the crash of another F-100.

NACA's Scott Crossfield flew the F-100A during October, November and December 1954, to define the flight boundaries where inertial coupling could occur. On one flight, with the original small vertical tail, he reported violent divergence in pitch and yaw during an abrupt aileron roll. Instruments recorded a −4.4G load and a sideslip angle of 26 degrees.

Crossfield had an ignominious start to his F-100A flight programme. On his first flight, the engine fire-warning light suddenly blazed brightly. Cutting power, Crossfield made a flawless dead-stick approach and landing (NAA pilots had doubted it possible; the F-100A had no flaps and landed 'hot as hell'), coasted off the lakebed, across the ramp, and into the front door of the NACA hangar, in what could only have been an attempt to gild the lily. But he had lost emergency braking power when he cut the engine. The F-100A rolled across the hangar, missing other NACA aircraft, and crunched its nose into the hangar side wall. USAF Major 'Chuck' Yeager, not missing the opportunity, commented sarcastically that the sonic wall was his, but the hangar wall was Crossfield's.

NACA and, later, NASA operated four different F-100s: The F-100A, two F-100C models (53-1712 and -1717), and a single JF-100C (53-1709). The first C model evaluated a pitching motion damper; the second flew chase, research support, and pilot proficiency. The JF flew in studies of variable-stability supporting X-15 and supersonic transport programmes.

Downed by Friendly Fire

Since the war in Vietnam, the USAF has placed heavy emphasis on training its pilots in the way they will have to fight, reflected in scenarios for countless Red Flag programmes of simulated combat, electronically scored.

But firing live missiles at live targets is a different matter. Factors conspire to reduce that essential element of pre-combat training to perhaps one firing each year, often against a small drone carrying a radar reflector and cruising at a known subsonic Mach number, altitude, and even heading. Those conditions do not resemble real combat.

But imagine a supersonic life-sized drone, capable of fighter manoeuvres, and looking like an enemy to radar and infrared detectors. The first of these 'real fighter' drones to be used extensively in fighter-pilot training was the PQM-102, a Sperry conversion of Convair F-102A interceptors. Now, the QF-100 is the real-world drone that gives the impression of a Warsaw Pact fighter to the hunting pilot.

The Air Force Armament Development and Test Center, Eglin AFB, Florida, awarded a contract to Sperry Flight Systems in August 1979, for full-scale engineering development of nine QF-100 drones, designated an interim multi-service target. In addition to simulating potential threats, the QF-100 system had to be compatible with all the existing ground and airborne equipment. Further, the drones

TOP
Before this F-100C (54-1964) was modified and marked as NASA-200, she sat on a rainy apron on a grey day, and was photographed
(Peter M Bowers/Maene Collection)

RIGHT
NASA 200 was an F-100C (54-1964) loaned to the Ames Research Center for tests of boundary-layer control systems. The airplane has a thicker inlet lip section, a drooped leading edge, and ducting carrying bleed air from the engine compressor to the wing leading edge just outboard of the fuselage
(NASA A24696)

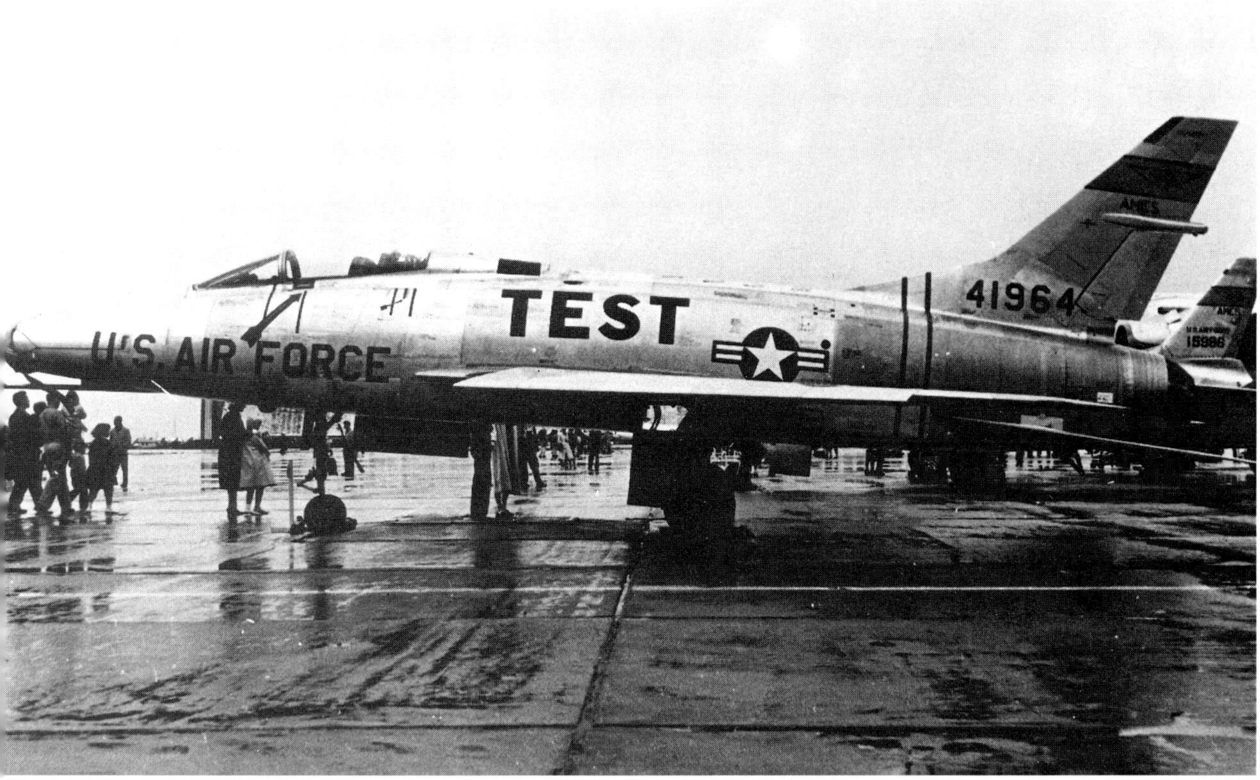
U.S. AIR FORCE
TEST
41964
AMES

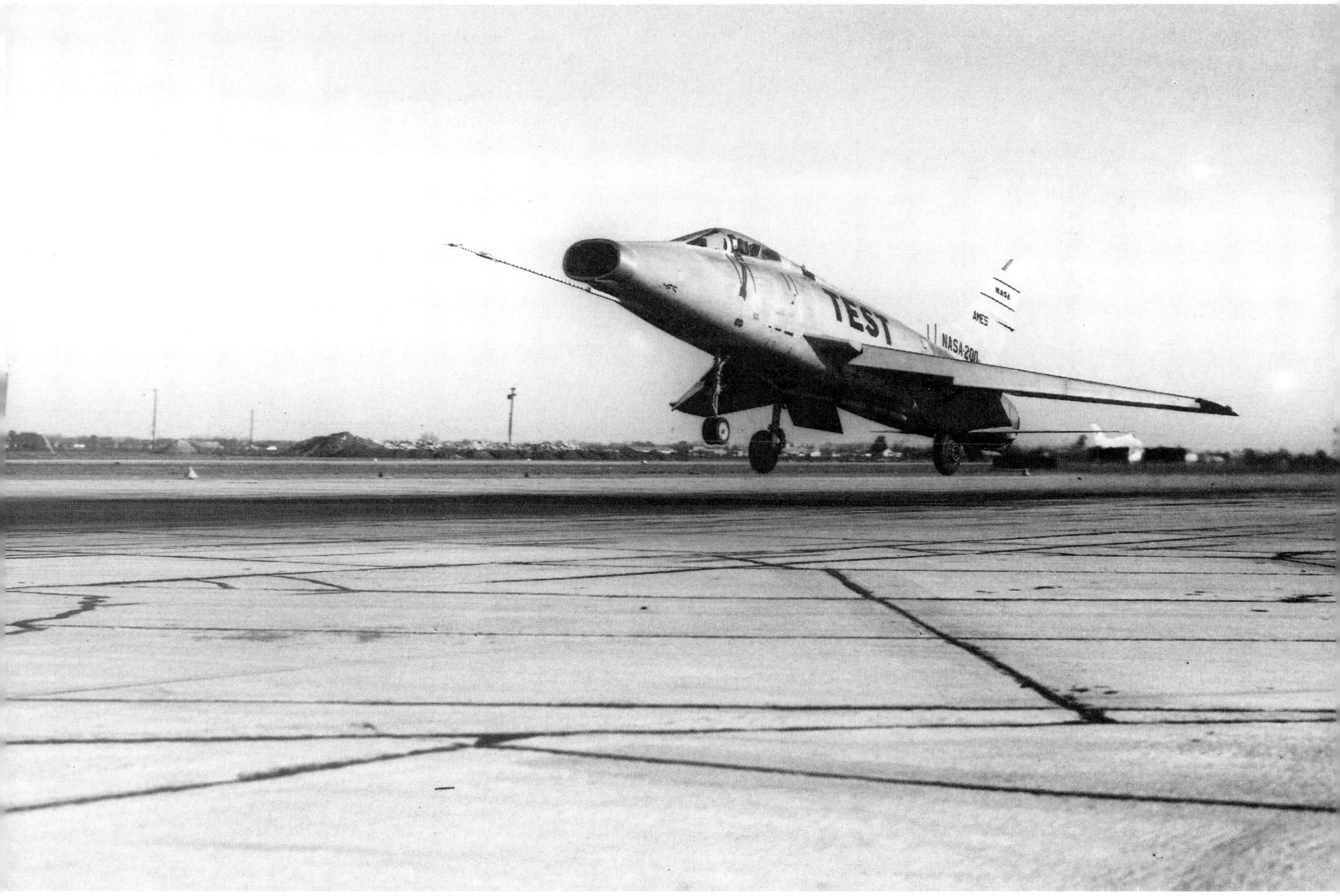
TEST
NASA 200
AMES

TOP LEFT
The first QF-100 drone completes its first flight, decelerating after landing, and rolling over the arresting gear. The specific airplane is a QF-100D, 55-3669. QF095, its identifier, is in white numerals on a red Day-glo nose panel
(Sperry/Montgomery Collection)

ABOVE
Red-tailed and red-nosed, this QF-100D sits on the ramp at Phoenix being readied for piloted test flights
(Sperry/Montgomery Collection)

LEFT
Over the runway threshold comes a QF-100D drone, ready for touchdown after completing an unmanned flight controlled by pilots on the ground
(Sperry/Montgomery Collection)

were also to be used to train US Army ground-to-air missile crews.

Training exercises use missiles programmed to miss, on the assumption that otherwise an expensive drone might be hit and destroyed each time. So the QF-100s have a non-cooperative scoring system that measures miss distance and scores the firing on its potential lethality.

Sperry began the programme at its Litchfield Park plant near Phoenix, Arizona, by developing nine F-100s in four different configurations. Two were YQF-100 developmental aircraft, with added cockpit controls so that they could be flown by pilots for system evaluation. Three were QF-100 models built to standard USAF target configuration, three more were built to Army requirements for multiple-target missions, and the ninth QF-100 was a two-seat version.

For the record, the eight F-100D development drones had AF serials 55-3610 and -3669; 56-2912, -2978, -2979, -3048, -3324, and -3414. The F-100F was 56-3984. In addition to those nine developmental drones, Sperry built 72 production systems, but was then outbid for a larger batch. The successful bidder was Tracor/Flight Systems Division, which received a contract for 209 QF-100 drone conversions over a four-year period. Aircraft for these conversions are being drawn from the F-100s preserved at the Aerospace Maintenance and Regeneration Center, Davis-Monthan AFB, Arizona.

Except for their brilliant red-orange markings, the QF-100 drones look like stock F-100Ds. They have a few extra blade antennas, and the airplane flies with cockpit empty, but otherwise it's a Super Sabre. The red-orange finish is applied to the nose, the vertical stabilizer and rudder, both top and bottom of the horizontal stabilizer and the wingtips, and (sometimes) the wing fence.

Drones are flown by two controllers from a mobile ground station positioned at the runway. One controller is responsible for pitch and throttle

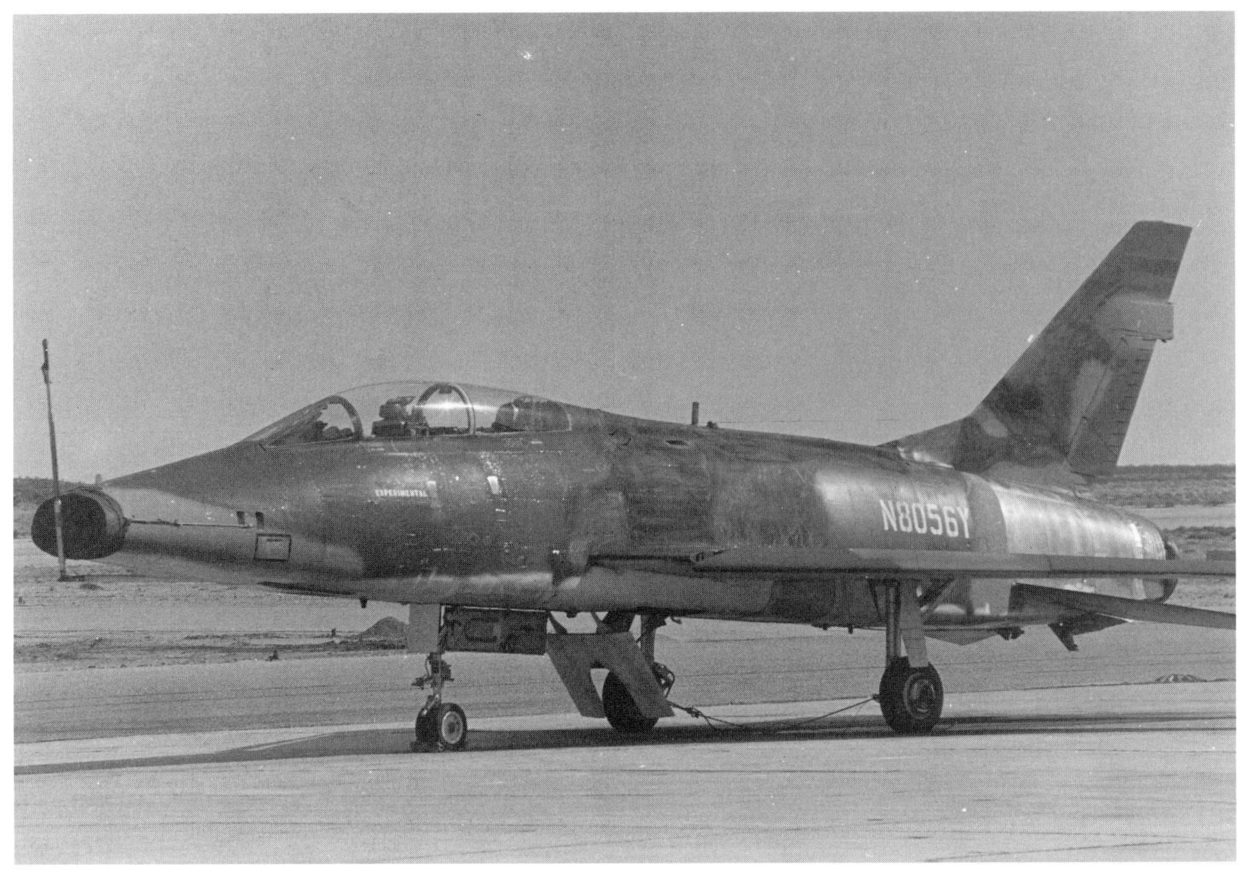

control; the other, for ailerons and rudder. After takeoff, when the drone is stabilized in climb, both controllers hand over the aircraft to a third controller in a fixed-base ground station. There, a dual redundant system is used to get the target to the mission area, and to select the manoeuvers—preprogrammed into on-board computers—that will be flown. If the drone survives the missiles, it is flown back to the handover point and the two controllers at the runway bring it back in and land it.

The drone missions have a new realism. The range now can put up a formation of two targets, and the capability to fly six is being developed in cooperation with the Army. Each drone can independently use chaff, flares, and electronic countermeasures against both IR- and radar-directed missiles. The QF-100s can fly as fast as Mach 1.3, and at altitudes between 200 and 50,000 ft (60–15,240 m). They can make high-G evasive manoeuvres, up to a demonstrated 8G, considerably more than human pilots could take routinely. During each mission, a drone typically makes three runs as a target. Its life expectancy is about ten flights.

Training missions are flown from Holloman AFB, NM, and from Tyndall AFB, Florida. The first unpiloted flight of a QF-100 was flown on 19 November 1981, from Tyndall. The drone flew at 35,000 feet (10,670 m) and 275 knots (509 km/h), and was attacked by a Convair F-106A Delta Dart interceptor flown by a pilot from the 475th Test Squadron of the Tactical Air Warfare Center at Tyndall AFB. A Lockheed T-33 chase aircraft, from the 95th Fighter Interceptor Training Squadron, also flew this mission. No missiles were launched; the F-106A carried a captive practice missile and only simulated firing.

Most recently, QF-100 drones were used in the AMRAAM (advanced medium-range air-to-air missile) programme. On 17 September 1985, an AMRAAM without an explosive warhead nailed a QF-100 drone flying above the White Sands (NM) Missile Range. The hunter was a General Dynamics F-16A flown by a pilot of the Air Force Armament Division's 3246th Test Wing. At the time of the engagement, the F-16 was at 20,000 feet (6095 m), travelling at Mach 1.2. The drone was at Mach 0.95, head-on to the shooter.

The last Super Sabre drone converted by Sperry at Phoenix was F-100D serial AF56-3162. It had been almost new when 1st Lieutenant James L Foster first climbed into it on a hot July, 1957, day at Cannon AFB, NB. In April, 1985, he said a final goodbye to 162. It was standing, partially stripped, in the Sperry Litchfield Park facility.

Foster, a retired USAF Colonel living in nearby Glendale, Arizona, found his airplane through the services of the indefatigable David W Menard, an expert on F-100 history. When Foster saw 162 for the

N8056Y is a retired F-100F, serial unknown, in the inventory of Flight Systems Incorporated, Kern County Airport, Mojave, California. FSI, a division of Tracor, converted military F-100Fs for target-towing, and for photographic support of flight testing, in addition to modifying a large number of D models to QF-100D drone configuration. This F-100F is shown before its modifications, updatings, and refinishings. FSI birds in service are invariably immaculate, glossy white with blue trim lines and are kept in beautiful condition
(David A Anderton)

BELOW
Thrust into the air by the combined urging of a powerful solid-propellant rocket, and the F-100D's J57 turbojet in full afterburner, 56-2904 becomes airborne in the initial test of the zero-length launch (ZEL) system. The picture has been retouched (heavily, but fairly well) to obliterate the dummy nuclear weapon carried under the left wing
(Rocketdyne 58-800)

last time, it had been converted, and bore the bright red-orange markings of a drone. But in its salad days, it had carried him into the blue for upwards of 350 hours. And one of those flights was a memorable deployment late in 1957 across the Pacific on MOBILE ZEBRA, a mass movement of F-100s, RF-101s, and B-66s to bases in the Philippines.

Interlude H: **Takeoffs from the World's Shortest Runway**

General O P Weyland, then commanding Tactical Air Command, said at a 1958 press conference: 'North American Aviation has developed and is now testing a Zero Launch System for the F-100 which so far has met with excellent success. . . We should have the ZEL system perfected and the launching equipment in the hands of our units in the near future.'

TAC's crystal ball was cloudy; the ZEL system never did become operational. But it seemed like a great idea at the time.

The NATO nightmare in the mid-1950s was about the Russian atomic bombs that would land on each airfield, wiping out all aircraft and rendering Allied air forces impotent (sound familiar?). One of the suggested counter-moves was to disperse NATO aircraft in hardened shelters at safe distances from targeted airfields, and launch them by means that were independent of runway conditions or runways themselves.

Today's partial solution is a VTOL aircraft; but then, such aircraft were only paper designs and experimental vehicles far from service use. Indeed, the only feasible way to launch a contemporary fighter, and not use 10,000 ft (3048 m) of concrete runway, was by some sort of rocket-propelled catapult.

What resulted was the concept of using a powerful solid-propellant rocket motor, attached directly to an F-100, producing enough thrust to accelerate the aircraft to a safe flying speed in very short distance. The concept was named Zero-Length Launch, or ZEL, for short.

(In another example of parallel development—or perhaps a borrowed idea—the Russians had arrived at a similar conclusion about the vulnerability of their airplanes and airfields. In 1956, the MiG design bureau produced five experimental MiG-19 aircraft, designated SM-30, '... with catapult launch and soft-field gear.' There's a picture of an SM-30, on the launcher, gear retracted, on page 180 of Bill Gunston's encyclopedic *Aircraft of the Soviet Union*, an Osprey book.)

A contract change notice on 12 October 1956, specified that NAA would build the last 148 F-100D aircraft with ZEL capability. Two F-100D test airplanes were designated: 56-2904 and -2947. Both had special modifications for the test programme, and were loaned to NAA by the Air Force for ZEL flights at AFFTC.

The company's Rocketdyne Division developed a solid-propellant rocket that produced 130,000 lb (58,957 kg) of thrust for four seconds, enough to accelerate an F-100 from zero to 275 knots (509 km/h). Since many questions were unanswered at the start of the programme, the first five launches were made with a dummy mass, airplane-shaped, to validate the concept and the system. The first such launch was made 12 December 1957, at the AFFTC.

On 26 March 1958, NAA engineering test pilot Al Blackburn climbed into 56-2904 parked on an inclined ramp, and item by item went through his check list. He started the engine, ran it briefly, pushed the throttle into full afterburner, fired the rocket and within four seconds was flying at 275 knots. The spent booster struck the aft fuselage after separation, but did no significant damage. Blackburn and the F-100D climbed away, entered the standard pattern, made the approach, and landed safely.

The second ZEL aircraft (F-100D 56-2947), flown by NAA engineering test pilot Al Blackburn, blasts out of a simulated hardened shelter in the only launch made from this type of site. From this angle, the size of the solid-propellant rocket is apparent. What also is apparent is the dummy nuclear weapon under the left wing, which looks to the uninitiated eye like a fuel tank. It isn't
(Smithsonian Institution Photo No 87–741)

The second flight, on 11 April, did not go as smoothly; the booster did not separate after burnout. Nothing Blackburn did could shake the empty booster casing loose. 'Actually I flew the airplane around for over an hour trying to shake the booster off,' Blackburn said. 'And because the booster hung well below the landing gear, I couldn't make a normal landing. I had to punch out, finally.' The F-100 went

into a flat spin and hit the ground about a mile north of Harper's Dry Lake. Despite a fire, it remained relatively intact, and that permitted a quick analysis of the problem.

The rest of the total of 20 manned launches were incident-free. Blackburn flew 16 of them, and USAF Captain Robert F Titus flew four. The tests were done at three different gross weights between 34,414 and 37,178 lb (15,607–16,861 kg), and with intentionally misaligned boosters. The test airplanes carried standard underwing stores. The configurations included a Mk 7 nuclear store on the left intermediate station and a 275 US-gal (1041-lit) drop tank on the right. On another run, 200 US-gal (757-lit) tanks at the inboard wing stations were added to the Mk 7 and the 275 US-gal drop tank loading.

There was a parallel between the ZEL launching system for the F-100 and a similar scheme for launching Martin Mace missiles then deployed in Europe. In a joint effort, Martin and North American developed the concept further, and fired airplane and missile from a launcher sited inside a simulated concrete hardsite shelter. The two companies also cooperated on development of a mobile launch system, a self-contained wheeled platform that could be towed at about ten mph over unimproved ground.

At the Air Force Fighter Weapons Meet in 1958, the Air Force demonstrated the ZEL F-100 system publicly for the first and only time. A North American ground crew drove the launch platform from Edwards AFB to Indian Springs gunnery range, part of the Nellis AFB complex in Nevada. There they loaded the F-100D on the 'world's shortest runway'—short steel cradles that retained the wheels of the Super Sabre—and drove to Range 1, where they set up for launch. Titus climbed in, started up, fired the rocket, and flew. And General Weyland held his press conference.

The last flight in the programme took place 26 August 1959. Blackburn again was the pilot; the flight was unremarkable except for two things: first, it was the only night launch of the F-100 ZEL programme and, second, it was the only launch from the simulated hardsite at Holloman AFB. The final report stated that any combat-ready pilot ought to be able to handle a ZEL takeoff. The system was reliable, and relatively simple to operate. It took a five-man launch crew two and one-half hours to get one plane loaded and launched. Re-cycling, with its obvious implications, apparently was not checked out.

Afterword: **A Few Last Thoughts**

In the Arthurian legend, the sword Excalibur takes on epochal dimension. Arthur's weapon, acquired by magic and returned by magic, is as much a part of the stories as any of the King's knights. You remember the name of Excalibur; but what about the many other swords at the service of the King that remain unidentified, unnamed?

Arthur dominated the legends; but his knights—Lancelot, Gawain, Gareth, Galahad, Bedivere, and the rest—were his strength and his support. Their swords righted the wrongs, defeated the invaders from the North, saved a country.

If you'll permit this romanticizing, then, consider the Super Sabre as the knight's sword—any knight, any sword. Another weapon in the arsenal, to be used as often as occasion demanded.

And, had you been one of Arthur's men, what kind of sword would you have asked the armourer to make for you? A strong blade, hard-edged, keen, yet light in your hands. A blade that could pierce mail, slash through the layers of leather and padded cloth, cleave a helmet. A blade that could strike the heaviest of armour without shattering or bending, that could be nicked and gouged, but still remain whole and still cut.

With swords like that, and not too long ago, brave men tried to right perceived wrongs, tried to defeat the invaders from the North, tried to save a country. As in legends, they failed. But as in legends, they failed nobly.

This book, then, was about the Super Sabre, the sword of fighting men.

When the squadron racked up 15,000 sorties, Lt Col Randy Steffens was there to hold the scorecard, since it was his most recent mission that made the big number. With him are the guys who kept his airplane up and running, airmen Ruedeman, McBride and Reed, here shown literally as Steffens' right-hand men. They are standing in front of F-100D 56-3025, Steffens' mount (Steffens Collection)

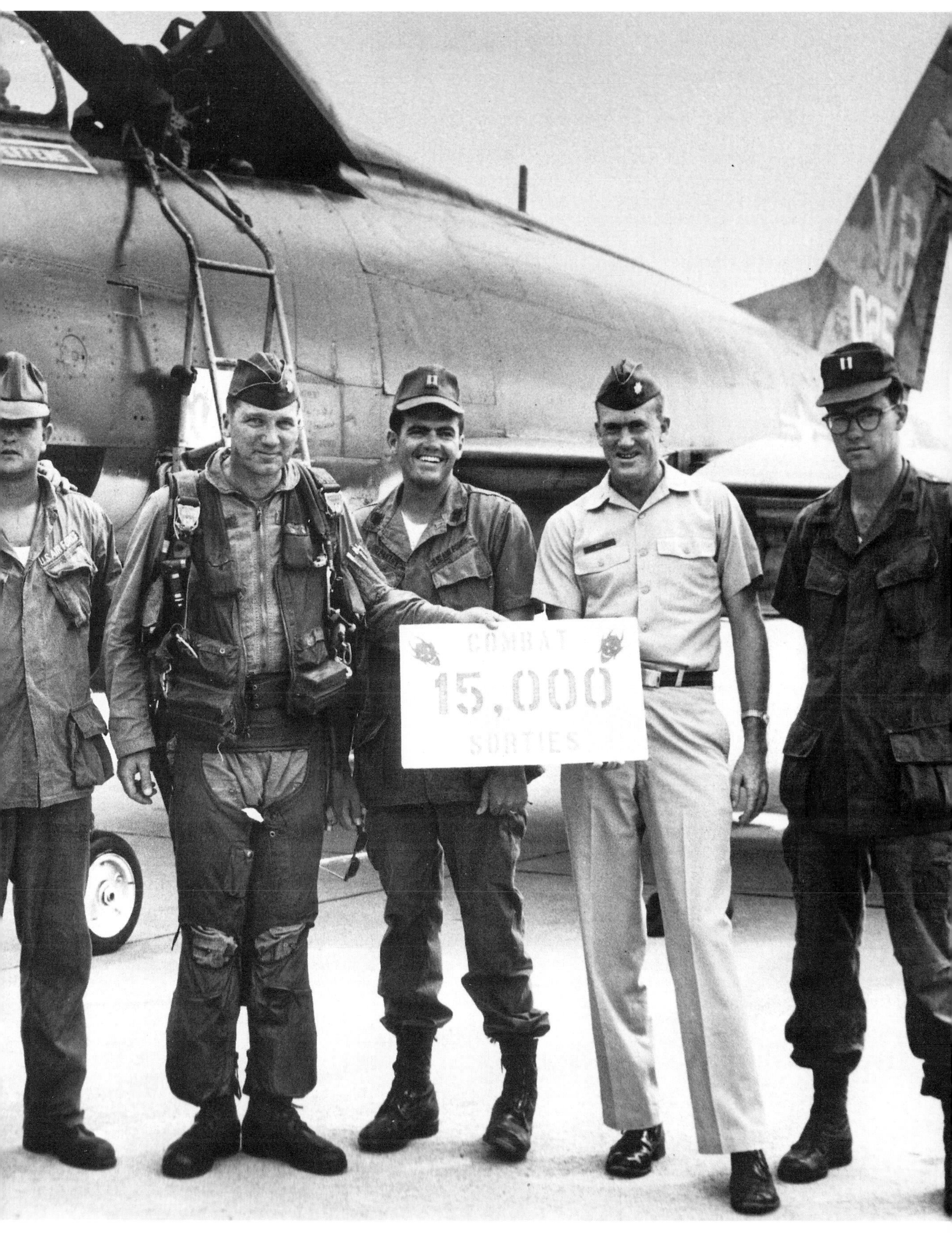
COMBAT
15,000
SORTIES

Glossary

AAA	Anti-aircraft artillery fire. Also: Triple-A
AFB	Air Force Base
ANG	Air National Guard
CIA	Central Intelligence Agency
CRT	Cathode ray tube
G	One gravity force
GM	General Motors
KP	Kitchen Punishment
NAA	North American Aviation, Inc.
NATO	North Atlantic Treaty Organization
POW	Prisoner of War
RTAFB	Royal Thai Air Force Base
SAM	Surface-to-air missile, usually refering to Soviet SA-2 *Guideline*
Tacan	Tactical air navigation system

Appendices

Appendix 1: **Design Proposals**

In continuing studies of the Super Sabre, NAA engineers investigated its potential as an interceptor, a fighter-bomber, a trainer, and a fast reconnaissance plane. They believed it would be a relatively simple task to accommodate those varied missions through minor modifications to the F-100, while still using many of its proven components. The result: a family of aircraft types, marketable at home and abroad, to help keep production lines filled and moving.

The following list of proposed designs in the early stages of the F-100 series is documented, but probably incomplete.

Type	*Design No*	*Date*
YF-100A	NA-180	24 Aug 1951[1]
F-100A	NA-192	24 Aug 1951[1]
F-100C	NA-214	1 May 1952[2]
F-100 Interceptor		5 Sep 1952
F-100A		7 Nov 1952
F-100 Interceptor		19 Jan 1953
F-100 Two-place interceptor		19 Jan 1953
F-100B Interceptor		22 May 1953
F-100B Interceptor		3 June 1953
F-100A Fighter-bomber		26 Aug 1953
F-100C	NA-214	2 Nov 1953[2]
F-100C	NA-217	2 Nov 1953[2]
F-100B Fighter-bomber		18 Nov 1953
F-100A Avon engine		27 Jan 1954[3]
TF-100C Trainer	NA-230	16 Jul 1954
F-100A 1956 Interceptor		19 Aug 1954
F-100C	NA-222	1 Nov 1954
F-100D	NA-223	1 Nov 1954
F-100D	NA-224	1 Nov 1954
F-100F	NA-243	

Notes:
1 = Revised on 1 May 1952
2 = Revised on 1 Feb 1954
3 = Revised on 22 Feb 1954

Air Force sources also identified four sub-types of F-100 that were proposed during the life of the Super Sabre, and carried along far enough so that they were assigned a model letter by the service. They were:

F-100J: An all-weather version offered to Japan through the Foreign Military Sales (FMS) programme;

F-100L: Replacement of the J57-P-21A by the J57-P-55;

F-100N: A simplified F-100D with fewer electronic systems;

F-100S: An F-100F airframe powered by a Rolls-Royce RB.168-25R Spey turbofan engine. This was a 1964 attempt by North American to establish a production line in France for 200 two-seat aircraft.

Appendix 2: **Models, Serial Numbers, Production**

Model (Quan)	*NAA Design*	*USAF Contract*	*USAF Serial No*
YF-100A (2)	NAA-180	AF 6545	AF52-5754 through -5755
F-100A (203)	NA-192	AF 6545	AF52-5756 through -5778
			AF53-1529 through -1708
F-100C (70)	NA-214	AF 26962	AF53-1709 through -1778
F-100C (381)	NA-217	AF 26962	AF54-1740 through -2120
F-100C (25)	NA-222	AF 28736	AF55-2709 through -2733
F-100D (183)	NA-223	AF 29150	AF54-2121 through -2303
(313)			AF55-3502 through -3814

Model (Quan)	*NAA Design*	*USAF Contract*	*USAF Serial No*
F-100D (221)	NA-224	AF 28736	AF55-2734 through -2954
F-100D (444)	NA-235	Af 31311	AF56-2903 through -3346
F-100D (113)	NA-245	AF 31388	AF56-3351 through -3463
F-100F (295)	NA-243	AF 31863	AF56-3725 through -4019
F-100F-20 (29)	NA-255	AF 35160	AF58-1205 through -1233
F-100F (9)	NA-261	AF 37687	AF58-6975 through -6983
F-100F (6)	NA-262	AF 38387	AF59-2558 through -2563

Production of all models of the F-100:

Fiscal Year Model	'53	'54	'55	'56	'57	'58	'59	'60	*Total*
YF-100	2								2
F-100A		15	165	23					203
F-100C			16	459	1				476
F-100D(I)				113	576	166	75	10	940
F-100D(C)				2	212	120			334
F-100F					14	227	53		294
F-100F(MAP)						14	16	15	45
Totals	2	15	181	597	803	527	144	25	2294

Maximum production rate of 66.9 aircraft/month occurred during FY 1957

Appendix 3: **Performance**

It does not libel manufacturers of military aircraft when I warn readers not to accept unquestioningly the performance figures found in brochures and press releases. All manufacturers of military equipment suffer under regulations specifying what they may or may not tell the public, and in how much detail. So it's often easier to describe an airplane's performance as 'supersonic', or 'in the 1,000-mph class'.

It's also simpler, because actual performance data are very dependent on aircraft weight, combat loads, fuel, ambient conditions, and a host of other factors. Further, there are substantial differences between a Phase IV flight-test performance of a clean, new airframe and engine just off the production line, and the combat performance of a scruffy operational fighter with several hundred hours in its logbook. Consequently, the Air Force and other customers for aircraft have developed standards to define and measure performance. For USAF combat aircraft, standard characteristic sheets summarize physical data of the aircraft, primary and secondary missions, and performance achieved under those conditions.

The official performance data for the F-100C, F-100D, and F-100F, taken from USAF Phase IV Performance flight tests, are reproduced below. Note that these are all based on the air superiority mission, a task that the Super Sabres were seldom assigned to carry out.

Bear in mind also that USAF test conditions at the Air Force Flight Test Center were considerably different from, and better than, conditions at Tuy Hoa in 1967. Perhaps no Super Sabre in combat operations in Vietnam ever duplicated the performance figures cited below.

Remember also that these figures are corrected to standard conditions at sea level: 59°F and a barometric pressure of 29.92 inches of mercury. In the heat and monsoons of Southeast Asia, conditions were far from those standards. Performance of jet aircraft deteriorates with increases in temperature, and the reduction is particularly noticeable—and critical—at takeoff, in low-altitude climb, and in stall characteristics.

F-100C

Air superiority mission

Basis: Takeoff weight (TOW), 36,549 lb (16,576 kg); combat weight 28,700 lb (13,016 kg); fuel load 2,222 US gal (8410 lit), with 47.4% external and droppable; 800 rds of 20-mm ammunition.

Combat radius: 542 nautical miles (1003 km) with 560-lb (254-kg) payload at 515 knots (953 km/h) in 2.60 hr. If wing tanks are jettisoned before combat, radius is reduced to 499 nm (923 km).

Ferry range: 1,776 nm (3291 km) with 2,222 US gal (8410 lit) fuel, at 515 kt (953 km/h) average in 3.60 hr at 36,549 lb (16,576 kg) TOW.

Speed: Combat, 775 kt (1434 km/h) at 37,000 ft (11,280 m), maximum (afterburner) power; maximum speed, 795 kt (1471 km/h) at 35,000 ft (10,671 m), maximum power; basic speed, same as maximum.

Climb: 3,400 feet/min (17.3 m/sec) at sea level, TOW and miliary power; 19,000 fpm (96.5 m/sec) at sea level, combat weight and maximum power.

Ceiling: 32,800 ft (10,000 m) at 100 fpm (0.5 m/sec) rate of climb, TOW and military power; 48,400 ft (14,756 m) at 500 fpm (2.5 m/sec) rate of climb, combat weight and maximum power.

Takeoff: 3,800 ft (1158 m) ground run; 5,900 ft (1798 m) to clear a 50-ft (15.2-m) obstacle.

Stalling speed: 158 kt (292 km/h), power off, landing configuration, takeoff weight.

Time to climb: 3.5 min, sea level to 35,000 ft (10,671 m), combat weight and maximum power.

F-100D

Air superiority mission

Basis: Takeoff weight (TOW), 38,048 lb (17,255 kg); combat weight, 30,061 lb (13,633 kg); fuel load 2,259 US gal (8550 lit), with 47.4% external and droppable; 800 rds of 20-mm ammunition.

Combat radius: 520 nm (965 km) with 560-lb (254-kg) payload at 510 knots (944 km/h) average in 2.67 hr. If wing tanks are jettisoned before combat, radius is reduced to 499 nm (923 km).

Ferry range: 1,712 nm (3176 km), with 2,259 US gal (8550 lit) of fuel, at 515 kt (953 km/h) average in 3.23 hr at 38,034 lb (17,249 kg) TOW.

Speeds: Combat, 757 kt (1404 km/h) at 36,500 ft (11,128 m), maximum (afterburner) power; maximum speed, 775 kt (1434 km/h) at 35,000 ft (10,671 m), maximum power; basic speed, same as maximum.

Climb: 3,300 ft/min (16.7 m/sec), at sea level, TOW and military power; 18,100 fpm (91.9 m/sec), at sea level, combat weight, and maximum power.

Ceiling: 34,000 ft (10,366 m), at 100 fpm (0.5 m/sec) rate of climb, TOW and military power; 46,900 ft (14,299 m) at 500 fpm (2.5 m/sec) rate of climb, combat weight, and maximum power.

Takeoff: 5,100 ft (1554 m) ground run; 7,650 (2332) to clear a 50-ft (15.2-m) obstacle.

Stalling speed, 155 kt (287 km/h), power off, landing configuration, TOW.

Time to climb: 3.5 min, sea level to 35,000 ft (10,671 m), combat weight and maximum power.

F-100F

Air superiority mission

Basis: Takeoff weight (TOW), 39,122 lb (17,742 kg); combat weight, 31,413 lb (14,246 kg); fuel load 2,259 US gal (8550 lit), with 47.4% external and droppable; 350 rds of 20-mm ammunition.

Combat radius: 500 nm (927 km), with 245-lb (111-kg) payload, at 505 kt (934 km/h) average in 2.93 hr. If tanks jettisoned before combat, radius is reduced to 469 nm (870 km).

Ferry range: 1,661 nm (3073 km), with 2,259 US gal (8550 lit) of fuel, at 510 kt (946 km/h) average in 3.22 hr at 39,122 lb (17,742 kg) TOW.

Speed: Combat, 755 kt (1400 km/h) at 34,300 ft (10,457 m), maximum (afterburner) power; maximum speed, 760 kt (1409 km/h) at 35,000 ft (10,671 m), maximum power; basic speed, same as maximum.

Climb: 3,100 fpm (15.7 m/sec) at sea level, TOW and military power; 17,400 fpm (88.4 m/sec) at sea level, combat weight and maximum power.

Ceiling: 33,900 ft (10,335 m), at 100 fpm (0.5 m/sec) rate of climb, TOW, and military power; 47,800 ft (14,573 m) at 500 fpm (2.5 m/sec) rate of climb, combat wt and max power.

Takeoff: 5,500 ft (1677 m) ground run; 8,200 ft (2500 m) to clear a 50-ft (15.2-m) obstacle.

Stalling speed: 157 kt (290 km/h), power off, landing configuration, TOW.

Model	**YF-100A**	**F-100A**	**F-100C**	**F-100D**	**F-100F**
NAA Design Number	*NA-180*	*NA-192*	*NA-214* *NA-217* *NA-222*	*NA-223* *NA-223* *NA-235* *NA-245*	*NA-243*
Dimensions:					
Wing span, ft/m	36.78/11.21	38.78/11.82	38.78/11.82	38.78/11.82	38.78/11.82
Length, ft/m	45.62/13.90	47.06/14.34	47.06/14.34	47.39/14.44	50.31/15.33
Height, ft/m	14.94/4.5	15.34/4.6	15.34/4.6	16.22/4.9	16.22/4.9
Weights:					
Empty, lb/kg		18,185/8248	19,270/8740	20,638/9360	21,712/9847
Combat, lb/kg		24,996/11,336	28,700/13,016	30,061/13,633	31,413/14,246
Takeoff, lb/kg	28,561/12,953	28,971/13,139	36,549/16,578	38,048/17,256	39,122/17,742
Powerplant:					
Engine: J57-	XJ57-P-7	P-7/-39	P-21	P-21/21A	P-21/21A
Int. fuel, US gal/lit		755/2858	1,142/4360	1,189/4500	1,189/4500
Ext. fuel, US gal/lit		550/2082	1,070/4050	1,070/4050	1,070/4500
Max. thrust, lb/kg	13,200/5986	14,800/6712	16,000/7256	16,000/7256	16,000/7256
Mil. thrust, lb/kg	8,700/3946	9,700/4400	10,200/4626	10,200/4626	10,200/4626
Nor. thrust, lb/kg		8,000/3628	8,700/3946	8,700/3946	8,700/3946

Appendix 4: **First Flights**

Type	*AF serial*	*Date*	*Pilot*
YF-100A	AF52-5754	25 May 1953	George Welch
F-100A	AF52-5756	29 Oct 1953	George Welch
F-100C-1	AF53-1709	9 Sep 1955	George Hoskins
F-100D	AF54-2121	24 Jan 1956	Daniel Darnell
TF-100C	AF54-1966	3 Aug 1956	Alvin White
F-107A	AF55-5118	10 Sep 1956	J Robert Baker
F-100F-1	AF56-3725	7 Mar 1957	Gage Mace

Appendix 5: **Flight-Test Phases**

At the time the YF-100A was in development, USAF required a standarized seven-phase flight-test programme for systematic evaluation of any new aircraft. New aircraft were tested by both the manufacturer and the Air Force at several locations: AF Flight Test Center (AFFTC) at Edwards AFB, California; Wright Air Development Center (WADC), at Wright-Patterson AFB, Ohio; Air Proving Ground Command (APGC), at Eglin AFB, Florida; and various manufacturers' facilities.

Phase I was exclusively the manufacturer's programme, including first flight and early evaluation of performance by company test pilots. Total flight time logged typically was 20 to 50 hours. The first YF-100A was flown 42 hr 35 min in its Phase I tests.

Phase II was the first USAF flight opportunity to verify that manufacturer's performance figures were accurate, and that the airplane met its contract requirements. USAF pilots also determined handling qualities, the pilot term for the way the airplane behaved and felt in flight. The YF-100A was flown for about 20 hr at AFFTC by several USAF engineering test pilots in completing this phase.

Phase III was a second series of manufacturer's tests which evaluated changes or suggestions made by the USAF during Phase II testing. The time flown depended on the number and nature of those changes.

Phase IV was the second series of USAF tests, flown by the first aircraft built to production standards. It required, typically, 150 hr at AFFTC in a detailed evaluation of performance, stability and control. Flight data were used to develop performance charts for the Pilot's Handbook for the type. The F-100A logged only 71 hr in Phase IV tests.

Phase V was the third series of USAF tests, and was dedicated to all-weather testing. Although later programmes might be flown at other bases as well, at the time of the YF-100A tests the Phase V flights were made at WADC where bad weather was available more often than it was in the California desert.

Phase VI was accelerated service testing, flown by USAF pilots at AFFTC with three or more early production airplanes. Pilots and maintenance personnel from user commands were invited to participate in this phase of flight test. Typical programmes simulated routine operations—gunnery, bombing, night and bad-weather flying—and were designed to prove overall suitability of new aircraft. Typical flight time logged would be about 150 hr on each airplane. Eight F-100As were assigned, and logged 552 hr during Phase VI tests.

Phase VII, the USAF's last round with a new airplane, was flown at APGC to assess the complete weapon system in conditions that simulated squadron service and combat environments. (In effect, Phase VI tests revealed how the airplane *flew* under operational conditions, and Phase VII showed how it *fought* in operational environments.)

Appendix 6: **Flight-Test Aircraft**

The two prototype YF-100As and the first 35 F-100As were assigned to flight test programmes at NAA facilities, USAF centres, and a privately-operated research laboratory. It was not regarded as exceptional to have 37 F-100s so assigned during the developmental life of the airplane. Further, production aircraft of all models occasionally were assigned to specific flight-test programmes by NAA, USAF, and NACA.

The following table summarizes the known flight-test programme assignments for F-100 aircraft.

Model	*AF Serial*	*Ship No*	*Assignment*
YF-100A	52-5754	1	EFT; Phase I and II
	52-5755	2	EFT
F-100A	52-5756	1	EFT; Phase I and III
	52-5757	2	EFT; Phase I and III
	52-5758	3	EFT; Phase I and III
	52-5759	4	EFT; Prototype for dry-wing F-100C
	52-5760	5	EFT; Phase I and III
	52-5761	6	EFT; Phase I and III
	52-5762	7	EFT
	52-5763	8	AFFTC/EAFB
	52-5764	9	EFT; crashed 12 Oct 1954
	52-5765	10	EFT
	52-5766	11	EFT
	52-5767	12	AFFTC/EAFB; Phase IV Stab & Control
	52-5768	13	EFT
	52-5769	14	AFAC/EgAFB
	52-5770	15	AFFTC/EAFB; Phase VI
	52-5771	16	do.(crashed during tests)
	52-5772	17	do.
	52-5773	18	do.
	52-5774	19	do.
	52-5775	20	ASD/WPAFB
	52-5776	21	CAL
	52-5777	22	AFAC/EgAFB
	52-5778	23	AFFTC/EAFB
	53-1529	24	AFFTC/EAFB;Phase VI
	53-1530	25	EFT
	53-1531	26	AFAC/EgAFB
	53-1532	27	do.
	53-1533	28	do.
	53-1534	29	do.
	53-1535	30	do.
	53-1536	31	Unknown-destroyed(?)
	53-1537	32	ASD/WPAFB
	53-1538	33	do.
	53-1539	34	do.
	53-1540	35	do.
F-100C	53-1710	2	AFFTC/EAFB; Phase II
	53-1713	5	AFFTC/EAFB; Phase VI
	53-1714	6	do.
	53-1716	8	do.
	53-1719	9	AFFTC/EAFB; Phase IV Performance
	54-1744	75	AFFTC/EAFB; Phase IV Stab & Control

Model	*AF Serial*	*Ship No*	*Assignment*
F-100D	54-2125	5	AFFTC/EAFB; Phase IV Performance
	55-3503	185	AFFTC/EAFB; Phase VI
	55-3505	187	AFFTC/EAFB; Category II
	55-3507	189	AFFTC/EAFB; Phase VI
	56-2904	719	EFT; ZEL launches
	56-2947	763	do.
TF-100C	54-1966	1	AFFTC/EAFB; Phase II
F-100F	56-3726	2	AFFTC/EAFB; Limited Phase IV
F-100F-20	58-1205	1	AFFTC/EAFB; Limited Category II
	58-1206	2	do.

Abbreviations:

EFT: NAA Engineering Flight Test
AFFTC/EAFB: Air Force Flight Test Center, Edwards Air Force Base
AFAC/EgAFB: Air Force Armament Center, Eglin AFB
ASD/WPAFB: USAF/Aeronautical Systems Division, Wright-Patterson AFB
ZEL: Zero-Length Launch

Appendix 7: **How to Tell the Huns Apart**

Each of the five basic models of the F-100 showed differences in dimensions, or weights, or thrust, or physical characteristics, from the other four models. Vertical tail shapes, sizes, and arrangement of rudder and fin varied from model to model. And the wing area and planform shape changed in the arrangement of leading-edge slats and by the addition of landing flaps to the D models.

The table overleaf summarizes the major physical characteristics of the five F-100 models.

Appendix 8: **Don Schmenk and SM 580**

It's a popular belief among model builders that a military pilot is assigned his own airplane. His name is on the canopy rail or on the fuselage side under the cockpit. His personally selected nose art is painted up front. He is photographed only in, or in front of, that particular plane.

But records can tell a different story. During the war in Vietnam, some pilots recorded combat missions on PACAF Form 20, a sheet divided into columns and spaces for date, aircraft number, times of departure and arrival, flying time, mission number, sortie, type and remarks. Form 20 was unofficial, but used within Pacific Air Forces; official records were on USAF Form 5.

Like other model builders, I knew of then-Captain Don Schmenk because of 'his' airplane—F-100D (55-3580) tail code SM 580—immortalized in Monogram's outstanding 1/48-scale plastic model kit. The little mouse and the names of Carol Ann and Mary Jane emblazoned on the nose of 580 were familiar. But Schmenk's Form 20 sheets, copies of which he loaned for research on this book, showed that he also had flown many other F-100s.

He did, in fact, fly 580 more often than he flew other aircraft. But on his 235 combat missions between 16 October 1969, and 15 August 1970, he flew 44 other F-100Ds and 14 F-100Fs. Schmenk flew 580 on 23 missions, just under ten percent of his total. He logged 20 missions in aircraft 945, 14 each in 859 and the two-seat 837, a dozen in 171, and 10 each in 601 and 879. During his ten months of combat, he flew the equivalent of more than two full squadrons of F-100s.

Schmenk's experience was probably typical of the fighter pilot in Vietnam, and should serve as a cautionary note to aircraft researchers and model-builders alike.

Appendix 9: **Survivor at the Smithsonian**

F-100D (AF56-3440), now in storage at the Paul E Garber Facility of the National Air and Space Museum, Silver Hill, Maryland, is on the list of aircraft waiting to be restored. (Knowing the exceptional job that the NASM does on all its restorations, I can hardly wait to see this one. But also aware of the competition for restoration work at the NASM, I will not hold my breath).

The NASM F-100D was a late-production model, number 1,250 in a line that stopped after 1,274 had been built. It has all the additional equipment and systems that had been factored into the D model along the way: Extra droppable fuel tanks, tail warning radar, autopilot, and bombing equipment.

The service record of 440 includes duty with five different regular USAF wings, five years of combat in South Vietnam, and six years with an ANG unit.

Manufactured at Columbus, 440 was delivered to the 506th Fighter Bomber Wing, TAC, in December 1957. In March 1958, 440 was transferred to the 413th Fighter Day Wing (later TFW) at George AFB, Calif. The 413th was redesignated the 31st TFW about a year later, and three years later moved to Homestead AFB, Florida, taking 440 along. From December 1957, 440 had deployed on many temporary duty (TDY) tours in Turkey, Italy and Spain.

During 1960, 440 was assigned to a special test project, painted gloss white, and flown to altitudes above 60,000 ft (in zoom climbs?) by then-Major Robinson Risner, who had to wear a partial-pressure flight suit because of the extreme altitudes.

In mid-1963, 440 went TDY to Japan on alert duty while the 8th TFW made its transition to the Republic F-105D. Then in 1965, 440 was flown to Bien Hoa AB, Vietnam, on TDY with the 307th TFS, 31st TFW, and later flew combat missions with that unit, and with the 308th, 531st, and 90th squadrons.

In July 1970, 440 was sent to the 524th TFS, 27th TFW, at Cannon AFB, New Mexico, the last regular USAF F-100 squadron. In June 1972, her next, and last, assignment was with the 107th TFS of the Michigan Air National Guard. After six years there, she was flown to Andrews AFB, Maryland, for inclusion in the aircraft collection at the National Air and Space Museum.

She was just four months short of her 21st birthday, and had flown a total of 6,159 hours. There are no immediate plans for restoration of 440. (But if everybody who loves F-100s sent a note to the NASM . . .)

Index